Sub National Constitutional Law in South Africa

Sub National Constitutional Law in South Africa

Rassie Malherbe
Dirk Brand

This book was originally published as a monograph in the International Encyclopaedia of Laws/Constitutional Law.

Founding Editor: Roger Blanpain
General Editor: Frank Hendrickx
Volume Editors: André Alen & David Haljan

Wolters Kluwer

Published by:
Kluwer Law International B.V.
PO Box 316
2400 AH Alphen aan den Rijn
The Netherlands
Website: www.wklawbusiness.com

Sold and distributed in North, Central and South America by:
Wolters Kluwer Legal & Regulatory U.S.
7201 McKinney Circle
Frederick, MD 21704
United States of America
Email: customer.service@wolterskluwer.com

Sold and distributed in all other countries by:
Turpin Distribution Services Ltd.
Stratton Business Park
Pegasus Drive, Biggleswade
Bedfordshire SG18 8TQ
United Kingdom
Email: kluwerlaw@turpin-distribution.com

Printed on acid-free paper

ISBN 97890-411-8741-3

e-Book: ISBN 97890-411-8764-2
web-PDF: ISBN 97890-411-8794-9

This title is available on www.kluwerlawonline.com

Printed and Bound by CPI Group (UK) Ltd, Croydon, CR0 4YY.

The Authors

Rassie Malherbe is an emeritus Professor of Public Law at the Rand Afrikaans University in Johannesburg and specializes in constitutional law, human rights, education law and the interpretation of statutes. He is a graduate of the University of Stellenbosch (LLB, 1975) and the Rand Afrikaans University (LLD, 1992). He publishes widely, both nationally and internationally, and is the author and co-author of numerous textbooks, articles and case notes in the fields of constitutional law, human rights and education law. He is a member of the editorial committee of the *Tydskrif vir Suid-Afrikaanse Reg/Journal for South African Law* and of the executive of the South African Education Law and Policy Association. He served as an adviser during the South African constitution-making process in 1995 and 1996.

Dirk Brand is a qualified (non-practising) lawyer of the High Court of South Africa, and is currently an Extraordinary Senior Lecturer at the School of Public Leadership, Stellenbosch University. He is a graduate of the University of Stellenbosch (LLB, 1983; LLD, 2005) and the University of the Free State (LLM – European Union Law – 1996). His doctoral thesis was published as 'Financial Constitutional Law – a

The Authors

Comparison between Germany and South Africa'. He has published a number of articles and contributions to books, mainly on constitutional law. Currently he also serves as a Co-chair of the Co-production Study Group of the International Institute of Administrative Sciences (IIAS) and member of the Advisory Board of the Ubuntu Centre for African Studies at the West University of Timisoara, Romania.

Table of Contents

List of Abbreviations

ACDP	African Christian Democratic Party
ANC	African National Congress
BCLR	Butterworths Constitutional Law Reports
CC	Constitutional Court
DA	Democratic Alliance
DP	Democratic Party
EC	Electoral Commission
EFF	Economic Freedom Fighters
FFC	Financial and Fiscal Commission
IFP	Inkatha Freedom Party
KNC	KwaZulu-Natal Constitution
NC	National Constitution
NCOP	National Council of Provinces
NNP	New National Party
PAC	Pan African Congress
RSA	Republic of South Africa
SA	South African Law Reports
SAJHR	South African Journal on Human Rights
SALGA	South African Local Government Association
SALJ	South African Law Journal
SCA	Supreme Court of Appeal
StellLR	Stellenbosch Law Review
THRHR	Tydskrif vir Hedendaagse Romeins-Hollandse Reg
TSAR	Tydskrif vir Suid-Afrikaanse Reg
WCC	Western Cape Constitution
ZACC	South African Constitutional Court Reports

List of Abbreviations

The overthrow of apartheid and the establishment of a non-racial, democratic constitutional order in South Africa was one of the most fascinating examples of peaceful constitutional engineering during the second half of the twentieth century. Not only was a political solution found to a complicated situation that had caused much suffering and travail, but also the solution included a constitution which provided for modern democratic structures at all levels of government. An integral part of the new system is the sub-national arrangements providing for nine provinces whose relationship with the national government is based on strong, constitutionally entrenched, semi-federal principles. Although only one province has adopted its own constitution so far, whereas the others continue to function in terms of the sub-national constitutional arrangements provided in the national Constitution, sub-national government is firmly established in South Africa and forms a prominent and influential part of day-to-day government.

Sub-national government in South Africa is described and analysed in this volume against the background of the intense process of negotiation and the dramatic constitutional transformation of the 1990s, within the framework of the national Constitution and the constitutional order which the Constitution provides nationally and sub-nationally, and with a view to determine its true nature and possible future development. Relevant issues such as judicial authority, citizenship and the position of aliens, the constitutional protection of fundamental human rights, the protection of minorities, and local government are explained in broad terms in order to complete the South African constitutional picture.

The authors of this volume wish to thank the editor of the *International Encyclopaedia of Constitutional Law*, Prof. André Alen and, in particular, the editors of the monographs on Sub-national Constitutional Law, professors Robert Williams and Alan Tarr of Rutgers University, Camden, New Jersey, for their invitation to include in the series this monograph on South Africa. We wish to thank everyone who has assisted us in various ways to obtain the necessary information and who has been involved in the preparation and publication of the volume. Without their tireless efforts this publication would not have been possible.

We believe that democratic government, however fragile, has come to the Southern African subcontinent to stay. We believe that much still needs to be done to secure continued democratic government in every sphere of government. Many structural and other mechanisms and steps, of which education, full restoration of law and order, and sustained economic growth are but a few, need to be employed and taken to support democracy and allow democratic constitutional values and processes to take root and flourish in a unique Southern African pattern. We believe that strong provincial government is one of the mechanisms that should remain a feature of the South African Constitution and should be encouraged, as an instrument to devolve power, bring government to the people, increase political openness and accountability, and overall reinforce democracy. Like the democratic order itself, provincial government is still a fledgling component of the new South Africa that needs to be nurtured. Much work lies ahead and many difficulties need to be overcome. The structures are in place, however, and the excellent people who are involved are giving their best for the sake of a better future. This monograph is presented as a confirmation of the authors' belief that South Africa will succeed in its democratic quest. It is dedicated to the people of South Africa.

Revised Edition / Second Edition

Since this monograph was published initially much progress has been made in South Africa's democracy journey. After more than two decades of constitutional democracy there is still much work to be done, although there are also some successes to celebrate. Many free and fair elections for all three spheres of government took place since 1994, something that is still lacking in some other parts of Africa. The independence of the judiciary, which has undergone significant transformation, is treasured and is still an outstanding feature of South Africa's constitutional system. The significance of independent institutions that must support and strengthen constitutional democracy, the so-called Chapter 9 institutions, is confirmed by the various contributions of institutions such as the Auditor-General, the Public Protector, and the Independent Electoral Commission.

In recent years there has been increasing pressure on the Rechtsstaat and the supremacy of the constitution, which is an issue of great concern. The Constitutional Court, which in 2016 found that the president acted in contravention of the constitutional requirements of the top political office in the country, reiterated the importance of the pillars of the constitutional democracy and that everyone including the president and the parliament are subject to the Constitution. The need for constitutional education as well as a general awareness of supremacy of the constitution is evident. The huge socio-economic inequality in the country and poor service delivery in local communities over many years are serious issues to be dealt with by all three spheres of government, but in which sub-national governments can play an important role to make a positive impact in society.

In the area of sub-national constitutional law there are no new provincial constitutions, as was predicted. However, sub-national government is still an important part of the constitutional landscape in South Africa despite poor performance in some cases. Some provinces have in different ways attempted to give more content to their legitimate constitutional space. The increasing role played by political parties other than the ANC and the steady decline in support for the ANC has an influence on the continuous development of constitutional democracy in South Africa. The local government elections in 2016 were quite significant in this respect and resulted in most of the major metropolitan councils being governed by the DA, either on its own or with coalition partners. This development will also impact on the future development of sub-national constitutional law.

General Introduction

1. The South African sub-national units, the provinces, are a prominent feature of the country's constitutional landscape. As in all composite states, the provinces form an integral part of the system of government and any description of the South African constitutional order would be incomplete without a full account of these sub-national units. There are nine provinces, but as explained later in this Introduction, they have been created only recently in terms of the new constitutional order that replaced the apartheid system at the end of the previous century. Until the 1990s, sub-national government comprised many different types and variations, underwent numerous adaptations and mutations according to the whims of the government of the day, and was, among other things, subject for many decades to the racial differentiation which characterized the apartheid structures. It is nevertheless notable that sub-national government in South Africa has strong historical roots, and that it is now equally powerfully imbedded in the Constitution. In this Introduction, the recent constitutional history of South Africa is recounted in broad strokes, with particular reference to the development of the provinces, and an overview of the provincial constitutional structure is provided by way of an introduction to the more detailed discussions that follow in later chapters.

§1. Types, Names and Territory of Sub-national Units

2. The South African national Constitution (NC) provides for one type of sub-national or regional unit, viz the provinces. As is evident from the historical background sketched below, that was not always the case and different types of sub-national structures existed under previous constitutions. The present nine provinces were created by the interim NC of 1993, which was the result of the negotiations of the early 1990s on the democratization of apartheid South Africa. The existence of these provinces was confirmed in the final NC of 1996.

3. The boundaries of the provinces are protected in the NC. In terms of the NC, the Republic has the following provinces:[1] Eastern Cape, Free State, Gauteng, KwaZulu-

1. *See* C. De Coning, *The Territorial Imperative: Towards an Evaluation of the Provincial Demarcation Process*, in *Birth of a Constitution* 189 (B. De Villiers ed., Juta 1994); D. Welsh, *The Provincial Boundary Demarcation Process* 223 (De Villiers ed., Juta 1994).

Natal,[2] Mpumalanga, Northern Cape, Limpopo,[3] North-West, and Western Cape.[4] The boundaries of the provinces are those determined by the interim NC.[5] Altering the provincial boundaries requires an amendment to the NC and must be approved by a two-thirds majority in the National Assembly and the support of six provinces in the National Council of Provinces (NCOP), whereas the legislatures of the provinces that are affected must also concur.[6]

4. The Interim NC made provision for the amendment of provincial boundaries in the case of certain contested areas. Provision was made for referenda to determine, for instance, whether Northern Cape wished to remain a separate province, whether Eastern Cape should be divided into two provinces, and whether a considerable number of specified border districts in various parts of the country wanted to be included in other provinces.[7] A referendum had to be called in the province or district in question if a petition containing a certain minimum number of signatures was lodged with Parliament within six months of the commencement of the NC.[8] The result of such a referendum would have been final. Although some attempts were made in certain districts, no provincial boundary was amended under the Interim NC.[9]

5. Apparently, the territory of the provinces includes the adjacent territorial waters and the air space,[10] but this is relevant for the exercise of provincial government authority only insofar as functional areas with regard to which authority can be exercised in the territorial waters or the air space have been allocated to the provinces.

§2. Historical Background

6. By way of background, a brief overview of the recent South African constitutional history is provided below, with special reference to the democratization of South Africa during the 1990s, and the creation of the sub-national units, the provinces. This overview should facilitate a proper understanding of sub-national constitutional law in South Africa.

2. The original name, Natal, was amended by s. 12 Act 2 of 1994.
3. The original name, Northern Province, was changed to Limpopo, which is also the name of the river that forms the border with Zimbabwe, by s. 3 of the Constitution Eleventh Amendment Act 2003.
4. Section 103(1). Section 104(2) provides for the change of the name of a province by Parliament at the request of the provincial legislature of that province. At least two-thirds of the members of the legislature must support the resolution. Towards the end of 1994, the Pretoria-Witwatersrand-Vereeniging legislature requested in terms of the Interim NC that the name of the province be changed to Gauteng.
5. Section 103(2) and Sch. 1A. *See* s. 124(2) and Sch. 1 of the Interim NC. Schedule 1 contained meticulous particulars on the demarcation of every province.
6. Section 74(3) and (8).
7. *See* s. 124(5) and (6) and part 2 Sch. 1.
8. Section 124(3).
9. Section 124(11). *See* e.g., *Bushbuck Ridge Border Committee v. Government of the Northern Province* 1999 2 BCLR 193 (T).
10. M. Chaskalson and J. Klaaren, *Provincial Government*, in *Constitutional Law of South Africa* 4.1–2 (M. Chaskalson et al. eds, Juta 1998).

I. The Democratization of South Africa

7. The democratization of South Africa remains one of the most fascinating examples of constitutional engineering during the latter half of the twentieth century. There are several reasons for this.[11] First, it involved the overthrow of the apartheid system that offended the world and occupied its attention for so long. Secondly, it took place quite peacefully, a rare achievement in the volatile twentieth century. Thirdly, as a truly democratic constitutional state was established, it was not, as in so many other instances in developing states, simply a case of power changing hands from one autocratic regime to another.

8. The South African sub-national system as it now exists is a direct product of the negotiations leading up, first, to the interim NC of 1993, and then to the NC of 1996, and the provinces form an integral part of the present South African constitutional order. A brief look at the negotiating process of the 1990s would be appropriate.

9. By the end of the 1980s, South Africa was on the brink of large-scale disruption and it was evident that only a quick end to apartheid could save the country from civil war. The turning point was in 1990, with the lifting of the ban on organizations like the ANC and the PAC and the release or return to South Africa of their leaders, which dramatically accelerated the process of constitutional change. Serious talks on the constitutional future commenced shortly after and in December 1991, the majority of political parties and organizations signed a declaration of intent in which they committed themselves to draw up a new democratic constitution through negotiation.[12] During the first half of 1992, negotiations took place on the principles to be included in a new constitution. Agreement on the particulars of an interim NC was reached during 1993. Although a contentious issue throughout the process, strong, entrenched sub-national or provincial government became a feature of the interim NC during this phase as a mechanism to prevent a centralized system. The interim NC and other laws necessary to facilitate the transitional process were adopted by Parliament at the end of 1993. It was also agreed that elections for the interim Parliament would take place during April 1994, after which the interim Parliament, acting as a Constitutional Assembly, would immediately begin to draft the final NC within two years. The interim NC was promulgated on 28 January 1994 and took effect on 27 April 1994.[13]

10. The first democratic elections in the history of South Africa took place from 26 to 28 April 1994. Over 20 million voters went to the polls for the first time. The elections led to the establishment of brand new, non-racial legislative, executive, and judicial institutions in the national and provincial spheres, a process that would continue for a considerable time.[14] Mr Nelson Mandela, who spent twenty-seven years in gaol

11. R. Malherbe, *The South African Constitution*, *Zeitschrift für öffentliches Recht* 61–62 (2000).

12. G.E. Devenish, *The Making of the Interim Constitution*, THRHR 613 et seq. (1997); D. Van Wyk, *Introduction to the South African Constitution*, in *Rights and Constitutionalism: The New South African Legal Order* 131 et seq. (D. Van Wyk et al. eds, Juta 1994); P. De Vos and W. Freedman (eds), *South African Constitutional Law in Context* 15–26 (Oxford U. Press 2014).

13. Constitution of the Republic of South Africa Act 200 of 1993, as promulgated in *Government Gazette* 15466 of 28 Jan. 1994.

14. For various reasons, the local sphere took a while longer and local elections were only held in November 1994 and early in 1995.

for his opposition to apartheid, was elected formally by Parliament as the first black President and he assumed office on 10 May 1994, after which the other members of the executive and other office-bearers were elected and designated.

11. From 1994 to 1996, the Constitutional Assembly concentrated on the drafting of the final NC, a process characterized by its comprehensiveness, inclusiveness and intensity, the dedication and perseverance of the negotiators, and the commitment of all major role players to adopt the Constitution by consensus.[15] Every aspect of the process was directed at the promotion of consensus. Apart from the monumental volume of paperwork generated during the process, and the numerous options on all issues developed by advisers (also on the issue of sub-national government), the negotiations included the various ingenious formal and informal multi- and bilateral mechanisms that were created for the purpose of fostering consensus, the remarkably impartial role played by the chairpersons of these forums, and the conduct of the parties towards one another. Although vigorous opponents, an underlying respect and tolerance characterized the negotiators, which facilitated compromise and consensus. To the inclusive and consensus-seeking way in which the process was conducted, one should, of course, add that the Constitution as a whole has turned out to be a commendable document, which boldly established a democratic order, and provided several creative mechanisms for the resolution or accommodation of the concerns of most stakeholders. Despite some difficulties on which consensus remained elusive right up to the end, it was therefore no real surprise when the NC was finally adopted with only two opposing votes.[16] Of course, the Constitution is a compromise document and no single party can claim it to be 'theirs' only. Also, nobody who regards the Constitution reasonably and rationally can argue convincingly that they disagree with so many aspects that their support for the system itself is in jeopardy. For this reason, it is not at all presumptuous to call the Constitution the 'birth certificate' of the new nation.[17]

12. The constitutional text eventually adopted was submitted to the Constitutional Court for certification, but the Court held that not all provisions complied with the constitutional principles included in the interim NC and declined to certify the text.[18] In October 1996, the Constitutional Assembly approved the necessary amendments, and it was referred back to the Court for certification. The Court certified the amended text on 4 December 1996,[19] and the Constitution of the Republic of South Africa 1996

15. For a full account of the process, *see* H. Ebrahim, *The Soul of a Nation: Constitution-Making in South Africa* (Oxford U. Press 1998). *See also* H. Ebrahim, *The Constitutional Assembly – Drafting South Africa's New Constitution*, in *International Roundtable on Democratic Constitutional Development* 22–32 (Commonwealth Secretariat 1995); Z. Yacoob, *The Constitution-Making Process: An Overview*, Hum. Rights & Const. L.J. S. Afr. 18 (1996).
16. The Constitution was adopted by 421 votes to 2, with 10 abstentions.
17. Ebrahim, *supra* 256.
18. *In re: Certification of the Constitution of the Republic of South Africa, 1996* 1996 10 BCLR 1253 (CC).
19. *In re: Certification of the Amended Text of the Constitution of the Republic of South Africa, 1996* 1997 1 BCLR 1 (CC).

took effect on 4 February 1997.[20] Various laws, most of which pursuant to specific provisions of the interim NC and the final NC of 1996, have been adopted since 1993 to give effect to the new constitutional order.

13. From a constitutional point of view, the constitutional principles and the certification function of the Constitutional Court are of particular interest.[21] This formed part of the deal that there would be a two-stage transitional period in which a power-sharing government would govern in terms of the interim NC while the non-racial Parliament elected in terms of that Constitution would draw up the final NC. Accordingly, a set of thirty-four constitutional principles was included in the interim NC with which the final NC had to comply before coming into effect. The Constitutional Court was assigned the responsibility to certify that the NC complied with those principles. The constitutional principles focused on the democratic and other principles agreed upon during the negotiations, and included a commitment to a democratic system of government based on universal adult franchise, regular elections, a multi-party system, common citizenship for all, an entrenched constitution as supreme law, a justiciable bill of rights, equality before the law and the prohibition of discrimination, an independent judiciary, separation of powers, three spheres of government, and the distribution of powers among these spheres.[22] The status and powers of the different spheres of government, specifically those of the provinces, and the relationship between these spheres received particular attention in the principles.

14. In the *Certification* case, the Constitutional Court described its certification function as unprecedented and proceeded to explain its approach to this task.[23] It saw its function as strictly confined to measuring the constitutional text against the principles and not to express any view on the merits of the choices made. The principles contained the fundamental guidelines and prescribed the boundaries within which the NC had to be drafted. Therefore, every provision of the text had to be tested against every principle. This implied for the Court that the principles had to be applied purposively to promote the objective of creating a democratic constitutional state.[24] They should also be interpreted holistically and not with technical rigidity.

15. Much debate ensued about the nature of the constitutional principles, particularly on the question as to their function once the NC was certified. Some felt that being of such fundamental nature, they would continue to exist and exert an

---

20. Proclamation R6 of 1997 (*GG* 17737 of 24 Jan. 1997). It is incorrect to refer to the NC as Act 108 of 1996. The NC was adopted by the Constitutional Assembly and not by Parliament and cannot be numbered like an Act of Parliament – E.F.J. Malherbe, *Die nommering van die Grondwet van die Republiek van Suid-Afrika 1996: vergissing of onkunde?* TSAR 140 (1998).
21. *See* the discussion by I.M. Rautenbach, *Rautenbach -Malherbe, Constitutional Law* 24 et seq. (LexisNexis 2012).
22. Schedule 4 of the interim NC. Quite a number of principles also dealt with the relationship between the national and provincial spheres of government and the distribution of powers between them.
23. *In re: Certification of the Constitution of the Republic of South Africa 1996* 1996 10 BCLR 1253 (CC) paras 1 et seq.
24. Paragraphs 34–43.

influence on future amendments to the NC.[25] Others were of the opinion that their function was a transitional function that had been fulfilled once the NC was certified.[26] The fear that the basic principles on which the NC is founded can be revoked easily and arbitrarily if the constitutional principles have ceased to exist after the certification of the NC is unfounded. That purpose served by the principles has now been assumed by the strict entrenchment procedures in the NC which are designed specifically to protect the underlying principles and values of the NC.[27] After all, by implication, if not expressly, certification of the NC as being in compliance with the principles, meant that the Constitutional Court had held that the principles were now contained, or given effect to, in the provisions of the NC. The point made here is not necessarily that even the basic features of the NC can now be amended as long as the required procedures are followed. The courts may still disallow amendments that destroy the very democratic fabric of our system. A basic features-doctrine can therefore still develop, but then on its own merits for which it is not necessary to keep alive the constitutional principles. According to the Constitutional Court, the principles may, however, still be relevant in the interpretation of the NC, as a reasonable interpretation of the NC that is in line with the principles should be preferred over one that is not in line.[28]

16. One may conclude on the negotiating process of the 1990s that it was hard and intense, but peaceful and generally successful. As pointed out, most role players were tremendously dedicated and acted surprisingly constructively. They were totally committed to reach consensus on all major issues and succeeded in most respects. It was a comprehensive and informed process liberally enriched by comparative knowledge, but in which local circumstances and preferences prevailed whenever appropriate. The result is a NC that satisfies the aspirations of most South Africans, and lays the foundation for a truly democratic constitutional state.

17. It is in terms and as a result of the process described above that the peculiar South African sub-national system, providing for nine constitutionally recognized provinces, has come into being.

---

25. A. Butler, *The 1996 Constitution Bill, Its Amending Power, and the Constitutional Principles*, Hum. Rights & Const. L.J. S. Afr. 24 (1996); A. Butler, *The Constitutional Court Certification Judgements*, SALJ 703 (1997). *See also* M. Wiechers, *Namibia: The 1982 Constitutional Principles and Their Legal Significance*, in *Namibia: Constitutional and International Law Issues* 1, 17–21 (D. Van Wyk et al. eds, University of South Africa, 1991 1991), where this view was propagated in respect of Namibia, where similar principles applied. *See generally* F. Venter, *Requirements for a New Constitution: The Imperatives of the Constitutional Principles*, SALJ 32 (1995).
26. E.F.J. Malherbe, *Die sertifisering van die 1996 Grondwet*, TSAR 356, 361–362 (1997); M. Chaskalson and D. Davis, *Constitutionalism, the Rule of Law, and the First Certification Judgement*, SAJHR 430 (1997); A. Butler, *The Constitutional Court Certification Judgements*, SALJ 703 (1997) (n 14).
27. Section 74 – Malherbe *supra* 358–359; *see* the discussion in II below.
28. *In re: Certification of the Constitution of the Republic of South Africa, 1996* 1996 10 BCLR 1253 (CC); 1996 4 SA 744 (CC) para. 42.

II. Development of the Provinces

18. Apart from the historical considerations, briefly related below, the reasons for the existence of a sub-national system in South Africa generally relate to the advantages of the vertical distribution of government authority. These advantages, which also apply to South Africa, can be summarized briefly as follows: the centralization of power is countered; the democratic principle to involve the people in government processes is furthered; more effective rendering of services takes place; cultural, religious, and ethnic differences can be managed better; and government at sub-national level leads to quicker decision-making, greater sensitivity to regional or local circumstances, and more direct control by the people over the exercise of government authority. In addition, the measure of mistrust between the negotiators during the 1990s reinforced the opposition of many parties to a more centralized system. On the other hand, a sub-national system may entail greater costs in respect of government and administrative structures, and may cause conflict between levels of government.[29] Added to these fears was the uneasiness of the ANC that strong provincial government could thwart its efforts to transform effectively the apartheid society.

19. As in other states, the special nature and form of the South African sub-national system is influenced by historical, demographic, economic, and social factors and circumstances. In many federations, the constituent states existed before the founding of the respective federations. That was also the position in South Africa at Union in 1910 with regard to the former four provinces. As former British colonies, they were the building blocks of the new national state created at the beginning of the twentieth century. In other cases, government institutions at regional level were created and developed after the establishment of the state to realize one or more of the general purposes mentioned above. Recent developments in some Western European states are examples in this regard.[30] The formation of the present nine South African provinces is another example.

20. The South African provinces exist in terms of the NC and, as such, are the product of negotiations, but they are also the result of a process which began at Union, and upon which historical, political, ideological, physical, economic, and ethnic factors have had a decisive influence over the years.

21. The Union of South Africa was created in 1910, when the two British colonies and two former Boer republics that existed at that time merged into one, unitary state and became the provinces of the new state. The provinces exercised authority at sub-national level over particular matters through their own legislative and executive structures.[31] These constituent units were the Cape Colony, Natal (the two British colonies), Transvaal, and the Orange Free State (the two former Boer

29. L. Schlemmer, *Regionalism in South Africa: Opportunities Missed?* in De Villiers, *supra* 243–245.
30. *See in general* about the developments in Western Europe, Council of Europe, *The Reforms of Local and Regional Authorities in Europe: Theory, Practice and Critical Appraisals* (1983). *See also* the contributions in B. De Villiers (ed.), *Evaluating Federal Systems* (Juta, 1994) and Department of Constitutional Development and Provincial Affairs, *Intergovernmental Relations: An International Comparative Study* (1998).
31. *See* the South Africa Act, Edw VII, C9.

republics), each with its distinct history, peoples, and economic, cultural and social circumstances. The political system, including the provincial system, created at Union was characterized by the fact, first, that it was a unitary system, that Parliament was supreme and that the provinces were subject to national legislation and, second, that it provided only for political participation by whites, setting in motion the development of the apartheid system. Since Union, South Africa has been characterized by the existence of different types of government institutions at sub-national level. The 1961 Constitution in terms of which South Africa left the British crown and became a republic, did not affect the provincial system.[32] In 1986, pursuant to the changes brought about by the 1983 Constitution,[33] in terms of which the Coloured and Indian minorities were included in the white dominated parliament and government, the elected legislative provincial councils, and executive committees were abolished and replaced by provincial executive committees appointed by the national government.[34]

22. In addition to the provinces, self-governing territories existed at sub-national level in which black communities in the rural areas exercised authority over a wide range of matters. As a part of apartheid policies, these territories came into being over the years in terms of various laws aimed at regulating the constitutional position of blacks separately.[35] The object was to lead these territories to full political autonomy and four of them even became independent in terms of legislation passed by the South African Parliament.[36] By the beginning of the 1990s, then, there were in South Africa four provinces, six so-called self-governing territories and four so-called independent states, each type with its own measure of autonomy and its own distinct relationship with the national government, leading to a quite complicated sub-national system.

23. All these sub-national institutions – provinces as well as self-governing and independent homelands – were abolished by the Interim NC and replaced by a uniform sub-national system. The Interim NC provided for a new demarcation of the country into nine provinces into which all previous sub-national institutions were integrated. The Interim NC contained considerable detail on this demarcation of the country into provinces, the legislative and executive institutions of each province, and their powers.[37] Essentially, this sub-national dispensation has been retained in the final NC. Based on the principle of co-operative government, discussed in Part I below, various particulars regarding the relationship between the provinces and the national and local spheres

32. *See* Act 32 of 1961.
33. Act 110 of 1983.
34. *See* the Provincial Government Act 69 of 1986.
35. The key instrument was the National States Constitution Act 21 of 1971. In past publications on South African constitutional law under the old system, extensive attention was given to the constitutional development of the black communities. *See* e.g., M. Wiechers, *VerLoren van Themaat Staatsreg* (Butterworth, 1981); D.H. Basson and H.P. Viljoen, *South African Constitutional Law* (Juta, 1988); G. Carpenter, *Introduction to South African Constitutional Law* (Butterworth, 1987); and L. Boulle, B. Harris and C. Hoexter, *Constitutional and Administrative Law* (Juta, 1989). *See also* F. Venter, *Suid-Afrikaanse Bantoestaatsreg* (LLD thesis University of Potchefstroom 1978).
36. Viz Transkei, Bophuthatswana, Venda and Ciskei. The international community never recognized the independence of any of them.
37. *See* the contributions in De Villiers *supra* ; G. Erasmus, *Provincial Government Under the 1993 Constitution: What Direction Will It Take?* SA Public Law 407 (1994).

of government have been added, however.[38] This will influence the further development of the provincial system.[39]

24. At first, during the negotiations of the early 1990s, there was neither consensus on nor any great enthusiasm for the idea of a number of sub-national units or provinces with constitutional status and powers. The ANC regarded the notion of provinces as contrary to its vision of a centrally controlled system and strongly believed that a system of relatively autonomous provinces could create footholds for the perpetuation of apartheid inequalities that would obstruct the ANC's commitment to eradicate all discrimination from the past and transform society on the basis of its policies of non-racialism and non-sexism. Other parties propagated strong provinces exactly because they opposed a centralized system in which one party dominated the whole country. This remained a bone of contention throughout the negotiation process on the interim NC. Apart from the actual provisions of the interim NC, one of the consequences of this difference of opinion was that several of the constitutional principles included in the interim NC with which the final NC had to comply, dealt with the status of the provinces, the distribution of powers between the national and provincial governments and the constitutional relationship between the different spheres of government.

25. Eventually, the provisions of the final NC dealing with sub-national government should be regarded as a compromise, and as such probably not really favouring one or the other of the original viewpoints. The constitutional status of the provinces and the relationship among the spheres of government are, of course, strongly influenced by the constitutional principle of co-operative government, which is discussed in Part I below. The way in which the provisions of the NC are fleshed out by national and provincial legislation and are applied by the courts on the basis of this principle is discussed in various other chapters.

§3. Overview of Provincial Constitutional Structure

26. As the provinces have been created by the NC, Chapter 6 of the NC makes full provision for the constitutional structures that had to be set up in every province. Eight of the nine provinces function in terms of the constitutional arrangements provided in the NC, which are discussed in full in Chapter 1 of Part II of this volume. However, the NC also provides that each provincial legislature may adopt a constitution for that province, which may differ from the provincial constitutional arrangements in the NC in respect of legislative and executive structures and processes. One province, Western Cape, has so far availed itself of the opportunity to adopt its own constitution, although another, KwaZulu-Natal, made a failed attempt to make a constitution. For a complete explanation of sub-national government in South Africa, both the developments in the latter two provinces and the arrangements applicable in all provinces except the Western

38. In terms of the Interim NC, the further development of the provincial system was to receive priority attention from the Constitutional Assembly, and the Constitutional Assembly had to consider any recommendations by the Commission on Provincial Government and any reaction by the provincial governments to such recommendations (s. 161(1)).

39. *See* the full explanation of the provincial system by D. Besdziek, *Provincial Government*, in *Government and Politics in the New South Africa* 147–192 (A. Venter ed., Van Schaik 1998).

Cape should be considered. The constitutional structures of the eight provinces are discussed in Part II. The failed KwaZulu-Natal Constitution is discussed in Chapter 1 of that Part. The Western Cape Constitution is discussed at some length in Chapter 2 of Part II.

27. In 2007, the national Department of Provincial and Local Government initiated a policy review process that focused on the future of provinces and local governments in South Africa.[40] Despite some political views about changes in the number and size of provinces, nothing changed after the end of this exercise.

28. The structures created for the provinces in terms of the NC broadly correspond with the national governmental structures discussed in Part I. Provision is made for provincial legislatures directly elected in terms of an electoral system based on proportional representation. Every provincial legislature, ranging in size from thirty to eighty members each, elects its own Speaker and Deputy Speaker. The provincial legislatures have the legislative powers allocated to them by the NC, which include the power to make laws on a number of exclusive matters and the power to make laws on a larger number of matters on which Parliament may also legislate, the so-called concurrent matters. The constitutional significance of these provisions is, first, that the powers of the different spheres of government are constitutionally entrenched and, secondly, that the courts are formally empowered to resolve disputes between the spheres on the constitutional distribution of their powers. The legislatures are elected for five years, but their terms may be cut short under certain circumstances, for example if a motion of no-confidence in the Premier is adopted, leading to his or her resignation, and the provincial legislature is unable to elect a new Premier within thirty days.

29. The executive authority of a province is vested in a Premier, who is elected by the provincial legislature from among its members. The Premier, who, in contrast to the national President, upon election retains his or her seat, exercises the executive authority together with the other members of the Executive Council, who are appointed by the Premier from among the members of the provincial legislature, but who retain their seats. Thus, the NC provides in each province for a parliamentary provincial government that is dependent on the support of the provincial legislature and can be removed from power by the adoption of a motion of no-confidence in the provincial legislature. The public administrations of the provinces form part of the national public service, although provincial governments are responsible for the members of the public service in their provincial administrations. In the relevant provinces, seven of them, there are also provincial houses for traditional leaders.

40. B. De Villiers (ed.), *Review of Provinces and Local Governments in South Africa: Constitutional Foundations and Practice*, Konrad Adenauer Stiftung, *Occasional Papers*, 2 (2008).

Part I. The National Context

30. Because the South African provinces are creatures of the NC and are dependent for their existence, their powers, and their structures on the NC (except, in the latter event, the Western Cape, which adopted its own constitution), the national context within which the provinces exist and function needs to be explained to some extent. Furthermore, the NC expressly envisages a particularly close relationship between the different spheres of government by providing that these spheres are 'distinctive, interdependent, and interrelated,' and that their relationship must be founded on the principle of co-operative government. The following topics are accordingly addressed in this Part: the form of the South African state (Chapter 1), an overview of the national Constitution and structure, in which some of the salient features of the national Constitution are explained briefly (Chapter 2), the constitutional relationship between the spheres of government (Chapter 3), and the exercise of judicial authority in South Africa (Chapter 4).

31. In terms of section 1 of the NC, the Republic of South Africa is one, sovereign democratic state. In fact, South Africa is a composite state with certain strong federal features. A closer examination reveals some unique features, but not more so than in many other systems. As mentioned in the General Introduction, during the negotiations of the early 1990s opinion differed strongly on the form that the new democratic state should take. Mainly for political reasons, some negotiators favoured a federal and others a unitary system. The result was a compromise, which was essentially confirmed in the final NC. Different opinions were subsequently expressed on the exact form of state that had in fact been adopted.

32. To furnish a conclusive answer to the question of whether South Africa is now a federation, simply from the provisions of the NC on the entrenched provincial system, would probably not be feasible. It would negate the complexity of modern forms of state *and* their dynamic nature and, in any case, the answer would change nothing of the constitutional arrangements and position explained in this publication. The answer may also differ to the extent that one chooses to concentrate on the formal constitutional distribution of powers (which, from the point of view of constitutional law, is the essential feature of a federation), or on the extent or even the volume of such powers, in other words, the extent of autonomy enjoyed by the provinces.

33. The difficulty to answer theoretical questions like these satisfactorily are aptly illustrated by the description of the system created in terms of the Interim NC in a single contribution as a 'federal political system', 'typical of regionalized unitary systems,' and a 'hybrid system.'[41] In a recent contribution, South Africa was referred

41. R. Watts, *Is the New Constitution Federal or Unitary?*, in *Birth of a Constitution* 75, 85–86 (B. De Villiers ed., Juta 1994). J. Klaaren, *Federalism*, in *Constitutional Law of South Africa* (M. Chaskalson et al. eds, Juta 1998) 5.1 refers to 'a federal system with unitary features.' *See also* D.H. Basson, *South Africa's Interim Constitution: Text and Notes* 185 (Juta 1994) who states: 'It would appear as if the interim Constitution provides for such a system which is neither fully federal nor fully unitary'; G. Devenish, *The Prospects for Constitutional Litigation in Relation to the Powers of the Central and Provincial Governments as Contained in the Interim Constitution, and Related Issues*, THRHR 34, 42 (1996):

[S]ome form of quasi-federalism will emerge from the jurisprudence of the Constitutional Court' and 'The interim Constitution does not create a conventional federation, nor is it manifestly a unitary state, but its exact configuration is somewhere between the two. Indeed it is a *via media*, the nature of which will only become clearer when the system is put into operation and the uncertainty resolved by the Constitutional Court.

to as 'quasi-federal', 'federal,' 'a highly centralized federal system,' 'a relatively centralized federal system,' and 'a multi-level system of government.'[42]

34. It seems as if a lot also depends on the dynamics of government and as if it is for various political and practical reasons quite possible for South Africa to develop either in a more federal or a more centralist direction. Without losing sight of these possibilities – it should be possible to discern certain tendencies – this publication focuses on the formal constitutional arrangements in respect of sub-national government and refrains from commentary which at this stage can be nothing but speculation.

42. R. Simeon, *Considerations on the Design of Federations: The South African Constitution in Comparative Context*, SA Public Law 42 (1998); De Vos & Freedman (*supra*) 59. However, *see* C. Tapscott, *Intergovernmental Relations in South Africa: A Comparative Analysis*, *Intergovernmental Relations: An International Comparative Study* 9, 27 (Department of Constitutional Development and Provincial Affairs 1998) who states that labels such as 'federal' and 'unitary' are less important than what actually happens in practice.

Chapter 2. Overview of National Constitution and Structure

35. The NC is a comprehensive and detailed document which provides for a complex democratic constitutional order. One may describe the NC as a compromise constitution (it is, after all, the product of intense negotiations), which establishes a constitutional democracy specifically aimed at fundamental social change in a post-apartheid era. For the purposes of this monograph, it would be appropriate to highlight a number of particularly significant features of the NC that have a direct or otherwise strong bearing on sub-national government.[43]

§1. Majority Government

36. The first, quite obvious, feature of the South African constitutional order is the fact that the country now has a democratic political system. Franchise has been extended to all adult citizens, irrespective of race, colour, or creed, resulting in a democratically elected national government that represents the majority of the people. An electoral system of proportional representation based on the simple list system has been adopted and seats in the national Parliament and the provincial legislatures are being allocated to political parties directly proportional to the percentage of votes each obtains in elections. Much has been written about alternative electoral systems that could be considered, for example, a mixed system as in Germany,[44] but it can be expected that the present system will be retained for the time being. In 2002 the Cabinet approved the appointment of a task team under the leadership of Dr Frederik Van Zyl Slabbert to investigate a new electoral system for South Africa. This task team recommended a mixed electoral system consisting of constituencies as well as proportional representation based on party lists, but the recommendations were not accepted by the national government.[45] The national and each provincial executive are appointed from among the members of the respective legislatures. In most cases strong majority governments are in power, but in the Western Cape a coalition government has been formed after the 1999 elections as no party was able to score an outright victory, and in KwaZulu-Natal the two strongest parties, the IFP and the ANC, entered into a voluntary coalition. The IFP also served in President Mbeki's national Cabinet after the 1999 elections. After the 2014 national and provincial elections the ANC governs eight out of the nine provinces while the Democratic Alliance, which is the main opposition party in parliament, governs the Western Cape. All governments are

---

43. *See* e.g., R. Malherbe, *A New Beginning: Introducing the South African Constitution and Bill of Rights*, Netherlands Q. Hum. Rights 45–65 (2000); *The South African Constitution*, Zeitschrift für öffentliches Recht 61–100 (2000).
44. *See* e.g., J. De Ville and N. Steytler (eds), *Voting in 1999: Choosing an Electoral System* (Butterworths 1996); G.E. Devenish, *Electoral Systems and Protection of Minorities in Order to Further Social and Political Stability and Integration: The South African Experience*, SA Public Law 111 (1998); M. Faure, *The Electoral Systems Issue in South African Politics*, Konrad Adenauer Stiftung, *Occasional Papers* (February 1999).
45. Report of the Electoral Task Team, January 2003 12.

parliamentary executives dependent on the support of their respective legislatures. During the 2016 local government elections the ANC lost significant support in many parts of the country and for the first time lost the control of most of the major metropolitan councils.

37. A majority national government coming to power has had the result that policies on many issues have changed dramatically. Driven by its determination to eradicate all forms of discrimination and create a non-racial and non-sexist society based on social justice, human dignity, equality, and freedom, the government is developing policies and frameworks directed at the transformation of most existing systems and institutions. Especially in the fields of social welfare, health care, education, land and labour relations, laws have been adopted that will have far-reaching consequences in the time to come. In South Africa's continuously evolving constitutional democracy the growth of opposition parties and the existence of more coalition governments at local level after the 2016 local government elections will have an influence on policy issues at national and provincial levels of government.

38. The national legislative and executive structures are explained briefly in the paragraphs that follow.

I. Parliament

A. Composition

39. Parliament consists of two Houses, the National Assembly, and the National Council of Provinces (NCOP). The National Assembly represents the people and ensures government by the people by:

- electing the President;
- providing a forum for the public consideration of issues;
- passing legislation; and
- overseeing and controlling the executive.[46]

40. The NCOP represents the provinces in Parliament and ensures that provincial interests are taken into account in national decision-making by:

- participating in the national legislative process; and
- providing a forum for the public consideration of issues affecting the provinces.[47]

41. The National Assembly consists of 400 members directly elected according to the system of proportional representation mentioned above. For the election of the National Assembly every citizen 18 years of age and older, and complying with certain basic voter qualifications, has the right to vote. In order to vote, one must register as a voter on the common voters' list and must be in the possession of a bar-coded identity document. Persons of unsound mind, or who apply for registration fraudulently, or

46. Section 42(3).
47. Section 42(4).

who are not ordinarily resident in the voting district in which they apply, may not register.[48]

42. The NCOP of ninety members is composed of ten delegates per province which consist of six permanent and four special delegates.[49] The permanent delegates are designated by each provincial legislature according to the proportional strength of the political parties in the legislature. The special delegates of each province consist of the provincial Premier and three other members of the legislature, usually members of the provincial executive, designated from time to time by the legislature. The purpose is to involve the provincial executives in the activities of the NCOP. This is a unique attempt analogous to the composition of the German *Bundesrat*,[50] to improve the direct involvement of the provinces in national decision-making.[51]

43. Members of Parliament must be qualified voters. In addition, they may not be insolvent, mentally ill, in public service or convicted of certain offences. Members vacate their seats when they cease to qualify, but members of the NCOP may be recalled by the party that nominated him or her.[52] The notion of an imperative mandate applied for a while to members of the National Assembly, as the interim NC provided that a member who changes party vacates his or her seat. This provision was retained in the final NC.

44. Parliament is elected for a term of five years, but can be dissolved earlier under certain circumstances:[53]

(a) When the National Assembly adopts a motion of no-confidence in the President, the President and ministers must resign and the National Assembly must elect a new President. If the National Assembly is unable to elect a new President within thirty days, Parliament must be dissolved for an election. As a matter of fact, the NC provides that Parliament must dissolve if a vacancy in the office of President exists for whatever reason, and the National Assembly fails to elect a President within thirty days.
(b) The President must dissolve Parliament if the National Assembly adopts a resolution to that effect, and three years have elapsed after the previous election.

48. Section 8(2) of the Electoral Act 73 of 1998. Despite the limitation it imposed on the right to vote, the requirement of a bar-coded ID was held to be constitutional in *New National Party of South Africa v. Government of the RSA* 1999 5 BCLR 489 (CC) on account of its salutary objective to eliminate fraud and other irregularities. In *August v. Electoral Commission* 1999 4 BCLR 363 (CC) the actions of the Electoral Commission to exclude prisoners from registration, and effectively disenfranchising them, was held to be unconstitutional – as the NC was silent on the issue, the Commission did not have statutory authorization for this action. In *Kham and Others v. Electoral Commission and Another [2015] ZACC 37* it was held that it is the duty of the Electoral Commission to ensure that voters are registered in the correct voting district where they are ordinarily resident, which is crucial in municipal elections.
49. Section 60.
50. Sections 50–51 of the German Constitution.
51. De Vos (*supra*) 134–142; C. Murray and R. Simeon, *From Paper to Practice: The National Council of Provinces after Its First Year*, 14(1) SA Public Law 96–141 (1999).
52. Section 62(4)(b) and (c).
53. Section 49.

B. Powers

45. The national legislative authority of the Republic is vested in Parliament.[54] Parliament has the power to amend the NC, pass legislation with regard to any matter (including those matters on which Parliament shares concurrent powers with the provinces, but excluding those matters under the exclusive jurisdiction of the provinces), and assign any of its powers, except the power to amend the NC, to any other legislature. Parliament may adopt legislation that is reasonably necessary or incidental to the effective exercise of its powers relating to the concurrent matters. Parliament may also, under the special circumstances explained before, intervene in provincial affairs by adopting legislation on the exclusive provincial matters. The relationship between Parliament and the provincial legislatures is discussed in more detail in Chapter 3 of this Part.

46. In the exercise of its legislative powers Parliament is subject to the NC, which is the supreme law of the Republic, and it must act in accordance with and within the parameters of the NC.[55] Any law made by Parliament that is inconsistent with the NC is invalid. It also means that Parliament may not delegate its legislative powers inconsistently with the NC. Delegation of subordinate legislative powers to the executive is in order, but the delegation of plenary legislative authority to amend the very law under which the delegation was made, would be unconstitutional.[56]

C. Functioning

47. The South African Parliament has a continuous session, starting on the day of its first sitting after an election and ending on the day it is dissolved for the next election. The National Assembly is chaired by its Speaker, who, together with the Deputy Speaker, is elected by the Assembly at its first sitting. The NCOP has a Chairperson and two Deputy Chairpersons all of whom are elected by the NCOP. One Deputy Chairperson rotates annually among the provinces.[57]

48. Parliament uses four types of committees,[58] ad hoc and standing committees of each House, and joint ad hoc and joint standing committees, both of which consist of members of both Houses. The standing committees of the National Assembly are the most important. They are appointed for the different portfolios of members of the executive, and have the responsibility to consider all bills introduced in Parliament, and to maintain oversight of the executive by conducting enquiries, hearing evidence, etc.

---

54. Section 43.
55. Section 44(4). Rules of Parliament may thus also be declared invalid in case of a conflict with any provision of the Constitution. *See Oriani-Ambrosini, MP v. Sisulu, MP Speaker of the National Assembly* [2012] ZACC 27; 2012 (6) SA 588 (CC); 2013 (1) BCLR 14 (CC); *Democratic Alliance v. Speaker of National Assembly and Others* [2016] ZACC 8.
56. *Executive Council of the Western Cape Legislature v. President of the RSA* 1995 10 BCLR 1289 (CC); 1995 4 SA 877 (CC). *See also* §4 of Ch. 4 below.
57. Section 64(3).
58. *See* the exposition of Rautenbach, *Rautenbach Malherbe Constitutional Law* 110–111 (2012).

D. *Legislative Process*[59]

49. Bills are classified on the basis of the difference in the legislative procedures that apply to each category. There are four types of bills: constitutional amendments, ordinary bills that affect the provinces, ordinary bills that do not affect the provinces, and money bills.[60] The basic procedures that apply to each category are explained in the NC itself, in particular when it comes to the relationship between the two Houses and the resolution of disagreements between the Houses. As a law could therefore be unconstitutional if the wrong procedure was followed in its adoption by Parliament, a 'tagging' or classification committee consisting of the Speaker and Deputy Speaker of the National Assembly and the Chairperson and Deputy Chairpersons of the NCOP classifies each bill introduced in Parliament and determines which procedure to follow in each case.[61] For the same reason, the committee also monitors amendments that may be adopted during the consideration of the bill.

50. The legislative process in Parliament can be explained briefly as follows:[62]

(a) Normally, bills, the great majority of which are initiated by the executive, are introduced in the National Assembly (although a bill affecting the provinces may also be introduced in the NCOP). Two things happen before introduction. First, all bills must be published for comment, unless good reasons are advanced why this could not have been done. Secondly, in order to allow committees an opportunity to plan their activities ahead, bills must also *before* introduction be submitted informally to Parliament for referral to the committees, unless it would result in prejudice to the state or the public.

(b) Upon introduction, a bill is regarded as having been read a first time and is formally referred to the relevant portfolio committee for consideration. (In the case of a money bill like the budget, there is a formal introduction in which the Minister of Finance gives his budget speech before introducing the bill.) The committee considers every aspect of the bill, may hear evidence on it, and may amend the bill before submitting it to the House. (Initially the finance committee was not allowed to amend the budget, but the NC now creates that possibility.[63])

(c) The House conducts a second reading debate in which only the principles of the bill are discussed; the assumption being that the detail was considered in the committee. (In the case of the budget, this is called the first reading debate.) Should a member put amendments on the order paper before the conclusion of the debate, the bill is referred back to the committee upon conclusion of the debate without a vote being taken. When the committee reports back, any new amendments are then considered before a vote on the second reading of the bill is taken. (In the case of the budget, the budget is divided into its different votes, each of which

59. Rautenbach (2012) (*supra*) 112–120.
60. Rautenbach (2012) (*supra*) 116–117.
61. The Joint Rules of Parliament provides for the tagging committee – r. 151–158, 160.
62. Sections 73–82 of the NC, read with the Rules of the two Houses and the Joint Rules of Parliament.
63. The Money Bills Amendment Procedure and Related Matters Act 9 of 2009 was adopted in terms of s. 77(3) of the NC.

are discussed separately over a period of a few months, before the budget is formally adopted after a brief second reading debate.)

(d) If the bill is adopted at second reading, it is referred to the other House where more or less the same procedure is followed.

(e) When the NCOP considers bills affecting the provinces, those bills are referred to the various provincial legislatures for consideration in order for the latter to confer mandates on their delegates in the NCOP in terms of section 65(2) of the NC. Section 65 provides that in the case of bills affecting the provinces, each province has one vote, and provincial legislatures must confer authority on their delegations in the NCOP to cast that vote on their behalf. In the case of other bills, the members of the NCOP vote individually.

(f) When there is a disagreement between the Houses on an ordinary bill affecting the provinces, a mediation committee is appointed to iron out the differences. Should the Houses still fail to reach agreement, the National Assembly may allow the bill to lapse, or may adopt a bill (either the bill as originally adopted by the Assembly, or the bill as recommended by the mediation committee) with a two-thirds majority, which is in the final analysis the way in which disagreements on this category of bills are resolved. A disagreement on other ordinary bills and on money bills is resolved by the National Assembly affirming its original adoption of the bill.

(g) Finally, the bill is submitted to the President for his assent, upon which the bill becomes a law. The President may refer the bill back if he has reservations on its constitutionality. If he is still not satisfied when Parliament resubmits the bill, he may refer it to the Constitutional Court for a decision.[64]

There is provision for a form of abstract control over laws in the sense that a third of the members of the National Assembly may within thirty days of the President's assent to a law apply to the Constitutional Court for an order declaring the law unconstitutional.[65]

The procedures relating to the consideration of constitutional amendments are discussed elsewhere.[66]

51. The classification of bills into bills affecting the provinces (section 76 bills), bills not affecting the provinces (section 75 bills), and mixed bills (bills with section 76 and section 75 components, which then have to be separated during the legislative process) have been criticized as too complicated. Some feel, for example, that this classification should be applied more flexibly.[67]

64. Section 79. In the one case so far in which the President exercised this power, the Court agreed with him and declared parts of the bill unconstitutional on the ground that it interfered with the constitutional powers of the provinces – *see Ex parte President of the Republic of South Africa In re: Constitutionality of the Liquor Bill* 2000 1 BCLR 1 (CC).

65. Section 80.

66. Section 2 below.

67. Department of Provincial and Local Government, *The Intergovernmental Relations Audit: Towards a Culture of Co-operative Government* (December 1999) 131.

II. The Executive

52. The national executive authority is vested in the President, who exercises the authority together with the other members of Cabinet.[68] The National Assembly elects the President by majority vote from among its members, and the President appoints the Cabinet from among the members of the Assembly.

A. The President

53. The President has the powers entrusted by the NC and other legislation, including the power to assent to bills adopted by Parliament, summon Parliament for an extraordinary sitting, make constitutional appointments, appoint commissions of inquiry, appoint, and receive diplomats, call a national referendum, pardon offenders. and confer honours. The Cabinet, chaired by the President, is responsible for implementing and initiating national legislation, developing and implementing national policy, and co-ordinating the functions of state departments and administrations.

54. At its first sitting after every election, the National Assembly elects a President as head of state and of government. The term of the President is, in other words, linked to that of Parliament. The President assumes office within five days and the term ends when the person next elected President assumes office. No one may hold office for more than two terms. The President may be removed from office for political reasons, and if the National Assembly adopts a motion of no-confidence in the President, the President and the other members of the Cabinet must resign. The President may also be removed for non-political reasons by a resolution adopted by the National Assembly with a two-thirds majority.[69] This may happen on the grounds of a serious violation of the NC or the law, serious misconduct, or inability to perform the functions of the office. In the first case of this nature in South Africa the Constitutional Court in 2016 ruled that the President failed to uphold, defend, and respect the Constitution when he did not comply with the remedial action taken against him by the Public Protector regarding the misuse of public funds for improvements at his private residence.[70] The subsequent process in the National Assembly to remove the President from office in view of the serious violation of the Constitution did not succeed due to the fact that the ANC had a large enough majority in the National Assembly to defeat the motion.

B. Cabinet

55. The Cabinet consists of the President, the Deputy President, and the ministers. The President appoints the Deputy President and any number of ministers from among the members of the National Assembly, and may appoint not more than two ministers from outside the National Assembly.[71] The President assigns to members of the Cabinet

68. Section 85.
69. Section 89.
70. *Economic Freedom Fighters v. Speaker of the National Assembly and Others; Democratic Alliance v. Speaker of the National Assembly and Others 2016 (5) BCLR 618 (CC); 2016 (3) SA 580 (CC).*
71. Section 91. For example, from the NCOP.

their responsibilities. A number of deputy ministers may also be appointed to assist ministers, but they are not members of the Cabinet. The majority of ministers that served under President Thabo Mbeki were members of the majority party in the National Assembly, the ANC (which after the 1999 elections held 62% of the seats), but in terms of an election pact between the ANC and the IFP, a few ministers from the IFP had been included in the Cabinet. After the 2014 elections all ministers in the Cabinet are members of the majority party in the National Assembly, the ANC. Members of the Cabinet are collectively and individually accountable to Parliament for the exercise of their powers, and must report regularly to Parliament. Members of the Cabinet must act in accordance with a code of ethics prescribed by-law.[72] They may not undertake any other paid work, act in any way inconsistent with their office, expose themselves to any risk of a conflict between their official responsibilities and personal interests, or use their position to enrich themselves or improperly benefit anybody else.[73]

III. Other National Structures

56. Other national constitutional structures that may be relevant are mentioned in §6 below.

§2. Constitutional Supremacy

I. Constitutional Supremacy versus Parliamentary Sovereignty

57. From a constitutional point of view the most significant feature of the NC is that it is the supreme law of South Africa. The adoption of the principle of constitutional supremacy[74] is without doubt the most fundamental and far-reaching change to the South African legal system during the previous century, if not ever. For nearly two centuries the legal system was dominated by parliamentary sovereignty, in terms of which Parliament was supreme and subject to no other authority, not even the courts.[75] Overnight, however, parliamentary sovereignty was abolished and the NC has become the supreme law of the Republic. All government bodies, including Parliament, are subject to the NC, and any law or conduct, including parliamentary legislation, inconsistent with it is invalid and can be struck down by the courts.[76] This also makes South Africa formally a constitutional state, in which everybody, including the state and all its organs, agencies and functionaries, is subject to the law. This is the critical constraint under which the majority government exercises its powers.

---

72. Executive Members' Ethics Act 82 of 1998, in terms of which a Code of Ethical Conduct and Disclosure of Members' Interests For Assembly And Permanent Council Members was adopted by Parliament on 13 Mar. 2014.
73. Section 96.
74. Section 2 of the NC.
75. *See* e.g., M. Wiechers, *Staatsreg* (1981) 22.
76. Section 2. *See* Rautenbach (2012) (*supra*) 8–10.

58. The result of this fundamental change was instantaneous and far-reaching. Whereas under parliamentary sovereignty the judiciary had very limited review powers over Parliament, the courts immediately assumed an active and resolute role in applying the NC as yardstick to all government actions. Consequently, numerous legislative provisions were struck down by the courts since the commencement of the interim NC.[77] The lead was provided unequivocally by the Constitutional Court when it stated early on in the *Western Cape* case: 'It is of crucial importance at this early stage of the development of our new constitutional order, to establish respect for the principle that the Constitution is supreme.'[78] Another significant case which drove home in quite stark terms the implications of constitutional supremacy was *De Lille v. Speaker of the National Assembly*, in which it was held that even the internal proceedings of Parliament were subject to the NC, and that in disciplinary proceedings against a member, the National Assembly had to comply *inter alia* with the rights to freedom of expression and just administrative action.[79] The importance of the founding values of the Constitution, in particular the principle of constitutional supremacy, was confirmed by the Constitutional Court as follows:

> One of the crucial elements of our constitutional vision is to make a decisive break from the unchecked abuse of state power and resources that was virtually institutionalised during the apartheid era. To achieve this goal, we adopted accountability, the rule of law and the supremacy of the Constitution as values of our constitutional democracy.[80]

II. Statutory Interpretation

59. Another significant consequence of constitutional supremacy has been its general effect on the interpretation and application of the laws. Traditionally, under

77. More than sixty legislative provisions have been invalidated so far. In terms of the interim NC, only the Constitutional Court had the jurisdiction to invalidate parliamentary legislation (s. 98(2)(c), read with s. 102(3)(c)). In terms of the 1996 NC jurisdiction in this regard has been extended to all high courts, but an order of constitutional invalidity by the Supreme Court of Appeal or any High Court must be confirmed by the Constitutional Court (s. 172(a), read with s. 167(5)).
78. *Executive Council of the Western Cape Legislature v. President of the Republic of South Africa* 1995 10 BCLR 1289 (CC); 1995 4 SA 877 (CC) par 100. *See* in this regard E.F.J. Malherbe, *Grondwetlike oppergesag in werking*' TSAR 175 (1996). *See also* J. Langa in *S v. Makwanyane* 1995 6 BCLR 665 (CC) par 220.
79. 1998 7 BCLR 916 (C). The decision was confirmed on appeal –*Speaker of the National Assembly v. De Lille* 1999 11 BCLR 1339 (SCA). *See* the discussion of the judgment by E.F.J. Malherbe, *Parlementêre voorreg en grondwetlike oppergesag: 'n bastion buig*, TSAR 145 (1999). *See also Economic Freedom Fighters v. Speaker of the National Assembly and Others; Democratic Alliance v. Speaker of the National Assembly and Others* 2016 (5) BCLR 618 (CC); 2016 (3) SA 580 (CC) par 1; *Democratic Alliance v. Speaker of National Assembly and Others* [2016] ZACC 8.
80. *Economic Freedom Fighters v. Speaker of the National Assembly and Others; Democratic Alliance v. Speaker of the National Assembly and Others* [2016] ZACC 11 para. 1.

parliamentary sovereignty, the function of the courts was limited to the strict application of the law as laid down by Parliament. In the interpretation and application of any law, therefore, the initial question always was 'What is the literal meaning of the words of the law?' or 'What was the intention of the legislature?' Now, when interpreting and applying ordinary laws, it is the duty of the courts in terms of section 39(2) of the NC first to ask 'What does the Constitution say?' and 'How do we give effect to the norms and values of the Constitution?'[81] The NC contains a number of basic values and ideals, particularly in the Preamble, section 1 and Chapter 2 (the Bill of Rights), which have been elevated to constitutional norms with which all conduct must conform. As a result, the literalist approach of the past is fast making way for a normative approach in terms of which the courts actively promote constitutional values and norms and pursue the ideals expounded in the NC.[82]

III. Constitutional Entrenchment

60. For obvious reasons, constitutional supremacy and entrenchment goes hand in hand. The South African NC is entrenched, with different methods and majorities applying to different provisions.[83] Most provisions of the NC can be amended by a two-thirds majority in the National Assembly, but any amendment to the Bill of Rights, and any amendment that affects the NCOP or the boundaries, powers, functions, or institutions of the provinces, requires a two-thirds majority in the National Assembly and the support of six of the nine provinces in the NCOP. Any amendment that affects a particular province requires the support of the legislature of that province as well, and creates a form of ratification of this kind of constitutional amendment.

61. Particularly significant are the procedures for the amendment of section 1, which requires a 75% majority in the National Assembly and the support of six provinces in the NCOP. Section 1 comprises the underlying values of the NC, and the obvious

81. Section 39(2) expressly provides that when interpreting any legislation, and when developing the common law or customary law, courts must promote the spirit, purport, and objects of the Bill of Rights, and this happens in particular in the case of laws affected by the Bill of Rights.
82. Much has been written on this subject already; *see* e.g., L.M. Du Plessis and H. Corder, *Understanding South Africa's Transitional Bill of Rights* 60 et seq. (Juta 1994); L.M. Du Plessis and J. De Ville, *Bill of Rights Interpretation in the South African Context (1): Diagnostic Observations*, Stell LR 63 (1993); *Bill of Rights Interpretation in the South African Context (2): Prognostic Observations*, Stell LR 199 (1993); *Bill of Rights Interpretation in the South African Context (3): Comparative Perspectives and Future Prospects*, Stell LR 356 (1993); D. Davis, M. Chaskalson and J. De Waal, *Democracy and Constitutionalism: The Role of Constitutional Interpretation*, in *Rights and Constitutionalism: The New South African Legal Order* 1 et seq. (D. Van Wyk et al. eds, Juta 1994); J. Kentridge and D. Spitz, *Interpretation*, in *Constitutional Law of South Africa* 11–10 et seq. (Chaskalson et al. eds, 1998); I.M. Rautenbach, *Introduction to the Bill of Rights*, in Butterworths editorial team *Bill of Rights Compendium* 1A-1 14–21 (Butterworths 1996); C.J. Botha, *Waarde-aktiverende Grondwetuitleg: Vergestalting van die Materiële Regstaat* (unpublished LLD thesis UNISA 1996). The so-called purposive approach of the courts as laid down in *S v. Makwanyane* 1995 6 BCLR 665 (CC) para. 9 has been reiterated on numerous occasions.
83. Section 74. *See* the discussion by Rautenbach (2012) (*supra*), 122–126.

intention is that these values should not be impaired or undermined lightly.[84] The stricter entrenchment of section 1 has far-reaching implications. Many provisions of the NC give effect to the values in section 1 and the logical inference is that those provisions cannot validly be amended according to the less strict procedures formally required by section 74 if such an amendment impairs the values in section 1. The stricter entrenchment requirements of section 1 therefore apply to section 1 as well as to those provisions of the NC that give effect to the values of section 1, conferring on section 1 a radiating effect over the whole NC.[85] One example would suffice. Given that human dignity is one of the founding values in section 1, it would not be possible to amend by a mere two-thirds majority the Bill of Rights in a way that compromises, violates or in any way impairs human dignity. This line of reasoning could furthermore lead to the conclusion that the stricter entrenchment of the values in section 1 could induce the development of a basic features-doctrine in South Africa in terms of which certain fundamentals of the NC cannot be amended at all.[86]

§3. Bill of Rights

62. The inclusion in the NC of an enforceable and justiciable Bill of Rights has been a momentous step. Both in terms of the particular rights protected by it and the provisions regarding the application of those rights, the Bill of Rights is one of the most sophisticated national human rights instruments in existence.[87] One of its noteworthy features is the fact that quite a number of social and economic rights have been included, *inter alia* the right of access to adequate housing, adequate health care, sufficient food, and water, social security, and children's rights. One may also refer to the educational rights, the rights relating to labour relations, the environmental rights, the cultural and minority rights, and the property rights, which include provisions relating to the redress of the plight of many people who were dispossessed of their land under apartheid.

84. Section 1 reads as follows:

The Republic of South Africa is one, sovereign, democratic state founded on the following values:
(a) Human dignity, the achievement of equality and the advancement of human rights and freedoms.
(b) Non-racialism and non-sexism.
(c) Supremacy of the constitution and the rule of law.
(d) Universal adult suffrage, a national common voters' roll, regular elections and a multi-party system of democratic government, to ensure accountability, responsiveness and openness.

85. Rautenbach (2012) (*supra*), 123; E.F.J. Malherbe, *Die wysiging van die Grondwet: die oorspoel-imperatief van artikel 1*, TSAR 191 (1999). G.E. Devenish, *A Commentary on the South African Constitution* 136 (Butterworths 1998) refers with caution to this viewpoint.
86. Malherbe (*supra*). *See* the opposing views by A. Butler, *The 1996 Constitution Bill, Its Amending Power, and the Constitutional Principles*, Hum. Rights & Const. L.J. S. Afr. 24–31 (1996) (n 14). *See also* Ch. 1 above.
87. For extensive discussions of the Bill of Rights, *see* e.g., Chaskalson et al., *Constitutional Law of South Africa* (Juta 1998); D. Davis et al., *Fundamental Rights in the Constitution: Commentary and Cases* (Juta 1997); I. Currie and J. De Waal, *The Bill of Rights Handbook*, 5th edn (Juta 2005); G.E. Devenish, *A Commentary on the South African Constitution* (Butterworths 1998).

With regard to the application of the Bill of Rights, one should mention, firstly, the fact of its express horizontal application.[88] Secondly, one finds in the Bill of Rights the most explicit and comprehensive general limitation provision of any existing human rights instrument. Based on the Canadian limitation provision, it includes all relevant factors developed by the Canadian and South African courts to determine whether a limitation of a right is reasonable and justifiable in an open and democratic society based on human dignity, equality, and freedom.[89] The Bill of Rights and the way in which it has been applied so far has already had a profound effect on the administration of justice, the development of the legal system, and, generally, on social change in South Africa.[90] The content and application of the Bill of Rights is discussed in more depth in Chapter 2 of Part IV.

§4. Independent Judiciary

63. Hand in hand with a justiciable Bill of Rights goes an independent judiciary with the constitutional authority to adjudicate all matters pertaining to the enforcement of the Bill of Rights and to invalidate all actions and conduct inconsistent with the NC in general and the Bill of Rights in particular. The NC is quite explicit about this status and role of the courts, and provides that the courts are independent and subject only to the NC and the law, which they must apply impartially and without fear, favour, or prejudice.[91] All high courts may strike down any action or conduct inconsistent with the NC.[92] A special Constitutional Court as the final arbiter in constitutional matters has been established, and when a high court invalidates a parliamentary or provincial law, the order must be confirmed by the Constitutional Court.[93] The independence of the judiciary is ensured *inter alia* by the procedures for the appointment of judges. The NC provides for a Judicial Service Commission, representative of all stakeholders in the administration of justice that plays an important part in the appointment, conditions of service and dismissal of all judicial officers.[94] The judiciary is discussed in more detail in §4 below.

---

88. Section 8(2). No other feature of the Bill of Rights elicited the same volume and intensity of debate – for an account *see* S. Woolman, *Application*, in Chaskalson et al. (*supra*) 10–1 et seq.
89. Section 36.
90. *See* e.g., R. Malherbe, *The South African Constitution*, *Zeitschrift für öffentliches Recht* 61–100 (2000); R. Malherbe, *Human Rights in South Africa: A Preliminary Assessment*, *Publiekrechtelike Kronieken* 150–168 (2000).
91. Section 165(2). *See* I. Mahomed, *The Role of the Judiciary in a Constitutional State*, 225(1) SALJ 111–115 (1998).
92. *See* ss 165, 167, 169 and 172.
93. Section 167(5). *See* Malherbe (*supra*) 82.
94. Section 178. *See also* ss 174–177.

§5. Three Spheres of Government

64. The three spheres of government, their powers, and their duty in terms of the principle of co-operative government to work together are entrenched in the NC. During the negotiations, the disagreement over the distribution of powers among the national, provincial, and local spheres of government was fuelled by the federal versus centralist debate and it became one of the most controversial aspects of the NC. Many of the constitutional principles consequently dealt with this matter and, eventually, most of the challenge to the Constitutional text submitted to the Constitutional Court during the certification process centred on it.[95] The end result is nevertheless that the South African NC displays particular federal characteristics and that it cannot be described simply as a unitary system.[96] This feature of the NC is the central focus of this volume and is discussed in depth in other chapters and also in §3 below. A particularly interesting feature of the NC is Chapter 3, which deals with the principle of co-operative government in terms of which the spheres of government have the constitutional obligation to co-operate. This principle is also discussed fully in other parts of this volume.

§6. Other Constitutional Structures

65. Another important feature of the NC is the provision it makes for the establishment of various independent institutions to support and promote the new democratic order.[97] They include the Public Protector, who acts as an ombudsman and may investigate anything improper in public affairs, the Auditor-General, the Human Rights Commission, the Commission for Gender Equality, the Electoral Commission, the Independent Broadcasting Commission, and the Commission for the Promotion and Protection of the Rights of Cultural, Religious, and Linguistic Communities. Although all these institutions have a specific role to play to support and promote constitutional democracy, the crucial role that the Auditor-General and the Public Protector play in strengthening good governance and constitutional democracy is emphasized.[98] A separate chapter of the Constitution deals with the different branches of the security services, which have the duty to uphold the NC and the law, and which must act in an impartial, accountable, and transparent manner.[99] State finances are also dealt with in the NC in some detail and provision is *inter alia* made for an independent Reserve Bank.[100]

95. *See In re Certification of the Constitution of the Republic of South Africa, 1996* 1996 10 BCLR 1253 (CC) paras 229 et seq.
96. *See* e.g., R. Watts, *Is the New Constitution Federal or Unitary?*, in *Birth of a Constitution* 75 (De Villiers ed., 1994).
97. Chapter 9 – the so-called institutions supporting constitutional democracy.
98. *See* T.N. Madonsela, *The Role of the Public Protector in Protecting Human Rights and Deepening Democracy*, Stell LR 1–15 (2012); De Vos & Freedman (*supra*) 257–265.
99. Chapter 11.
100. Chapter 13.

66. Bodies such as the Human Rights Commission and the Commission for the Promotion and Protection of the Rights of Cultural, Religious and Linguistic Communities are discussed in Part IV.

§7. Accommodation of Diversity

67. Through mechanisms such as the Bill of Rights and the recognition of values such as human dignity, equality, non-racialism, and non-sexism, the NC aspires to nation building. In various intricate ways it also attempts to accommodate the diversity of interests in South African society and to ensure justice for all.[101] Examples are the provision for eleven official languages and the establishment of the Pan South African Language Board to promote multilingualism, the electoral system of proportional representation, the nine provinces, and their representation in the NCOP, the recognition of traditional leaders and indigenous law, and the protection of rights concerning language, culture, religion, education, women, children, and so on.[102] Given the intensity of the separation between black and white by the end of the 1980s, South Africa has come a long way to reconcile the differences and embark on the long road to nation-building. Nobody would deny that a hard, up-hill battle still lies ahead, and the struggle to get to grips with the past as illustrated by the activities of the Truth and Reconciliation Commission provided ample evidence in this regard. However, the NC has laid a workable foundation from which to proceed peacefully and constitutionally. As a matter of fact, the NC itself probably provides the most suitable vehicle for nation building in South Africa. It is supported by most South Africans and may become a symbol around which a common national identity and patriotism can develop.[103] It may nevertheless be argued that in view of some recent developments in international law, further attention needs to be given to proper mechanisms for the protection of minorities in South Africa, a matter which is discussed further in Chapter 3 of Part IV.[104]

101. I.M. Rautenbach and E.F.J. Malherbe, *What Does the Constitution Say?* 4–5 (J.L.Van Schaik 1998).

102. *See* the remarks by Albie Sachs, *Member of the Constitutional Court*, in *The Constitutional Protection of Multiculturalism*, Konrad Adenauer Stiftung, *Seminar Report* (May 1998) 8, 12–15. Some of these aspects are discussed in Ch. 3 of Part IV below.

103. *See* A. Venter, *Questions of National Identity in Post-Apartheid South Africa*, Konrad Adenauer Stiftung, *Occasional Papers* (July 1998) 13–14.

104. *See* e.g., F. Venter, *The Protection of Cultural, Linguistic and Religious Rights: The Framework Provided by the Constitution of the Republic of South Africa, 1996*, SA Public Law 438 (1998); H.A. Strydom, *South African Constitutionalism between Unity and Diversity: Lessons from the New Europe*, SA Public Law 373 (1997); *Minority Rights Protection: Implementing International Standards*, SAJHR 373 (1998).

Chapter 3. Relationship Between National and Sub-national Units

68. As South Africa can be described as a composite state, made up of different sub-national components, called provinces, the NC contains particular and very extensive provisions that determine and explain the relationship between the national and provincial spheres of government. Before any discussion of the sub-national or provincial system, this constitutional relationship needs to be explained in some depth.

§1. Constitutional Distribution of Powers

69. As mentioned in Chapter 2 above, the fact that the powers of the different spheres of government are set out and entrenched in the NC is one of the most salient features of the South African constitutional system. Together with the principle of co-operative government, this feature determines the nature and content of the relationship between the spheres of government.

I. General

70. The legislative authority of Parliament and each provincial legislature is entrenched in the NC. There is, in other words, a constitutional distribution of government authority between the provinces and the national sphere and, as this distribution forms part of the supreme and entrenched NC, the courts are constitutionally empowered to exercise control over it. The legislative powers of Parliament are discussed in Chapter 2 above. The NC provides that a provincial legislature is subject only to the NC and the provincial constitution (if there is one).[105] A provincial legislature has legislative authority over the following matters:[106]

- The adoption of a constitution for the province.[107]
- A list of functional areas in respect of which the legislature has exclusive legislative authority.
- A list of functional areas in respect of which the legislature has concurrent legislative authority (together with Parliament).
- Any other matter that Parliament by-law assigns to the legislature.[108]
- Any matter on which provincial legislation is envisaged in the NC.[109]

105. Section 104(3).
106. Section 104.
107. *See* Part II Ch. 1.
108. Section 44(1)(a)(iii). Parliament can, of course, withdraw the authority.
109. *See* e.g., ss 120(2) and 140(3).

- Any matter that is reasonably necessary for, or incidental to, the effective exercise of a power concerning the functional areas on which the legislature has exclusive legislative authority.
- The delegation to a municipal council of any legislative authority, except the authority to adopt a provincial constitution.

A provincial legislature may recommend to Parliament the adoption of a law on a matter on which the province has no legislative authority. A provincial legislature may by resolution adopted by a two-thirds majority request Parliament to change the name of the province.[110]

II. Exclusive and Concurrent Powers

71. A provincial legislature has exclusive legislative authority which it exercises on its own and concurrent legislative authority which it shares with Parliament. The legislature has *exclusive legislative authority* over the list of functional areas in Schedule 5 of the NC.[111]

Schedule 5 contains the following functional areas: abattoirs, ambulance services, archives, libraries, and museums (excluding national archives, libraries, and museums), liquor licences, provincial planning, provincial cultural affairs, sport, recreation and amenities, provincial roads and traffic and veterinary services. In addition, a provincial legislature can make laws on a variety of local government matters.[112]

A provincial legislature shares *concurrent legislative authority* with Parliament over the list of functional areas in Schedule 4 of the NC.[113] The list is more extensive than in the case of the exclusive powers.

Schedule 4 contains the following functional areas: administration of indigenous forests, agriculture, airports (excluding national and international airports), animal control and diseases, casinos, racing, gambling and wagering (but not lotteries), consumer protection, cultural affairs, disaster management, education (excluding tertiary education), environment, health services, housing, indigenous law and customary law, industrial promotion, language policy, nature conservation (excluding national parks, botanical gardens and marine resources), media service, police (to the extent that the NC confers legislative authority on the provinces), pollution control, population development, property transfer fees, provincial public enterprises, public transport, public works, regional planning and development, road traffic, soil conservation, tourism, trade, traditional leaders, urban and rural development, vehicle licensing and welfare services. This concurrent list also includes a large number of local government matters.

110. A 104(2).
111. Section 104(1)(b)(ii), read with Sch. 5.
112. *See* Ch. 12.
113. Section 104(1)(*b*)(i), read with Sch. 4. *See* U. Leonardy and D.J. Brand, *The Defect of the Constitution: Concurrent Powers Are Not Co-operative or Competitive Powers*, (4) TSAR 657–670 (2010) for a discussion about the complexities relating to the way concurrent powers were designed in the NC.

Apart from the exceptional case of laws that are adopted in the exercise of the national government's powers of intervention,[114] legislation of the national government on exclusive provincial matters will be unconstitutional and can be *declared invalid* by the courts. This corresponds to the position in states such as the USA and Canada.[115] Note, however, the views of the Constitutional Court in *Ex parte President of the Republic of South Africa In re: Constitutionality of the Liquor Bill*[116] on the potential for overlap between the two categories of functional areas, in the sense that some of those functional areas cannot be strictly separated even though formally they fall into different categories.

72. A provincial legislature has full legislative authority over the matters indicated in the NC and may adopt laws in that regard from the commencement of the NC. For the sake of efficiency, the Interim NC as well as the NC provided that the President could assign existing laws to the provinces on matters in respect of which the provinces would henceforth have legislative authority.[117] This had the advantage that serious legislative voids were prevented and that the provinces could take up the administration of matters under their authority right from the start. In principle, this arrangement does not inhibit the legislative authority of the provinces. Hence, a province may adopt its own legislation on a matter under its authority, or may continue to administer the applicable 'national law,' if and insofar that law has been assigned to the province.[118]

73. It is a question whether a national law that has been assigned to a province becomes a provincial law that can be amended or repealed by the provincial legislature. In the case of a matter within the exclusive authority of the provinces (Schedule 5), Parliament lost its legislative authority in terms of the NC, and it is evident that the provincial legislature can deal with the law as it deems fit. In the case of a concurrent matter (Schedule 4), Parliament retains its legislative authority. A provincial legislature should, however, be able to adopt its own law on the matter, replacing the national law that has been assigned to the province. May the provincial legislature also amend the law as it deems fit? On the face of it, it should be possible. The law, or the part in question, became a provincial law on its assignment – hence the provision that the President, when assigning it, may amend the law to fit the province.[119] In *Ex Parte Western Cape Provincial Government: In Re DVB Behuising (Pty) Ltd v. North West Provincial Government*[120] the Constitutional Court held that a provincial legislature had the implicit power to repeal its provincial legislation, including legislation assigned to it by the national government. However, such assigned legislation may be repealed

114. Section 44(2).

115. *See* P.W. Hogg, *Constitutional Law of Canada* 390 et seq. (Carswell 1992) on the doctrines which develop e.g., in Canada to lessen the impact of judicial review in this regard.

116. 2000 1 BCLR 1 (CC). *See* the discussion of this judgment by E.F.J. Malherbe, *Die Drankwetsontwerp: vooraf kontrole en grondwetlike gesagsverdeling verder omlyn*, THRHR 321 (2000).

117. Section 235 of the Interim Constitution and item 14 of Sch. 6 of the Constitution. Note that laws assigned in terms of the Interim Constitution are deemed to be assigned in terms of the Constitution (item 14(5) of Sch. 6).

118. Section 125(2).

119. Item 14(2) of Sch. 6. *See also In re: Kwazulu-Natal Amkhosi and Iziphakanyiswa Amendment Bill of 1995: In re: Payment of Salaries, Allowances and other Privileges to the Ingonyama Bill of 1995* 1996 7 BCLR 903 (CC), 1996 SA (CC), 1996 4 SA 653 (CC) para. 12.

120. 2000 4 BCLR 347 (CC).

by a province only to the extent that it deals with matters administered by that province. To the extent that the legislation includes exclusive national matters on which parliamentary legislation will prevail over provincial legislation, the province may not repeal the legislation.

May Parliament amend the law? To the extent that the law in question became a provincial law upon its assignment, it does not, on the face of it, seem possible. Parliament should, however, be able to re-enact a new, amended law, or to amend a part of the law that has not been assigned. However, as it concerns a concurrent matter, these questions should all be answered within the framework of the principle of co-operative government. This requires that the matter be proceeded with by way of consultation, cooperation, and co-ordination between the province and the national government (and other provinces, if necessary).

74. The subjects in Schedules 4 and 5[121] comprise *functional areas* and not necessarily specific matters.[122] This implies that a province does not necessarily exercise complete authority over every area. In the case of the exclusive matters, the provinces take full responsibility. If justified in terms of its powers of intervention, Parliament will, however, be able to make laws on those matters if a province fails to do so.[123] In the case of the concurrent matters, the provinces and Parliament share legislative authority and Parliament will make provision whenever a province does not. A province may, for example, decide not to take up agriculture completely, with the result that the remainder of matters falling under that functional area remains under the jurisdiction of the national government.[124] The fact that the schedules refer to functional areas also means that in jurisdictional disputes it will always have to be settled whether a law falls within a particular functional area, before its constitutionality is investigated further.[125]

75. From the possibility that a province does not exercise complete authority over a particular functional area, it follows that the extent of the legislative powers of the provinces may eventually differ. From this, an asymmetrical relationship between the national and provincial spheres of government may develop in terms of which some provinces enjoy more autonomy than others. The notion of *asymmetry* entails that differences among regional units with regard to factors such as size, population figures, resources, and financial and administrative capacity should be reflected in

---

121. With regard to the powers which the provinces have in terms of the two schedules, the Constitutional Court held as follows in *In re: Certification of the Constitution of the Republic of South Africa, 1996* 1996 10 BCLR 1253 (CC), 1996 4 SA 744 (CC): 'Our analysis has led us to conclude that the powers of the provinces in terms of the New Text Schs 4 and 5 are marginally less than or inferior to the powers enjoyed by the provinces in terms of the Interim Constitution sch 6' (para. 457).
122. Section 104(1)(*b*). Section 126(1) of the Interim Constitution also referred expressly to 'matters which fall within the functional areas specified in Schedule 6.'
123. Section 44(2).
124. G.E. Devenish, *A Commentary on the South African Constitution* 43–44 (Butterworths 1998) is of the same opinion.
125. That is also the approach in Canada –*see* Hogg (*supra*) 376. *Also see* J. De Ville, *Guidelines for Judicial Review on 'Division of Powers' Grounds*, Stell LR 139, 147 (1995).

their powers or extent of autonomy within the country.[126] In most states, the sub-national units are formally regarded as equal, and they have the same powers, but in countries such as Canada, Malaysia, and Spain constitutional provision is made for different degrees of autonomy for sub-national units.[127]

III. Pre-eminence in Respect of Concurrent Powers

76. Whenever levels of government share *concurrent legislative authority*, an arrangement is required for those cases in which their legislation on the same matter are in conflict. Section 146 of the NC contains an extensive arrangement in this regard. Of course, when a conflict occurs, the question to be determined before section 146 is applied is whether both legislatures have acted within their respective spheres of competence when enacting the laws.[128] To determine this question, the purpose and effect of a particular law should be considered.[129] Section 146 provides that national legislation on a concurrent matter that applies uniformly to the country as a whole, prevails over conflicting provincial legislation if it complies with any of certain conditions (if it does not comply, the provincial legislation prevails).[130] The conditions are the following:[131]

(a) The national legislation deals with a matter that cannot be regulated *effectively* by provincial legislation.[132]
(b) The national legislation deals with a matter that, to be dealt with effectively, requires *uniformity* and the national legislation does that by providing norms and

126. *See* the various contributions in B. De Villiers (ed.), *Evaluating Federal Systems* (Juta, 1994), particularly those of A. Mullins and C. Saunders, *'Different Strokes for Different Folks?': Some Thoughts on Symmetry and Difference in Federal Systems*, 41 et seq.; J.P. Boase, *Faces of Asymmetry: German and Canadian Federalism*, 90 et seq.; D.J. Brand, *Asymmetry in Federal Systems – Constitutional Arrangements in South Africa*, in *Asymmetries in Constitutional Law* 117–131 (F. Palermo, C. Zwilling and K. Kössler eds, EURAC Research 2009).
127. *See* e.g., iro Canada L. Brown-John, *Asymmetrical Federalism: Keeping Canada Together?* in De Villiers (*supra*) 111 et seq.; and iro Spain R. Agranoff, *Asymmetrical and Symmetrical Federalism in Spain: An Examination of Intergovernmental Policy*, in De Villiers (*supra*) 61 et seq.
128. *See* J. Klaaren, *Federalism*, in Chaskalson et al. (*supra*) 5.5–6.
129. *In re: Kwazulu-Natal Amkhosi and Iziphakanyiswa Amendment Bill of 1995: In re: Payment of Salaries, Allowances and other Privileges to the Ingonyama Bill of 1995* 1996 7 BCLR 903 (CC), 1996 4 SA 653 (CC) para. 19. *See also Ex Parte Western Cape Provincial Government: In Re DVB Behuising (Pty) Ltd v. North West Provincial Government* 2000 4 BCLR 347 (CC) para. 37.
130. Section 146(5). *See* with regard to this construction U. Leonardy, *Constitutional Provisions on Devolution and Federalism*, in *Birth of a Constitution* 157 (De Villiers ed., 1994, Juta).
131. *See* the discussion of the criteria contained in s. 146 by De Ville, *Guidelines for Judicial Review on 'Division of Powers' Grounds*, Stell LR 152–156 (1995). *See also* F. Venter, *Aspects of the South African Constitution of 1996: An African Democratic and Social Federal* Rechtsstaat? Zeitschrift für ausländisches öffentliches Recht und Völkerrecht 51, 63–72 (1997).
132. According to Klaaren (*supra*), 5.14 this conditions reminds of the subsidiarity principle.

standards, frameworks or national policies.[133] The second part is important and national legislation that contains too much detail and thus goes further than merely establishing norms and standards, or frameworks, or national policy, will not prevail under this condition.

(c) The national legislation is *necessary* for:

- the maintenance of *national security*;
- the maintenance of *economic unity*;
- the protection of the *common market* in respect of the mobility of goods, services, capital, and labour;
- the promotion of *trade* across provincial boundaries;
- the promotion of *equal opportunity or equal access* to services; or
- the protection of the *environment*.

(d) National legislation also prevails if it is aimed at the prevention of unreasonable action by a province that is prejudicial to the economic, health or security interests of another province or the country, or impedes the implementation of national economic policy.[134] The requirement that the national legislation must apply uniformly to the whole country does not apply here, because the national legislation must indeed in such a case be able to apply to the actions of a single province.[135]

77. Formally, section 146 imposes no conditions on the exercise of their legislative authority by Parliament or the provinces in respect of the concurrent matters and it does not limit their legislative authority.[136] Both levels of government may freely make laws in this regard. Section 146 only provides which law *prevails* in the case of a

---

133. *Cf.* s. 75 of the German Constitution which provides for so-called framework legislation that provides only general rules within which the states may adopt detail legislation. Previously, instead of the criterion of effectiveness, this condition merely referred to the interests of the country. This led the Constitutional Court to the conclusion in *In re: Certification of the Constitution of the Republic of South Africa, 1996* 1996 10 BCLR 1253 (CC), 1996 4 SA 744 (CC) that, in comparison with the Interim NC, the overrides have been expanded to some extent in favour of the national government (paras 337, 480).

134. Section 146(3).

135. It seems as if a different point of departure from the Interim NC applies in s. 146. Previously, the provincial law prevailed *unless* the national law complied with the stated criteria (s. 126(3) of the Interim NC). Now the national legislation prevails *if* it complies with the criteria. There is no difference, not even with regard to the burden of proof. The NC lays down criteria for national legislation only, and in every dispute it will have to be determined whether in fact the national legislation complies with them. There will always be a burden of proof on those who allege that the national legislation must prevail to establish that the national legislation complies with the criteria. It would have made a difference only if particular criteria were laid down for provincial legislation as well.

136. That was also the position iro concurrent powers under the Interim NC – *In re: National Education Policy Bill No 83 of 1995* 1996 4 BCLR 518 (CC), 1996 3 SA 289 (CC) para. 14.

conflict.[137] From this, it can *inter alia* be inferred that the American 'field pre-emption' doctrine does not apply in South Africa. According to the doctrine, a national law may regulate a particular field so completely that it leaves no room for a province also to adopt a law on that matter, and that any provincial law in that regard will automatically be inconsistent with the national law and, accordingly, invalid. According to the South African approach to the concurrent powers, Parliament cannot exclude the legislative powers of the provinces over these matters[138] and a province will still be able to adopt legislation on the matter. Section 146 will be invoked only in the case of a conflict. The approach is confirmed by section 149, which provides that when, in the case of a conflict, legislation prevails, the other legislation is not invalid, but is inoperative as long as the conflict continues.[139]

78. In other states with a constitutional distribution of powers between the levels of government, similar criteria as in section 146 are employed to determine when national legislation will prevail. Uniformity, effectiveness, protection of the national economy and the common market and the promotion of inter-provincial commerce are well-known concepts for this purpose in states such as the USA, Germany, Canada, and Australia.[140] Sometimes, however, the courts experience difficulties to adjudicate the question whether particular legislation is *necessary*– the requirement in paragraph (c) above. The American Supreme Court has adopted the attitude that it is a question better dealt with by the political structures than through the judicial process.[141] The German Federal Constitutional Court follows a similar approach.[142] In an obvious attempt to alleviate the burden on the courts in answering this question, the South

---

137. That was also the position in terms of the Interim NC –*Premier of KwaZulu-Natal v. President of the Republic of South Africa* 1995 12 BCLR 1561 (CC), 1996 1 SA 769 (CC) para. 25; *The Executive Council of the Western Cape Legislature v. President of the Republic of South Africa* 1995 10 BCLR 1289 (CC), 1995 4 SA 877 (CC) para. 90.

138. Klaaren (*supra*) 5.9 refers to a 'total jurisdictional veto.'

139. *See* below and *see In re: National Education Policy Bill No 83 of 1995* 1996 4 BCLR 518 (CC), 1996 3 SA 289 (CC) paras 16–20 where this approach was applied already in the case of the Interim NC. Klaaren (*supra*) 5.9–10 is therefore not correct when he avers that the doctrine will probably be applied in South Africa.

140. *See* e.g., iro the USA P. Hay and R.D. Rotunda, *The United States Federal System: Legal Integration in the American Experience* (Oceana Publications, 1982); iro Germany D.P. Currie, *The Constitution of the Federal Republic of Germany* 33 et seq. (University of Chicago Press 1994); iro Canada Hogg (*supra*) 371 et seq.; iro Australia P.H. Lane, *A Manual of Australian Constitutional Law* 39 et seq. (Law Book Company 1991). *See also* the discussion of the provision in the American Constitution on inter-state commerce, the so-called commerce clause by G. Devenish, *The Prospects for Constitutional Litigation in Relation to the Powers of the Central and Provincial Governments as Contained in the Interim Constitution, and Related Issues*, THRHR 48 et seq (1996).

141. *See* e.g., *Garcia v. San Antonio Metropolitan Transit Authority* (1985) 469 US 528. This decision was strongly criticized. *See* e.g., J.E. Hicks, *Garcia v San Antonio Metropolitan Transit Authority: Federalism Revisited*, Okla. City U. L. Rev. 393 (1986); C.L. Cantrell, *Judicial Review in American Federalism: An Uncertain Future*, Det. C.L. Rev. 995 (1986); W.P. Denny, *Breakdown of the Political Safeguards of Federalism: A Response to Garcia v San Antonio Metropolitan Transit Authority*, J.L. & Pol. 749.

142. D.P. Kommers, *The Constitutional Jurisprudence of the Federal Republic of Germany* 98 (Duke University Press 1989).

African NC provides that in a dispute over the question whether national legislation is necessary, the court must have due regard to the approval or rejection of the legislation by the NCOP.[143]

79. The initial constitutional text provided that national legislation on the aspects mentioned in paragraph (c) which had been approved by the NCOP, had to be presumed to be necessary.[144] This created a rebuttable presumption which, admittedly, did not exclude the jurisdiction of the courts over this particular aspect, but put the burden of proof on somebody who disputed the necessity of the national legislation.[145] The provision was unnecessary and undesirable. Section 148 provides in any case that if the court is unable to resolve a dispute concerning a conflict between national and provincial legislation, the national legislation will prevail. That gives sufficient recognition to the difficulties that the courts may experience in jurisdictional disputes, but quite correctly leaves it to the discretion of the courts whether or not they are prepared to deliver judgment in a particular case. Eventually, the rebuttable presumption proved to be one of the grounds on which the Constitutional Court refused to certify the initial constitutional text.[146]

80. A few additional remarks should be made about the exercise of concurrent legislative powers:

- Section 146 refers throughout to 'legislation,' which includes subordinate legislation such as proclamations and regulations. This implies that a regulation may prevail over a law of an elected legislature. In view of the constitutional status of Parliament and the provincial legislatures, that is in principle undesirable. In a clumsy attempt to avoid such a result, section 146(6) provides that subordinate legislation will be able to prevail over an Act only if it has been approved by the NCOP. Therefore, if the intention is that a particular regulation by the national government, for example, should prevail over provincial laws, the functionary concerned must refer it to the Council for approval. (If the Council does not take a decision within thirty days after the regulation has been referred to it, the regulation must be deemed to have been approved by the Council. If the Council does not approve the regulation, it must, within thirty days, supply reasons for the decision to the body that has referred the regulation to the Council.)
- National legislation may also prevail over a provincial constitution. If a provincial constitution contains provisions on a concurrent matter, section 146 applies and

143. Section 146(4).

144. In the Afrikaans text the term 'geag word nodig te wees' was used. The Afrikaans text did not reflect the English accurately. In previous versions of the bill, the term 'must be regarded as necessary' was used, and as an irrebuttable presumption that could indeed have been translated as 'geag word nodig te wees.' The use of the term 'must be presumed to be necessary' in the final text, indicated, however, an intention to create a rebuttable presumption and not an irrebuttable presumption.

145. According to the Constitutional Court this was a difficult, even formidable, onus –*In re: Certification of the Constitution of the Republic of South Africa, 1996* 1996 10 BCLR 1253 (CC), 1996 4 SA 744 (CC) paras 336 and 337, n 277.

146. *In re: Certification of the Constitution of the Republic of South Africa, 1996* 1996 10 BCLR 1253 (CC), 1996 4 SA 744 (CC) para. 480.

national legislation will prevail over the provincial constitution if it complies with the conditions set out above.[147]

- Whenever a court considers an alleged conflict between national and provincial legislation, it must prefer any reasonable interpretation that avoids a conflict.[148] Various doctrines have been developed in other states concerning the questions what a conflict is and how the courts can avoid a finding that there is a conflict.[149]
- A decision by a court that legislation prevails over other legislation does not invalidate that other legislation, as long as it has been enacted within the sphere of competence of the legislature in question and is otherwise valid. The legislation is inoperative, however, as long as the conflict remains.[150] The legislation therefore remains valid and will apply in respect of those parts not declared subordinate.[151] If the conflict is removed through amendment or repeal, the legislation of which the application has been suspended, will simply become operative again.

§2. Financial Relations between the Spheres of Government

81. A multi-sphered system of government each with constitutionally allocated powers requires proper financial arrangements to ensure sufficient and equitable funding of the activities of each sphere of government. Various competing principles impacted on the design of financial intergovernmental relations in South Africa. For example, fiscal autonomy, which implies devolution of authority, stands in contrast to the principle of equity that requires some nationally determined minimum standards. In search for a balance between such competing principles and opposing views the Financial and Fiscal Commission (FFC) played a significant role as an independent constitutional

147. Section 147.
148. Section 150. *Cf.* ss 35(2) and 232(3) of the Interim NC. The NC does not contain such a provision elsewhere any more. Section 126(5) of the Interim NC provided that the legislation had to be construed as being consistent with each other, unless they were, expressly or by necessary implication, inconsistent with each other. *See* in this regard De Ville (*supra*) 156–159.
149. *See* with regard to Canada Hogg (*supra*) 419 et seq. and with regard to Australia Lane (*supra*) 210 et seq.
150. Section 149. This approach can already be found in *In re: The National Education Policy Bill No 83 of 1995* 1996 4 BCLR 518 (CC), 1996 3 SA 289 (CC): 'If the conflict is resolved in favour of either the provincial or the national law the other is not invalidated; it is subordinated and to the extent of the conflict rendered inoperative.'– P Chaskalson para. 19. *See also* De Ville (*supra*) 159. *See* Hogg (*supra*) 395–396, 434 for the application of this approach in Canada.
151. *See Papachristoforou v. MEC for Finance and Economic Affairs, North West Province* 1998 10 BCLR 1237 (B) in which on the basis of this principle it was held that the provincial Gambling Act in question prevailed over the national Gambling Act, but that the latter would still apply in those provinces that have not enacted their own gambling laws.

institution to inform the drafting of the NC.[152] The end product, of which the basic framework is contained in the NC, provides a system of intergovernmental financial and fiscal relations with the following characteristics:

- major taxation powers are vested in the national government;[153]
- all spheres of government have a right to an equitable share of the revenue raised nationally;[154]
- some flexibility and autonomy in expenditure for provincial and local government;[155]
- national standards for budgets, treasury control, and procurement;[156]
- borrowing powers for national, provincial, and local governments.[157]

82. The matters discussed in this section are part of a distinct part of constitutional law, namely financial constitutional law, which includes the constitutional allocation of functions and financial resources to the respective levels or spheres of government, financial intergovernmental relations, the way in which the law deals with policy issues relating to financial intergovernmental relations and the justiciability of the legal provisions dealing with financial intergovernmental relations.[158]

83. The provinces have limited taxation powers, and are entitled to an equitable share of the national revenue. The national revenue is divided in a similar way in Argentine, Brazil, Malaysia, Mexico, and India.[159] A provincial legislature may impose taxes, levies, or duties, excluding income tax, value-added tax, general sales tax, property rates, and customs duties.[160] A provincial legislature may however impose flat-rate surcharges on taxes imposed by national legislation, except in the case of corporate taxes, value-added tax, property rates, and customs duties. The Constitutional Court confirmed that provinces also have an implied power to enact legislation authorizing user charges.[161] Although it is not mentioned expressly as in the Interim NC, a province will still be entitled to impose taxes on casinos, gambling, wagering,

152. The FFC, which was established in terms of s. 198 of the Interim NC, produced a *Framework Document for Intergovernmental Fiscal Relations in South Africa* in June 1995 to fulfil their constitutional mandate, viz to influence the development and maintenance of intergovernmental financial and fiscal relations in South Africa. For a detailed discussion of the system of financial intergovernmental relations in South Africa *see* D.J. Brand, *Financial Constitutional Law – a Comparative Study between Germany and South Africa,* Konrad Adenauer Stiftung, Johannesburg (November 2006).
153. Sections 228, 229 of the NC.
154. Sections 214, 227.
155. Section 227(1)(a), (4).
156. Sections 215–217.
157. Section 230.
158. D.J. Brand, *Financial Constitutional Law – a Comparative Study between Germany and South Africa*, Konrad Adenauer Stiftung, Johannesburg (2006) 25.
159. Tapscott (*supra*) 9, 23–25.
160. Section 228(1)(*a*).
161. The NC does not refer to the imposition of user charges any more – s. 156(3) of the Interim NC. *See In re: Certification of the Constitution of the Republic of South Africa, 1996* 1996 10 BCLR 1253 (CC), 1996 4 SA 744 (CC) para. 438.

lotteries, and betting.[162] However, the taxing powers of a provincial legislature must be regulated in terms of an Act of Parliament.[163] The Act must be adopted according to the procedures for bills affecting the provinces, in terms of which the NCOP can compel the National Assembly to adopt the bill with a two-thirds majority.[164] Such an Act was adopted in 2001, namely the Provincial Tax Regulation Process Act 53 of 2001, which in fact restrict the potential tax raising scope of provinces. A provincial legislature may not exercise its power to impose taxes in a way that materially and unreasonably prejudices national economic policy, economic activities across provincial boundaries, or the national mobility of goods, services, capital, or labour. A province may raise loans for capital or current expenditure within the framework of reasonable conditions prescribed by an Act of Parliament.[165]

84. In terms of the NC, the annual Division of Revenue Act provides for the equitable distribution of the national revenue among all three spheres of government and for any other allocations to the provinces and municipalities.[166] This Act may be adopted only after consultation with the provinces and organized local government

162. The Constitutional Court held that the power to impose gambling taxes has, in effect, been transferred from an exclusive to a concurrent power – *In re: Certification of the Constitution of the Republic of South Africa, 1996* 1996 10 BCLR 1253 (CC), 1996 4 SA 744 (CC) paras 441–442.

163. The Act may be adopted only after consideration of recommendations by the FFC (s. 228(2)(*b*)).

164. Section 76(4)(*b*). The requirement laid down by the Interim NC that the Act had to be adopted by both Houses sitting separately and which afforded the Senate a veto, was deleted – s. 156(1) and (1A) of the Interim NC. The Constitutional Court was unable to find that, in comparison with the Interim NC, this change constituted a diminution of provincial powers – *In re: Certification of the Constitution of the Republic of South Africa, 1996* 1996 10 BCLR 1253 (CC), 1996 4 SA 744 (CC) para. 413.

165. Section 230(1). The recommendations by the Financial and Fiscal Commission must first be considered, but the requirement that the Act must be adopted by both Houses sitting separately has also been deleted here – s. 157(1) and (1A) of the Interim NC. The Borrowing Powers of Provincial Governments Act 48 of 1996 regulates the borrowing powers of provinces.

166. The *Intergovernmental Fiscal Relations Act* 97 of 1997 provides for the procedures relating to the division of revenue among the three spheres of government. *See* ss 214(1) and 227(1) of the NC. The actual distribution of income takes place annually in terms of a special division of revenue Act, and the annual submission of the FFC makes a significant contribution in the final determination of the actual division of revenue. *See* D. Brand, *The South African Constitution: Three Crucial Issues for Future Development*, Stell LR 182, 188 et seq (1998). on the requirements with which such an Act must comply; RSA Dept. of Finance, *Intergovernmental Fiscal Review 1999* 2.6. *See* on intergovernmental fiscal relations, and particularly on the performance of certain structures such as the statutory Budget Council, Department of Provincial and Local Government, *The Intergovernmental Relations Audit: Towards a Culture of Co-operative Government* 139–167 (December 1999).

and after consideration of the recommendations of the Financial and Fiscal Commission (FFC).[167] Factors that must be taken into account when the distribution is made, include:

- the national interest and needs;
- the assurance that the provinces and municipalities are able to provide basic services and to perform their functions;
- the fiscal capacity and efficiency of provinces and municipalities and their developmental and other needs;
- economic disparities;
- obligations of provinces and municipalities; and
- the desirability of stable and predictable allocations and the need for flexibility.

85. Additional revenue generated by provinces or municipalities may not be deducted in the determination of their share, but the national government also need not compensate provinces or municipalities that do not raise income in accordance with their capacity.[168] In contrast to the Interim NC, the NC does not set out that a province's share of the national revenue must be based on a percentage of individual income tax and of value-added tax (or other sales tax) collected nationally, as well as a percentage of the national fuel levy, and that a province is entitled to the transfer duty on property transactions in the province concerned.[169] However, an equitable share as required by the NC can hardly be determined without taking into account these sources of revenue. All revenue received by a province must be paid into a provincial revenue fund and money may be withdrawn from it only in terms the NC or of an Act of the relevant provincial legislature.[170] The form and other particulars with regard to the budget of a province must be prescribed by national legislation.[171] There is national treasury control over the finances of the provinces.[172]

86. Although provinces have very limited own sources of revenue, they have some degree of autonomy in deciding over their expenses. Expenditure assignment is based on the division of functions in Schedules 4 and 5 of the NC. Provinces were able to draft their own budgets for the first time in 1997, after a developmental period within which provincial budgets merely amounted to the total of nationally determined

---

167. *See* with regard to the functions of the FFC ss 220–222 of the NC and the Financial and Fiscal Commission Act 99 of 1997, and with regard to the FFC as it has functioned in terms of the Interim Constitution, J. Mokgoro, *Interprovincial Fiscal Equalization: The Role of the Financial and Fiscal Commission*, in *Birth of a Constitution* 281 (De Villiers ed., Juta 1994). The FFC plays an important role in the overall functioning of the financial intergovernmental relations and *inter alia* provides regular reports on financial and fiscal matters (*see* www.ffc.co.za).
168. Section 227(2).
169. Section 155(2)(*a*), (*b*), (*c*), (*d*) and (*e*) of the Interim NC. According to the Constitutional Court, the absence of these particulars carries no weight at all –*In re: Certification of the Constitution of the Republic of South Africa, 1996* 1996 10 BCLR 1253 (CC), 1996 4 SA 744 (CC) para. 426.
170. Section 226(1) and (2). A province's share of the national income must be transferred to the province promptly and without deduction – s. 227(3).
171. Section 215.
172. Section 216. The Public Finance Management Act 1 of 1999 (as amended by Act 29 of 1999) gives effect to s. 216 of the NC.

allocations for various functional areas.[173] Although provinces now have freedom to set their own budgets, there are a number of constraints that reduce the scope of provincial prioritization, for example the fact that personnel expenses which form a large percentage of provincial expenditure depend on nationally determined conditions of service.[174] Provinces must also, within their available resources, give effect to the constitutional obligation to progressively realize specific socio-economic rights that fall within their jurisdiction.[175]

§3. Co-operative Government

87. As mentioned, the Constitution introduces a principle of co-operative government which determines the relationship among the different spheres of government. In terms of the principle of co-operative government, this relationship is one of close co-operation within a larger framework that recognizes the distinctiveness of every component as well as the interrelatedness and interdependence of all components. In addition to co-operation, the relationship among the spheres of government is characterized by consultation, co-ordination, and mutual support.[176]

88. The NC envisages legislation for the establishment of structures and institutions in which governments in the various spheres will co-operate and through which the principle will be given effect.[177] In the meantime, extensive statutory and informal structures for intergovernmental relations have been developed.[178] These include an intergovernmental forum in which the provincial premiers meet with national ministers and the President (President's Coordinating Council), committees in which

173. J.H-G. Wehner, *Fiscal Federalism in South Africa* 46 (M.A. dissertation University of Stellenbosch 1999).
174. RSA Dept. of Finance, *Intergovernmental Fiscal Review 1999* 2.5; FFC, 'Submission on the 2016 Fiscal Framework and Revenue Proposals' 21 (2016).
175. Section 26 and 27. *See Government of the Republic of South Africa v. Grootboom* 2000 BCLR 1169 (CC); *Soobramoney v. Minister of Health, KwaZulu-Natal* 1997 12 BCLR 1696 (CC), Brand (2006) (*supra*) 256–266.
176. On co-operation among the spheres of government, the Constitutional Court already stated in terms of the Interim NC in *In re: The National Education Policy Bill No 83 of 1995* 1996 4 BCLR 518 (CC) para. 34 iro of the exercise of the concurrent powers: 'Where two legislatures have concurrent powers to make laws in respect of the same functional areas, the only reasonable way in which these powers can be implemented is through cooperation.' In *In re: Certification of the Constitution of the Republic of South Africa, 1996* 1996 10 BCLR 1253 (CC), 1996 4 SA 744 (CC) para. 290 it was stated: 'Intergovernmental cooperation is implicit in any system where powers have been allocated concurrently to different levels of government.'
177. Section 41(2). Although the provinces are directly involved in this legislation, it is not provided that this legislation must be adopted in accordance with the procedure prescribed by s. 76 and in which the NCOP plays a stronger role on behalf of the provinces. Such an Act was adopted by Parliament, namely the Intergovernmental Relations Framework Act 13 of 2005.
178. *See* in general on intergovernmental relations, also in other states, B. De Villiers, *Intergovernmental Relations: A Constitutional Framework*, in *Birth of a Constitution* 256 et seq. (De Villiers ed., Juta 1994), and *Intergovernmental Relations:* Bundestreue *and the Duty to Co-operate from a German Perspective*, SA Public Law 430 (1994). *See* iro local government Part III.

ministers and members of provincial executive councils meet,[179] a technical intergovernmental committee, consisting of senior officials, other technical committees assisting the political office-holders, and the Budget Council, in which the Minister of Finance and the members of the provincial executive councils entrusted with finance serve.[180] These bodies are supported by agreements and continuous liaison on matters of mutual interest among and within the spheres of government. Investigations so far show that many practical as well as conceptual difficulties exist in respect of the conduct of intergovernmental relations and that some of these structures and processes require extensive overhaul to improve their performance.[181] Within each province there are also intergovernmental relations structures in which a premier and the executive council member responsible for local government meet with the mayors of municipalities, and technical intergovernmental fora at senior management level.

89. The NC gives expression in different ways to the idea of a close co-operative relationship among the spheres of government.[182] As a result, there is no watertight separation between the spheres of government and their powers and functions. The Constitutional Court has nevertheless held that the principle does not invade provincial autonomy.[183]

90. (a) *Chapter 3 of the NC sets out the principles of co-operative government:*[184] *Governments at the three spheres of government are distinctive, interdependent and interrelated.*

They must preserve the peace, national unity, and indivisibility of the Republic, be loyal to the Constitution and the Republic and must secure the well-being of the people. They must implement effective, transparent, accountable, and coherent government. They must respect the constitutional status, institutions, powers and functions of government in other spheres, and must exercise their powers in a manner that does not encroach on the geographical, functional, or institutional integrity of government in other spheres.[185] They may not assume powers which the NC does not confer on them. They must co-operate in mutual trust and good faith by fostering friendly relations, assisting and supporting one another, informing one another and consulting on mutual interests, co-ordinating their actions and legislation, adhering to

179. Called MINMEC's. There is one MINMEC envisaged in the NC, viz the one on police referred to in s. 206(8) of the NC.

180. *See* e.g., B. De Villiers, *Intergovernmental Relations in South Africa*, SA Public Law 197 (1997); Brand (*supra*) 184–188. The budget council is also statutory –*see* s. 2 of the Intergovernmental Fiscal Relations Act 97 of 1997.

181. *See* e.g., the audit initiated by the Department of Provincial and Local Government, *The Intergovernmental Relations Audit: Towards a Culture of Co-operative Government* (December 1999).

182. *See infra* . *See* with regard to local government, Part III.

183. *In re: Certification of the Constitution of the Republic of South Africa, 1996* 1996 10 BCLR 1253 (CC), 1996 4 SA 744 (CC) paras 287–292, 469.

184. Sections 40 and 41.

185. Section 41(1)(*e*) and (*g*). According to the Constitutional Court in *In re: Certification of the Constitution of the Republic of South Africa, 1996* 1996 10 BCLR 1253 (CC), 1996 4 SA 744 (CC) para. 245, the fact that this directive applies to all three spheres of government does not have the result that constitutional principle XXII, which provides that the national government may not encroach on provincial government, is not complied with.

agreed procedures, and avoiding legal proceedings against one another. For this purpose, bilateral meetings and other mechanisms and avenues are used to resolve conflicts, but sometimes disputes still need to be referred to the courts. This is not totally wrong, because the courts do have the constitutional duty to help shape the system of co-operative government. In the case of a constitutional law or action, the matter can, after all, only be resolved by the courts and not by political action.[186] Although some principles in Chapter 3 appear to be unjusticiable and look more like guidelines for conduct (e.g., when can it be said that a particular government does not foster friendly relations with other governments, or that it does not assist and support them?), as a whole they constitute a framework for the conduct of governments in the various spheres towards one another.[187] Some also provide a specific norm against which the constitutionality of a government's actions can be measured. It will definitely be possible to determine whether a government encroaches on the geographical, functional or institutional integrity of government in another sphere and this norm should be taken into account when, for example, a court must resolve a jurisdictional dispute in terms of section 146.[188]

91. (b) *Co-operative government is strengthened by the provision that is made for participation by governments in decision-making in other spheres of government.*

As the second House of Parliament, the NCOP represents the provinces in the national legislative process.[189] Furthermore, the Council is representative of the governments of each province due to the fact that the Premier and a few members of the executive council are members.[190] In their turn, permanent members of the Council may attend their provincial legislatures.[191] Representatives of organized local government are also entitled to sit in the NCOP and to participate as observers.[192] From the point of view of a strict separation between the spheres of government, this type of representation could be questioned.[193] However, the co-operative model adopted in South Africa does not entail such a strict separation; on the contrary, it requires a much closer relationship. Representation of the provinces and local government in the NCOP

---

186. *See* the comments in this regard in Department of Provincial and Local Development, *The Intergovernmental Relations Audit: Towards a Culture of Co-operative Government* (December 1999) 176.
187. *See Uthukela District Municipality v. President of the Republic of South Africa* 2002 (11) BCLR 1220; 2003 (1) SA 678 (CC).
188. After all, this norm is a constitutional principle (principle XXII) with which the present NC as well as future actions of the national government must comply.
189. The Constitutional Court was, however, unable to find that, in comparison with the former Senate, the Council would be able to exercise more influence on behalf of the provinces – *In re: Certification of the Constitution of the Republic of South Africa, 1996* 1996 10 BCLR 1253 (CC), 1996 4 SA 744 (CC) para. 333. *See* on the participation of the German states in the federal legislative process G.B. Oschatz, *Position and Responsibilities of the German* Länder, Konrad Adenauer Stiftung, *Occasional Papers* (January 1994) 3–7.
190. *See* Ch. 2, §1, I above.
191. Section 113.
192. Section 67. *See* the Organized Local Government Act 52 of 1997.
193. It may also be questioned whether this aspect is in accordance with constitutional principle XVI in terms of which government must be structured at national, provincial and local levels.

will, without doubt, contribute to greater understanding and co-operation among the spheres of government.

92. There has been some debate on the question to which extent the NCOP succeeds in representing provincial interests effectively, and proposals to strengthen the position and role of the Council are continuously made.[194] The procedures of Parliament have also been adapted to make the NCOP more effective.[195] A report has found, for example, that the NCOP does not focus strongly enough on provincial issues; that its permanent members are too few to consider matters effectively (the special members do not make any significant contribution to NCOP activities); that provincial legislatures are unable to confer meaningful mandates on their delegates in the NCOP on bills affecting the provinces; and that the NCOP tends on all legislation to become a rubber-stamp of the National Assembly.[196] It has even been found that the executive intergovernmental structures and processes tend to eclipse the function of the NCOP. To be precise, when legislation is tabled in the NCOP, it has gone through such an extensive process of talks and negotiations at executive level among the spheres of government, that it is almost a *fait accompli*, leaving the NCOP with very little opportunity to make further inputs on behalf of the provinces. Whereas the NCOP does have various important constitutional review functions in respect of intergovernmental relations, proposals have been made, for example, to the effect that the NCOP should make a concerted effort to focus more strongly on provincial issues, and that the special delegates to the Council should be replaced by about 40 permanent members, which would increase the capacity of the Council to perform its functions effectively.[197]

93. (c) *Governments in the various spheres of government are constitutionally obliged to assist one another.*

In the determination of each province's and municipality's share of the national income, the Act of Parliament regulating it must ensure that they are able to provide basic services and perform the functions allocated to them.[198] The national government must also assist the provinces through legislative and other measures to develop the administrative capacity that is required for the effective exercise of their powers and performance of their functions.[199] This corrects a deficiency in the Interim NC. Numerous functions have been transferred by the national government to the nine provinces without them having the administrative infrastructure required to perform those functions effectively. Now the national government is obliged to assist the provinces

194. For example, by C. Murray and R. Simeon, *From Paper to Practice: The National Council of Provinces after Its First Year*, SA Public Law 96 (1999). *See also* on the potential role of the NCOP E.F.J. Malherbe, *The South African National Council of Provinces: Trojan Horse or White Elephant?* TSAR 77 (1998), and *see* the proposals by B. De Villiers, *National-Provincial Cooperation: The Potential Role of Provincial Interest Offices: The German Experience*, Konrad Adenauer Stiftung, *Occasional Papers* (January 1999).
195. *See* the Rules of the National Council of Provinces (March 1999).
196. *Intergovernmental Relations Audit* (*supra*) 113 et seq.
197. *Intergovernmental Relations Audit* (*supra*) 130–133.
198. Sections 214(2)(*d*) and 227(1)(*a*). *See* the discussion in §1 above.
199. Section 125(3). *See* §2 above.

in this regard.[200] The national and provincial governments have a similar obligation towards local government.[201]

94. (d) *Co-operation among the spheres of government is promoted by the authorization of governments to delegate powers to governments in other spheres.*

There is a general authorization to delegate executive functions and to perform agency services for other governments.[202] The authorization is not without limits and must be exercised within the parameters of the NC. In addition, Parliament may delegate any legislative power, except the amendment of the NC, to a government in another sphere.[203] In turn, a provincial legislature may assign any legislative power to a municipality.[204] A member of the Cabinet may also assign to a member of a provincial executive council or a municipality a power or function that must be exercised or performed in terms of an Act of Parliament.[205] A member of an executive council may assign any power to a municipality.[206]

95. (e) *The national government is expressly authorized under certain circumstances to intervene at legislative as well as executive level in provincial matters.*[207]

Parliament may in terms of section 44(2) adopt *legislation* on a matter over which the provinces have exclusive powers, if it is necessary to maintain national security, economic unity or essential national standards, or to determine minimum standards for the rendering of services, or to prevent unreasonable action taken by a province which is prejudicial to the interests of another province or the country.[208] Parliament must adopt such legislation in accordance with the procedures set out in section 76, which enables the NCOP to enforce a two-thirds majority in the National Assembly. The dispute in *Ex parte President of the Republic of South Africa In re: Constitutionality of the Liquor Bill*[209] concerned the meaning and scope of the exclusive provincial functional area 'liquor licences.' The Liquor Bill proposed to regulate the production, distribution and sale of liquor, including the licensing thereof. The Constitutional Court held that 'liquor licences' referred only to the retail selling of liquor intra-provincially. Insofar as the Bill provided for the licensing of the production and distribution of liquor, the Court held that the national government made out a

200. *Cf.* the dictum in this regard by the Constitutional Court in *In re: Certification of the Constitution of the Republic of South Africa, 1996* 1996 10 BCLR 1253 (CC), 1996 4 SA 744 (CC) para. 267: 'In a situation such as that which exists in South Africa, where newly established provinces may not yet have the administrative infrastructure to enable them to carry out the functions they have to perform in terms of the New Text, the provision serves a necessary governmental purpose.'
201. Section 154. *See* Part III.
202. Section 238. *See* Rautenbach, (2012) (*supra*) 219.
203. Section 44(1)(*a*)(iii). *Also see* s. 104(1)(*b*)(iii).
204. Section 104(1)(*c*). Although it is not mentioned as such in s. 44(1)(*a*)(iii), the legislature will not be able to delegate the power to amend the provincial constitution.
205. Section 99. This takes place by agreement and in accordance with the law in question and must be promulgated by the President by proclamation. *Also see* s. 125(2)(*c*).
206. Section 126. The requirement that it must take place by agreement and in accordance with the law and that it must be promulgated by the Premier also applies here.
207. *See* with regard to local government Part III.
208. Section 44(2).
209. 2000 1 BCLR 1 (CC). *See* the discussion of the judgment by Malherbe (*supra*).

convincing case why that was a matter which was necessary to be regulated nationally. However, the national government failed to show that it was necessary for the purposes of section 44(2) to regulate the licensing of the intra-provincial retail selling of liquor as well. To that extent the Bill was declared unconstitutional.

96. When a province does not fulfil an *executive* obligation, the national government may intervene by taking any appropriate steps to ensure that the obligation is fulfilled.[210] This may include a directive to the province in which the steps that are required to fulfil the obligation are mentioned. The national government may also itself assume the responsibility for the obligation to the extent that it is necessary to maintain economic unity, national security, or standards, or to prevent the province from taking unreasonable steps that are prejudicial to the interests of another province or the country. If the national government itself assumes the responsibility, a notice to that effect must be tabled within fourteen days in the NCOP. The intervention ends unless the Council approves it within thirty days, and the Council must review the intervention regularly.[211]

97. With regard to *finance*, strict treasury control over the provinces is imposed by the NC. The NC provides that there must be transparency and control over expenditure in every sphere by introducing recognized accounting practices, uniform expenditure classifications and uniform treasury norms and standards.[212] The treasury may, with the concurrence of the Minister of Finance, stop the transfer of funds to any government on account of serious or persistent material breach of these directives.[213] The transfer of funds may not be stopped for longer than 120 days and will lapse retrospectively unless Parliament approves it within thirty days. Parliament may, however, renew the decision to stop the transfer of funds for a maximum of 120 days at a time. Before Parliament may decide, the Auditor-General must report and the province must be given the opportunity to state its case before a committee of Parliament.

98. The powers of the national government to intervene in provincial affairs appear to be far-reaching, but are strictly defined and obviously intended to be exercised in exceptional circumstances only.[214]

---

210. Section 100(1). There have been a few cases where the national government intervened in provinces due to the failure of the respective provincial governments to fulfil their executive obligations, e.g., in Limpopo and the Eastern Cape. *See* D.J. Brand, *Die finansiële krisis in provinsies en munisipaliteite: Verg dit grondwetlike of politieke oplossings?*, LitNet Akademies, Jaargang 9(3) 26 Oktober 2012; National Treasury, *Media statement – Joint ministerial team on Limpopo section 100 intervention*, 19 Jan. 2012.

211. Section 100(2).

212. Section 216(1).

213. Section 216(2).

214. *See In re: Certification of the Constitution of the Republic of South Africa, 1996* 1996 10 BCLR 1253 (CC), 1996 4 SA 744 (CC) paras 254–257, 262–266. This was reiterated in *Ex parte President of the Republic of South Africa In re: Constitutionality of the Liquor Bill* 2000 1 BCLR 1 (CC).

99. The principle of co-operative government has been compared with the German principle of *Bundestreue*,[215] and it has been pointed out that federal comity as practised in Germany has strongly influenced the South African constitutional provisions in this regard.[216] However, the direction in which this prominent feature of the NC will develop is uncertain. A number of factors impact on this issue. On the one hand, there are the financial and administrative difficulties encountered by the provinces, as well as a continuing tendency from the side of the national government to regulate matters as far as possible from the top. Both these factors reinforce centralism. On the other hand, one witnesses a strong desire by a few provinces to stand on their own feet and demonstrate their autonomy.[217] Some also feel that the way in which the courts define and apply the principle may have a decisive influence on the future unfolding of the sub-national system.

§4. Status of the Provinces

100. Within the framework of co-operative government, the provinces enjoy constitutional status and protection. The provinces enjoy considerable status in terms of the NC, and they form a prominent and integral part of the exercise of government authority in the Republic. The fact that the NC refers to *spheres* of government instead of *levels* of government indicates an intention to move away from a hierarchical relationship among the spheres of government to one of greater equality. Of course, the mere use of the concept 'sphere of government' is in itself insufficient, and one needs to analyse all relevant provisions of the NC in order to determine the actual status of the provinces.[218]

101. The relevant provisions of the NC can be summarized as follows. The existence and powers of the provinces are entrenched in the NC. The provinces have exclusive powers over a limited number of matters. Under certain circumstances, provincial laws on concurrent matters are subject to laws of Parliament, but Parliament does not have unlimited authority over those matters. A provincial law will prevail if a conflicting Act of Parliament on the same issue does not comply with the prescribed criteria. Disputes in this regard are resolved by the Constitutional Court, which may have the result that an Act of Parliament becomes inoperative if it does not conform to the requirements of section 146. The provinces are represented in the NCOP and,

215. *See* e.g., B. De Villiers, *Intergovernmental Relations: The Duty to Co-operate: A German Perspective*, SA Public Law 430 (1994); Bundestreue: *The Soul of an Intergovernmental Partnership*, Konrad Adenauer Stiftung, *Occasional Papers* (March 1995); *Intergovernmental Relations: A Constitutional Framework*, in *Birth of a Constitution* 256 et seq (De Villiers ed., Juta 1994).

216. *See* e.g., F. Venter, *Aspects of the South African Constitution of 1996: An African Democratic and Social Federal* Rechtsstaat?, Zeitschrift für ausländisches öffentliches Recht und Völkerrecht 51, 61 (1997); Malherbe (*supra*) 77, 85.

217. *See* Brand (*supra*) 182.

218. *See* e.g., the undue weight attached to the term 'sphere' by J. Meyer, *Local Government Law 1997* 6 (Butterworth 1998). *Cf.* the more balanced comments by G. Pimstone, *The Constitutional Basis of Local Government in South Africa*, Konrad Adenauer Stiftung, *Occasional Papers* (March 1998) 4–5.

through their representatives, they take part in the adoption of all laws.[219] Furthermore, the provinces have direct control over the way in which their representatives vote in the Council.[220] Especially in respect of laws affecting the provinces, the Council can exercise considerable influence and can force the National Assembly to adopt such legislation by a two-thirds majority. Constitutional amendments must be referred to the provincial legislatures for comment and constitutional amendments affecting the provinces must be approved by six out of the nine provinces in the Council. A constitutional amendment that affects the boundaries or powers of a particular province must also be adopted by the relevant provincial legislature.[221] The national government must act in accordance with the principles of co-operative government and, among other things, may not encroach on the geographical, functional, or institutional integrity of the provinces. In particular respects, the national government must assist the provinces to act effectively. It is evident that the provinces enjoy material constitutional protection and that the national government does not have an unlimited discretion to legislate on provincial matters or to encroach arbitrarily on the constitutional position and status of the provinces.

102. On the other hand, the provinces may also not act arbitrarily and they are also subject to the principles of co-operative government. It has been pointed out that the national government does have wide and far-reaching powers to intervene in provincial affairs and even to cut off provincial funds. In comparison with the Interim NC, their authority over Acts of Parliament with regard to provincial finances has also been diminished because the NCOP, in contrast to the former Senate, does not have to adopt it in a separate sitting and thus, in effect, exercise a veto over it.[222] The approval of the relevant provincial legislature when an ordinary bill before Parliament affects a particular province has also been deleted.[223] In addition, their powers over certain aspects were limited. They lost concurrent legislative power over certain matters, as well as the power to appoint provincial public protectors and provincial service commissions.[224] Unlike the Interim NC, the NC does not make provision for a Commission on Provincial Government which can give advice on the further development of the provincial system.[225]

103. To reiterate a previous statement, it is clear that South Africa is a composite state with constitutionally entrenched sub-national units. The relationship between these units and the national government displays strong federal characteristics, but,

---

219. *See* e.g., R. Watts, *Provincial Representation in the Senate*, in *Birth of a Constitution* 125 (De Villiers ed. 1994 Juta) on the significance of a second chamber in this regard.
220. Section 65. *See* Ch. 2, §1.II.A above.
221. Section 74(3) and (4).
222. Sections 155–157 of the Interim NC. The Constitutional Court's argument in *In re: Certification of the Constitution of the Republic of South Africa, 1996* 1996 10 BCLR 1253 (CC), 1996 4 SA 744 (CC) paras 411–422 why this is no diminution of their powers, is unconvincing.
223. Section 61 of the Interim NC.
224. *See* ss 114, 213 and 217 of the Interim NC. *See In re: Certification of the Constitution of the Republic of South Africa, 1996* 1996 10 BCLR 1253 (CC), 1996 4 SA 744 (CC).
225. *See* ss 163–173 of the Interim NC. *See also* Rautenbach, *Rautenbach-Malherbe Constitutional Law* (2012) (*supra*) 194–195. This in itself does not necessarily affect the provinces detrimentally, but the abolishment of the Commission after only two years, with a majority of the provinces still struggling to get on their feet, can be questioned.

as a nation's development into a particular form of state depends on a number of dynamic and other factors, it is much too early to suggest that South Africa has become a federation under the present constitutional dispensation. The first two decades of constitutional democracy in South Africa has shown that there is a continuous tension between ideas of centralization and decentralization influenced by the opposing political forces in the country.

Chapter 4. Judicial Authority in South Africa

104. In this part, the judicial system of South Africa is discussed with special reference to the legal system, the judicial authority vested in the courts, the different courts found in South Africa, and the constitutional jurisdiction of the courts. Special attention is given to the Constitutional Court, which is the highest court in constitutional matters. Finally, the powers of the courts to review administrative action are explained briefly.

§1. The Legal System

105. The South African legal system forms part of the Western legal systems and is to a large extent the product of a synthesis between Roman Dutch law and English law.[226] In addition, South Africa has developed its own legal tradition, influenced by extensive comparative studies, indigenous law, and the recent adoption of the principle of constitutional supremacy.[227] The latter development has probably been the single most significant influence ever on the legal system. Parliamentary sovereignty was replaced by a supreme constitution and Parliament is now subject to the NC in all respects, even its internal procedures and affairs.[228] Any law adopted by Parliament may be declared unconstitutional and invalid if the courts found it to be inconsistent with the NC. Since its commencement numerous provisions in parliamentary legislation have been struck down by the courts on the basis of their inconsistency with the NC.

106. Parallel to the main legal system, a body of customary or indigenous law developed almost as a separate legal system. Customary law applies to traditional communities only. The NC recognizes the existence of customary law and provides that traditional communities that observe customary law may continue to do so. The courts may apply customary law whenever appropriate, but the objective is that in its application, the courts must in due course bring customary law in line with the NC. The NC also gives some form of recognition to Muslim personal and family law, but the implications and legal ramifications in this regard require further study and analysis.[229]

§2. Judicial Authority: The Courts

107. In terms of section 165(1) of the NC, the judicial authority of the Republic is vested in the courts. The courts are independent and subject only to the Constitution and the law, which they must apply impartially, and without fear, favour, or prejudice. No one may interfere with the functioning of the courts, and all organs of state must

226. L.M. Du Plessis and A.G. Du Plessis, *Introduction to the Law* 18 (Juta 1990).

227. R. Malherbe, *The Legal System and the Judiciary*, in *Government and Politics in the New South Africa* 82, 86 (A. Venter ed., Van Schaik 1998).

228. *De Lille v. Speaker of the National Assembly* 1998 7 BCLR 916 (C); 1998 3 SA 430 (C).

229. Section 15(3).

assist and protect the courts to ensure their independence, impartiality, dignity, accessibility, and effectiveness.

108. South Africa has a nationally organized judiciary, regulated by the national government, and with a court system that functions within a strict hierarchical structure. No judicial powers and functions have been allocated to the provinces or local governments, and only Parliament may legislate on judicial matters.

109. The following courts exist in South Africa and, as mentioned, they stand in a hierarchical relationship: magistrates' courts, which are lower courts, High Courts, the Supreme Court of Appeal, the Constitutional Court, and a number of special courts. The High Court consists of the provincial and local divisions established in different parts of the country.

The President of the Republic appoints all judges on the advice of the Judicial Service Commission.[230] The Commission, which is a constitutional body, consists of the Chief Justice, the President of the Supreme Court of Appeal, other judges, the Minister of Justice, advocates, attorneys, a teacher of law, and several members of both Houses of Parliament.[231] In principle, the jurisdiction of the High Courts is unlimited, and they have jurisdiction in all constitutional matters, except matters under the exclusive jurisdiction of the Constitutional Court.[232] When a High Court strikes down a parliamentary or provincial law, or any conduct of the President, the Constitutional Court must confirm the order.

The Supreme Court of Appeal, seated in Bloemfontein, is the highest court of appeal, except in constitutional matters. The Court hears appeals on constitutional matters, but when it declares a parliamentary or provincial law, or any conduct of the President, unconstitutional, the Constitutional Court must confirm the order.

110. The Constitutional Court seated in Johannesburg and specially established when the supreme Constitution was adopted, is the highest court in all constitutional matters. Constitutional matters include the interpretation, protection, and enforcement of the Constitution. The Constitutional Court consists of a President, a Deputy President and nine other judges.[233] The President of the Republic, acting together with the other members of Cabinet, appoints the judges after consulting the leaders of all the political parties in Parliament.[234] In the case of the President and Deputy President of the Court, the President must also consult the Judicial Service Commission. In the case of the other judges, the President must also consult the President of the Court, and must make the appointments from a list of names submitted by the Judicial Service Commission.

111. The administration and governance of all superior courts has been consolidated under the auspices of the Chief Justice since 2013 to give effect to specific provisions in the Constitution dealing with the judiciary.[235]

112. There are various special courts to try cases in certain specialized fields. Examples are labour courts, water courts, income tax courts, land claims courts, children's courts, and small claims courts.

230. Section 174(6).
231. Section 178.
232. *See* below.
233. Section 167(1).
234. Section 174(3) and (4).
235. Sections 165–180; see also Superior Courts Act 10 of 2013.

§3. Constitutional Jurisdiction

113. As mentioned, magistrates' courts do not have jurisdiction in constitutional matters, but all High Courts, the Supreme Court of Appeal, and the Constitutional Court do have constitutional jurisdiction. All courts with constitutional jurisdiction interpret and enforce the NC, as well as any provincial constitution. It is accepted that the courts follow a so-called generous and purposive approach to the interpretation of the NC which gives expression to the underlying values of the NC.[236]

The following sources are employed and rules applied in the interpretation of the NC: the text of the NC, as the natural starting point;[237] the values underlying an open and democratic society based on human dignity, equality and freedom must be promoted, particularly when the Bill of Rights is interpreted;[238] giving expression to the underlying values of the NC requires a generous and purposive approach to interpretation;[239] international law must be considered and foreign law may be considered;[240] the interpretation given to the NC when the Constitutional Court certified it;[241] clear, undisputed and relevant background information on the constitutional negotiations;[242] and the South African history of human rights violations.[243] Public opinion is not decisive in the interpretation of the NC.[244]

A dispute on the single provincial constitution, the Western Cape Constitution (WCC), has not arisen yet, but it may be taken for granted that a similar approach will be adopted to the interpretation of that NC. It should, of course, be taken into account that a particular relationship exists between the NC and the WCC as explained elsewhere, which may impact on the interpretation of the WCC.

114. A few rules apply to the interpretation of other laws. When interpreting any law, or when developing the common law, every court must promote the spirit,

236. *S v. Makwanyane* 1995 6 BCLR 665 (CC) para. 9.

237. Rautenbach, *Introduction*, in Butterworths editorial team *Bill of Rights Compendium* 1A-14 (Butterworths 1996). *See also* L.M. Du Plessis and H. Corder, *Understanding South Africa's Transitional Bill of Rights* 95–98 (Juta 1994). However, in the words of the President of the Constitutional Court, the text 'must not be construed in isolation, but in its context' (P. Chaskalson in *S v. Makwanyane* (*supra*) para. 10. *See also* D.P. Mahomed, para. 266).

238. Section 39(1)(a). These values are to be found particularly in the Preamble and s. 1. It is argued, furthermore, that constitutional interpretation must not only reflect these values, but must actively promote them (C.J. Botha, 'Maatskaplike geregtigheid, die "animering" van fundamentele grondwetlike waardes en regterlike aktivisme: 'n nuwe paradigma vir grondwetuitleg,' in G. Carpenter (ed.), *Suprema Lex: Essays on the Constitution presented to Marinus Wiechers* 57 (Butterworths 1998).

239. *S v. Makwanyane* (*supra*) para. 9.

240. Section 39(1)(b) and (c).

241. *See In re: Certification of the Constitution of the Republic of South Africa, 1996* 1996 10 BCLR 1253 (CC).

242. That is, the legislative history –*S v. Makwanyane* (*supra*) paras 17–19.

243. This was reiterated in a number of cases –*see* the references by Rautenbach (*supra*) 1A-19.

244. The Constitutional Court declared: 'Public opinion may have some relevance to the enquiry, but in itself, it is no substitute for the duty vested in the Courts to interpret the Constitution and to uphold its provisions without fear or favour. If public opinion were to be decisive there would be no need for constitutional adjudication.' (*S v. Makwanyane* (*supra*) para. 88).

purport, and objects of the Bill of Rights.[245] This rule is directed at bringing the whole legal system in conformity with the Bill of Rights. Laws must also be interpreted in conformity with the Bill of Rights – the so-called reading down principle, which provides that any reasonable interpretation that is not inconsistent with the Bill of Rights must be followed.[246]

115. As the highest court in all constitutional matters, the Constitutional Court is also the highest court of appeal in such matters. It hears appeals on constitutional matters from the Supreme Court of Appeal as well as directly from the High Courts.[247] The Constitutional Court has exclusive jurisdiction in certain constitutional matters:[248]

- Only the Constitutional Court may decide disputes between national or provincial organs of state concerning their constitutional status, powers, or functions. Disputes between national or provincial organs of states and municipalities, or disputes between national or provincial organs of state about other matters may be resolved by other courts. The several cases so far between the national and provincial governments concerning the constitutional distribution of powers between them had accordingly been brought directly to the Constitutional Court.
- Only the Constitutional Court has prior control to pronounce on the constitutional validity of a bill referred to the Court by the President of the Republic or the Premier of a province.
- Only the Constitutional Court has abstract control over a law referred to the Court by a third of the members of the National Assembly or by a fifth of the members of a provincial legislature.
- Only the Constitutional Court may decide on the constitutionality of amendments to the NC.
- Only the Constitutional Court may decide that Parliament or the President of the Republic has failed to fulfil a constitutional duty.[249] It seems as if other courts may enquire into this matter, but they may not decide that such an obligation was not fulfilled.
- Only the Constitutional Court may certify provincial constitutions or constitutional amendments.

245. Section 39(2).
246. This rule was expressly contained in s. 35(2) of the interim NC, and applied e.g., in *Bernstein v. Bester NO* 1996 4 BCLR 449 (CC). It has been omitted from the final NC, so that the corresponding common law rule now applies –*Ynuico Ltd v. Minister of Trade and Industry* 1995 11 BCLR 1453 (T).
247. In terms of s. 8(3) of the NC, any court has the power to develop the common law in order to give effect to a right in the Bill of Rights. In *Amod v. Multilateral Motor Vehicle Accidents Fund* 1998 10 BCLR 1207 (CC) the Constitutional Court stated that on the assumption that the jurisdiction of the Constitutional Court to develop the common law was no different to that of the Supreme Court of Appeal, it would prefer in such cases that the matter first be dealt with by the Supreme Court of Appeal before it reached the Constitutional Court. When the development of the common law was not involved, however, considerations of time and costs could make it desirable for the appeal to be brought directly to the Constitutional Court.
248. Section 167(4).
249. *Economic Freedom Fighters v. Speaker of the National Assembly and Others; Democratic Alliance v. Speaker of the National Assembly and Others* [2016] ZACC 11.

116. Regarding access to the courts in constitutional matters, the NC makes wide provision. Particularly in the case of an alleged infringement of a right in the Bill of Rights, any one of the following persons has a right of access to the courts:[250] anyone acting in their own interest; anyone acting on behalf of somebody who cannot act in their own name; anyone acting in the interest of a group or a class of persons; anyone acting in the public interest; and any association acting on behalf of its members. Individuals may also have access to the courts when a dispute over the distribution of powers between the national and provincial governments affects them. In exceptional cases, direct access to the Constitutional Court may be granted.[251]

117. When deciding a constitutional matter, a court may make any order that is just and equitable.[252] The court may grant appropriate relief, which includes all existing statutory and common law remedies, including a declaration of rights. Declaring a law invalid may have serious implications for existing legal relationships and the administration, and various ways exist in which a declaration of invalidity may be avoided, or its extent and effect may be limited. For example:

- A case may be decided on grounds other than constitutional grounds.[253]
- A law may be interpreted not to be inconsistent with the NC. It is accepted that if a provision in a law could reasonably have more than one meaning, the meaning which is not inconsistent with the NC should be followed.
- A law may be declared invalid only to the extent of its inconsistency. The bad provision may thus be severed from the rest.[254]
- A court may limit the retrospective effect of invalidity, and may even suspend its order of invalidity to allow the competent legislature to correct the defect.[255]

§4. JUDICIAL CONTROL OF ADMINISTRATIVE ACTION

118. There is extensive judicial control of administrative action in South Africa. Over many years a number of rules for valid administrative actions have been developed as part of administrative law and the courts have the inherent jurisdiction to review any administrative action on the basis of these rules.[256] These review powers are exercised in respect of administrative action in all spheres of government. In addition,

250. Section 38.
251. Rautenbach (2012) (*supra*) 181–182.
252. Section 172(1)(b). *See* De Vos & Freedman (*supra*) 393–406.
253. *See* e.g., *S v. Vermaas; S v. Du Plessis* 1995 7 BCLR 851 (CC) para. 13; *National Coalition for Gay and Lesbian Rights v. Minister of Home Affairs* 2000 1 BCLR 39 (CC) para. 24; *De Kock NO v. Van Rooyen* 2006 6 BCLR 714 (SCA) para. 29.
254. *Ferreira v. Levin NO; Vryenhoek v. Powell NO* 1996 1 BCLR 1 (CC) para. 157.
255. *See* e.g., *Executive Council of the Western Cape Legislature v. President of the Republic of South Africa* 1995 10 BCLR 1289 (CC) paras 102–107, and *Dawood v. Minister of Home Affairs; Shalabi v. Minister of Home Affairs; Thomas v. Minister of Home Affairs* 2000 8 BCLR 837 (CC).
256. *See* e.g., Rautenbach (2012) (*supra*) 154–161; Y. Burns, *Administrative Law under the 1996 Constitution* (Butterworths 1998); De Vos & Freedman (*supra*) 581–584.

the NC provides for a right to just administrative action, which confers constitutional status on most of these common law rules.

119. Section 33 of the NC provides in particular that everyone has the right to administrative action that is lawful, reasonable and procedurally fair, and that everyone whose rights have been adversely affected by administrative action has the right to written reasons. This provision encompasses and codifies many of the above-mentioned common law rules. The right to lawful administrative action guarantees the application of the rule of law and the principle of legality to administrative action. In addition, it entrenches the principle that all administrative actions must be authorized by-law.[257] The right to reasonable administrative action constitutionalizes the requirement of 'reasonableness,' which is a longstanding principle in South African administrative law. The right to procedurally fair administrative action and the right to written reasons in turn elevate the rules of natural justice to a constitutional right.[258] Section 33, and its predecessor in the Interim NC, section 24, have been applied in numerous cases since the inception of a supreme Constitution.[259] In terms of the NC, the Promotion of Administrative Justice Act has been adopted to give further effect to the rights in section 33.[260]

257. *See* e.g., *Fedsure Life Assurance Ltd v. Greater Johannesburg Transitional Metropolitan Council* 1998 12 BCLR 1458 (CC).
258. Rautenbach (2012) (*supra*) 438–450.
259. *See* the references in Rautenbach (2012) (*supra*) 445–449; Currie & De Waal (*supra*) 642–682. *See* for a discussion of s. 24 J. De Ville, *The Right to Administrative Justice: An Examination of Section 24 of the Interim Constitution*, SAJHR 268 (1995).
260. Act 3 of 2000.

Part II. Sub-national Constitutional Arrangements

Chapter 1. National Rules

§1. Provincial Constitutional Arrangements in National Constitution

120. As mentioned before, only one South African province has its own constitution, and the constitutional arrangements of the other eight provinces are based on the provision made in this regard in the NC. In this Chapter, the constitutional arrangements of these other eight provinces as provided for in Chapter 6 of the NC are discussed and, where appropriate, briefly compared to the Western Cape Constitution (WCC), the particulars of which are discussed in Chapter 2 of this Part. Although individually the traditional authorities cannot really be regarded as sub-national authorities, and in some respects rather resemble local authorities, their constitutional position should also be referred to in this Chapter, as the NC organizes them into a national and several provincial representative bodies. Accordingly, the following aspects will be touched on in this Chapter: the provincial legislative and executive structures provided for in Chapter 6 of the NC, the provisions of the NC dealing with traditional authorities, and the requirements of the NC for the adoption of provincial constitutions. This includes a brief discussion of the failed KwaZulu-Natal Constitution.

I. Provincial Legislative Authority

121. Every province has its own directly elected legislature vested with the legislative authority of the province.[261] This reintroduced elected legislative structures to the provinces after the provincial councils of the former four provinces had been abolished in 1986. The partly elected legislatures of the former homelands were abolished when those territories were integrated into the new provinces by the Interim NC.

261. Section 104(1).

A. Composition

122. Every provincial legislature is elected directly by the voters according to an electoral system that provides, in general, for proportional representation. A provincial legislature must consist of at least thirty and at most eighty members. The exact number of members of each provincial legislature was determined by the Electoral Commission according to a formula prescribed in the Electoral Act.[262] The number of members of each provincial legislature is presently as follows: Eastern Cape – sixty-three, Free State – thirty, Gauteng – seventy-three, KwaZulu-Natal – eighty, Mpumalanga – thirty, Northern Cape – thirty, Limpopo – forty-nine, North West – thirty-three and Western Cape – forty-two.[263] The members are elected in terms of an electoral system prescribed by the Electoral Act, which are based on that province's segment of the national voters' roll, and which results, in general, in proportional representation.[264] As in the case of the National Assembly, the simple list system is used.

123. The qualifications for members of provincial legislatures are similar to those for members of the National Assembly.[265] As in the case of Parliament, a member of a provincial legislature loses membership if the member ceases to be eligible and is absent without leave under circumstances for which the rules provide.[266] The filling of vacancies is determined by national legislation.

124. A provincial legislature is elected for five years,[267] but under the following circumstances the *term* may be shorter:

- If a legislature at any time during the term adopts a motion of no-confidence in the Premier, the Premier and the other members of the executive council *must* resign.[268] If the legislature fails to elect another Premier within thirty days, the acting Premier must dissolve the legislature.[269]
- The Premier must dissolve the legislature if the legislature adopts with an absolute majority a resolution to that effect and three years have passed already since the previous election.[270]

262. Section 105(2) of the NC and Sch. 3 of the Electoral Act 73 of 1998. The formula entails that one seat is awarded per 100,000 inhabitants, with a minimum of 30 and a maximum of 80 (item 2).
263. Government Notice 1317 of 11 Jun. 1999 (*Government Gazette* 20201 of 11 Jun. 1999). Actually, the number of members of the Western Cape legislature was fixed at 42 by s. 13 of the WCC. This was challenged by the Electoral Commission (EC), but confirmed by the Constitutional Court –*Premier of the Province of the Western Cape v. The Electoral Commission* 1999 11 BCLR 1209 (CC).
264. Section 105(1). The minimum voting age is 18 years (s. 105(1)(*c*)).
265. Section 106. In terms of the Interim NC, at least 90% of the candidates of each party had to reside in the province in question (s. 132(3), read with s. 40(2)–(5)).
266. Section 106(3).
267. Section 128(1).
268. Section 141(2). If the motion of no-confidence excludes the Premier, it does not affect the term of the legislature and the Premier must only reconstitute the executive council (s. 141(1)).
269. The same potentially unfair arrangement applies as in the case of Parliament –*see* Part I, Ch. 2, § I.A.
270. Section 109(1).

125. After the dissolution of the legislature, an election must be held within ninety days, and if the result is not announced within the prescribed period, or is set aside by a court, another election must be held within a further period of ninety days.[271] A provincial legislature remains competent to function from its dissolution until the day before the polling day.

B. Powers

126. The legislative powers of provincial legislatures have been discussed in Part I and it is unnecessary to repeat them here. Suffice to say that their powers are constitutionally entrenched and that, because of the constitutional distribution of powers between the national and provincial spheres of government, and the extensive provisions of the NC in that regard, the powers of the provincial legislatures cannot properly be understood in isolation from those of the national Parliament.

C. Functioning

127. A provincial legislature functions for all intents and purposes like the National Assembly. The provisions in the NC with regard to the functioning of a provincial legislature largely correspond to those applicable to the National Assembly.[272] A provincial legislature also has a continuous session and sits on the days and at the times that it determines for itself.[273] At its first sitting, every legislature elects a speaker and a deputy speaker, who perform the same functions with regard to the provincial legislature as the speaker and deputy speaker with regard to Parliament. A legislature makes its own rules of procedure and determines the powers and privileges of its own members, of which the most prominent, the freedom of speech of members, is guaranteed in the NC.[274] A province's permanent delegates to the NCOP may participate in the proceedings of the provincial legislature, but may not vote in it.[275] A legislature may also require a permanent delegate to attend the legislature.[276] The quorum of a legislature is a majority of all members if a vote is taken on a bill and one third when a vote is taken on any other question.[277] Decisions are taken by a majority of votes.[278] The public

271. Section 108 (3).
272. Sections 110–124. *See* Part I, Ch. 2, §1.I.C.
273. Section 110(1).
274. Sections 116 and 117. Section 117(1)(*b*) provides that a member shall not be liable to any action by reason of anything he or she has said in, produced before, or submitted to, the legislature. A legislature or a committee may summon any person to give evidence (s. 115). *See Democratic Alliance v. Speaker of National Assembly and Others* [2016] ZACC 8.
275. Section 113.
276. This relates to the provision that a permanent delegate can lose membership of the NCOP if he or she has lost the confidence of the legislature (s. 62(4)(*c*)).
277. Section 112(1)(*a*) and (*b*).
278. Section 112(1)(*c*). The presiding member has no deliberative vote, but must cast a deciding vote in the case of an equality of votes, and may cast a deliberative vote if a two-thirds majority is required (s. 112(2)).

has free access to a provincial legislature and legislatures must facilitate public involvement in the legislative and other processes.[279]

128. The NC does not contain much detail on the legislative process in a provincial legislature and every legislature determines its own procedures.[280] It is nevertheless provided that only a member of the executive council of the province, or a committee or a member of the legislature may introduce a bill, and that only the member of the executive council responsible for finance may introduce a money bill.[281] Like the President,[282] the Premier must assent to a bill adopted by the legislature, unless the Premier refers the bill back because he or she is of the opinion that it is unconstitutional.[283] The provision is identical to the provision which applies to Acts of Parliament and in which case unconstitutionality relates to the NC.[284] In the case of the provinces, it could be argued that unconstitutionality may relate either to the NC or to the relevant provincial constitution. The legislature must reconsider the bill in the light of the Premier's reservations and if the Premier still has reservations when the bill is resubmitted to him or her, the Premier must assent to it, or refer it to the Constitutional Court for a decision. If the Court decides that the bill is constitutional, the Premier must assent to it.[285] After assent, the bill becomes an Act and it must be published promptly. It takes effect when published or at a later date determined in terms of the Act.[286] At least one-fifth of the members of a legislature may within thirty days of the assent to an Act apply to the Constitutional Court for an order declaring that Act unconstitutional.[287]

279. Section 118. Access may be regulated (s. 118(*b*)).
280. The procedures of the majority of legislatures are based on standard rules provided by Parliament, although, in some cases, unique rules have been adopted –*see* e.g., the *Standing Orders of the Gauteng Legislature*, April 1996. The procedures with regard to money bills must be determined by-law – s. 120(2). A provincial Act must determine the procedure by which money bills may be amended by a provincial legislature – s. 120(3).
281. Section 119. A money bill is a bill that appropriates money or imposes taxes, levies or duties (s. 120(1)(*a*)).
282. *See* Part I, Ch. 2, §1.I.D.
283. Section 121(1).
284. Section 79(1).
285. Section 121(2) and (3).
286. Section 123. Provincial acts must also be entrusted to the Constitutional Court for safekeeping (s. 124). *See* in respect of Acts of Parliament s. 82.
287. Section 122. The same provisions further apply as in the case of Acts of Parliament (*see* s. 80), but in the case of Parliament at least one-third of the members of the National Assembly must support the application (s. 80(2)(*a*)). The provision in the Interim NC in terms of which a pending bill could be referred to the Constitutional Court has been omitted –*see Killian v. Gauteng Provincial Legislature* 1999 2 BCLR 225 (T) in which it was held that the speaker of the legislature could commit the legislature to pay the costs in such a case.

II. Provincial Executive Authority

A. General

129. The executive authority of a province vests in the Premier who exercises his or her powers together with an executive council. The provisions of the NC in respect of the provincial executive authority correspond in principle to the provisions of Chapter 5 of the NC in respect of the national executive authority.[288]

130. The Premier, together with the other members of the executive council, exercises the executive authority by:[289]

- initiating, preparing and implementing provincial legislation;[290]
- implementing national legislation within the exclusive and concurrent functional areas;
- administering national legislation outside those areas that has been assigned to the province in terms of an Act of Parliament;[291]
- developing and implementing provincial policy;
- co-ordinating the functions of provincial departments and administration; and
- performing other functions assigned to the province.

131. The NC may confer executive authority on a province directly. An example is the executive authority of the provinces in respect of police.[292] A province has executive authority over national legislation within the exclusive and concurrent functional areas only to the extent that the province has the administrative capacity to assume effective responsibility.[293] However, the provision puts an obligation on the national government to assist the provinces by way of legislation and other measures to develop the administrative capacity that is required for the effective exercise of their powers. This obligation, which did not exist under the Interim NC, may be regarded as a consequence of the principle of co-operative government. A dispute between the national government and a province over the question whether the province has the administrative capacity to administer a particular national law, must be referred to the NCOP for resolution within thirty days.[294] How the NCOP must resolve the dispute,

288. *Cf.* ss 125–141 on the provincial executive authority with ss 83–102 on the national executive authority. *See* the discussion in Part I, Ch. 2, §1.II.

289. Section 125(2).

290. The implementation of provincial legislation is an exclusive provincial matter – s. 125(5).

291. The distinction made in *Zama v. Minister of Safety and Security* 1994 4 BCLR 91 (D), 1994 4 SA 699 (D) 703C-F between the exercise of executive authority and the administration of a law, is nullified by this provision.

292. Section 206(4). *See* in general ss 206 and 207. This is one of the powers which has been added pursuant to the refusal by the Constitutional Court to certify the initial text –*In re: Certification of the Constitution of the Republic of South Africa, 1996* 1996 10 BCLR 1253 (CC), 1996 4 SA 744 (CC) paras 391–401.

293. Section 125(3). On the assignment of national legislation to the provinces, *see* D. Brand, *Development of Concurrent Legislation – a New South African Perspective*, Konrad Adenauer Stiftung, *Seminar Report: Sub-national Constitutional Governance* (1999) 37, 39.

294. Section 125(4).

is not clear. On the assumption that a province's peers in the Council will be able to render an objective judgment, the idea is probably that the Council must investigate the dispute and resolve it by resolution.

132. This matter illustrates the fact that a province does not automatically enjoy full executive authority over every functional area mentioned in Schedules 4 and 5. The national government continues to administer existing national legislation on each of these subjects until the President transfers it to a province.[295] A similar arrangement applied in terms of the Interim NC, but subject to the condition mentioned above, namely that a province had to have the administrative capacity to exercise the power in question.[296] A transfer of legislation in terms of the Interim NC remains effective.[297] The condition in respect of the administrative capacity of provinces is meaningful from a practical point of view. It may prevent the discontinuation of a service to the public on account of the incapacity of a province, and it is flexible because a province may request the transfer of only certain powers in accordance with internal needs and circumstances. However, the condition does not exclude the legislative authority of a province and carries the potential of conflict between the spheres of government. In terms of section 104 a provincial legislature has full legislative authority over any matter within the functional areas in the schedules.[298] The exercise of this legislative authority does not depend on the transfer of national legislation in those areas by the President. It could have the result, for example, that if the President should refuse to transfer a particular law on the ground that the province in question does not have the required administrative capacity to execute it, the provincial legislature could adopt its own law on that subject for the provincial executive council to execute. The national government would not be able to prevent it, unless it could justify an intervention in terms of section 100.[299] A provincial legislature may amend as it deems fit any national law which has been transferred.[300]

B. The Premier

133. After every election, the Premier of a province is elected by the provincial legislature from among its members.[301] Unlike the national President, the Premier retains his or her seat in the legislature. The Premier assumes office within five days by taking an oath or solemn affirmation and the term of office continues until a vacancy

295. Item 14(1) Sch. 6.
296. Section 235(8) of the Interim NC.
297. Item 14(5) Sch. 6.
298. *See* Part I, Ch. 3 §1.
299. *See* Part I, Ch. 3 §3.
300. *In re: KwaZulu-Natal Amakhosi and Iziphakaniyiswa Amendment Bill of 1995: In re: Payment of Salaries, Allowances and other Privileges to the Ingonyama Bill of 1995* 1996 7 BCLR 903 (CC), 1996 4 SA 653 (CC) para. 12; *Ex parte Western Cape Provincial Government: In Re DVB Behuising (Pty) Ltd v. North West Provincial Government* 2000 4 BCLR 347 (CC). *See also* Part I, Ch. 3 §1.
301. Section 128(1). The same procedure is followed as in the case of the President (s. 128(2)). The election must take place within thirty days after the office has become vacant (s. 128(3)). In Brazil and the USA the governors of the states are directly elected, and in Argentine and India the Premiers are appointed by the national government.

occurs or a succeeding Premier assumes office.[302] The term of the legislature is five years and normally the Premier's term corresponds to that. The Premier may not serve more than two terms,[303] and may be removed from office by the legislature on the grounds of misconduct, inability to perform the functions of office, or a serious violation of the law.[304]

134. The Premier has the powers and functions entrusted to the office by the NC and other laws and is responsible for:[305]

- assenting to and referring back bills;
- the referral of bills to the Constitutional Court;
- summoning the legislature to an extraordinary sitting;
- the appointment of commissions of inquiry;[306] and
- calling referenda.

135. The provision that the Premier exercises the executive authority *together* with the other members of the executive council corresponds to the position in terms of the Interim NC. In terms of the latter, the Premier had to exercise most of the powers 'in consultation with' the executive council.[307] The expression 'together with' as it is now used in the NC does not change this position, and the relationship between the Premier and the other members of the executive council remains the same. The provision still indicates that the Premier requires the concurrence of the executive council, but that the council expresses its concurrence in accordance with its own decision-making procedures.[308] No fixed rules of law exist in this regard. The procedures and the extent of concurrence required depend on the leadership position of the Premier (within the province and within his or her party) which enables him or her to play a strong dominating role, but at the same time does not allow without political risk the Premier to take decisions totally without the concurrence of the members of the executive council. This position is confirmed by the provision that the members of the executive council, which includes the Premier, are collectively and individually accountable to the provincial legislature.[309] A written decision by the Premier concerning a function

302. Sections 129 and 130(1).
303. Section 130(2). When a vacancy is filled, the period until the next election of a Premier is not regarded as a term.
304. Section 130(3). In the case of misconduct or a serious violation of the law, no benefits may be received from the office and no other public office may be held.
305. Section 127(2).
306. The Constitutional Court confirmed the right of a premier to appoint a commission of inquiry on questions of police efficiency in *Minister of Police and Others v. Premier of the Western Cape and Others* [2013] ZACC 33; 2013 (12) BCLR 1365 (CC); 2014 (1) SA 1 (CC).
307. Section 147(2) of the Interim NC.
308. Section 233(3) of the Interim NC provided that where in the NC it was required that a decision be taken in consultation with another functionary, that other functionary's concurrence was required, but that where such other functionary was a body of persons, concurrence was determined in accordance with that body's own decision-making procedures.
309. Section 133(2).

which falls under another member of the executive council must be countersigned by that other member.[310]

136. Whenever necessary, a member of the executive council designated by the Premier, or a member designated by the other members of the council, or the speaker (until the legislature designates another member), acts as Premier in this order.[311]

C. *The Executive Council*

137. The executive council of a province is the 'cabinet' of the province and fulfils the same function in the province as the Cabinet at national level. The council consists of the Premier as chairperson and at least five and at most ten members appointed by the Premier from among the members of the legislature.[312] The Premier assigns their powers and functions to the members of the council and may dismiss them. According to the courts, this includes the less far-reaching sanction of temporary suspension.[313] The Premier may assign the duties of one member of the executive council to another, and by so doing bring about a reshuffle of the council, and may also temporarily assign a member's duties to another in his or her absence.[314]

138. Before assuming office, a member of the executive council must take an oath or solemn affirmation. A member must act in accordance with a code of ethics that must be prescribed by national legislation and, specifically, may not undertake any other paid work, act in any way that is inconsistent with the office, expose himself or herself to a situation that may lead to a conflict of interest, or abuse the position for personal enrichment.[315] The members of the executive council are responsible for the functions of the executive authority which the Premier assigns to them and are collectively and individually accountable to the legislature for the performance of those functions.[316] This includes the Premier as a member of the council. The council must act in accordance with the NC[317] and must provide the legislature with regular and full reports on matters under their control. Subordinate legislation issued by members of the council is accessible to the public, and must be tabled in the provincial legislature and be approved by it in the way determined by provincial legislation.[318] If the legislature by a majority of all members adopts a motion of no-confidence in the executive council, including the Premier, the Premier, and the other members of the council must resign.[319] If the motion of no-confidence excludes the Premier, the Premier must reconstitute the executive council. When the legislature is dissolved for

310. Section 140(1).
311. Section 131.
312. Section 132(1).
313. *Mpehle v. Government of the Republic of South Africa* 1996 7 BCLR 921 (Ck) 930.
314. Sections 137 and 138.
315. Section 136. The Executive Members' Ethics Act 82 of 1998 applies to members of provincial executive councils.
316. Section 133(1) and (2).
317. And certainly also in accordance with the provincial constitution, if there is one.
318. Section 140(2) and (3).
319. Section 141(2).

an election, the executive council remains competent to function until a Premier is elected and assumes office.[320]

139. The administrations of the provinces form part of the national public service[321] and a national Public Service Act has been adopted to structure the public service in the national and provincial spheres of government.[322] Hence, the provinces have only limited powers with regard to the structures of their own administrations. In terms of the NC, the provinces do have authority over their own staff.

§2. Comparison of Provincial Constitutional Arrangements

140. By definition there are no significant differences among the constitutional arrangements of the eight provinces which function directly according to the provisions of the NC. It should also be taken into account that although constitutionally possible, asymmetry among the provinces in respect of their powers is presently not widely canvassed and is not yet a recognized feature of South African sub-national constitutional law. This is, however, a distinct possibility for the future, given the fact that in terms of their resources and administrative capacity some provinces are simply more capable than others to take control of certain functional areas.[323]

141. Due to the fact that the Western Cape adopted its own constitution, a number of differences between the Western Cape and the other provinces may, however, be pointed out.[324] First of all, as mentioned in paragraph 122 above, the Western Cape has fixed the number of members of its Provincial Parliament in its Constitution, and the Electoral Commission has no authority in this regard as in the case of the other provinces.[325] Secondly, there are certain important differences in respect of the executive authority. The number of members of the Western Cape executive differs from those of the other executive councils. In addition, the Western Cape executive may include a maximum of two members who are not members of the legislature.[326] This feature corresponds to the position in the national Cabinet and enables the Premier to bring into the executive expertise not available in the legislature. The names of the legislative and executive structures of the Western Cape have been changed, and the legislature

---

320. Section 134.
321. Section 197.
322. Act 103 of 1994. In *Premier of the Province of the Western Cape v. President of the RSA* 1999 4 BCLR 382 (CC), 1999 3 SA 657 (CC) it was confirmed that the provinces do not have executive powers over the structure of their administrations. That is why a Premier has to request the President if he or she wishes to restructure the provincial administration. On the other hand it was held (paras 84–88) that the power of the national minister to transfer a provincial function to the national sphere infringed the executive powers of the provinces and was unconstitutional.
323. *See* the discussion on asymmetry in Part I, Ch. 3 §1.II; D.J. Brand, *Asymmetry in Federal Systems – Constitutional Arrangements in South Africa*, in (F. Palermo, C. Zwilling and K. Kössler eds) (*supra*) 117–131.
324. These differences are made particularly clear in Ch. 2 of this Part.
325. This was confirmed in *Premier of the Province of the Western Cape v. The Electoral Commission* 1999 11 BCLR 1209 (CC).
326. This provision only applied until the second election in terms of the WCC which took place in 2014 – *see* Sch. 2 Annexure A of the WCC.

is called the Provincial Parliament, the executive council is called the Provincial Cabinet, and the members of the Cabinet are called Provincial Ministers. An interesting innovation in the WCC is the inclusion of a set of directive principles of provincial policy, which is not legally enforceable, but is supposed to guide the provincial government in its policy-making function.

142. Other differences between the Western Cape and the other provinces include the provision in the WCC for three provincial official languages, Afrikaans, English, and isiXhosa, whereas the other provinces operate under section 6 of the NC, which provides for eleven official languages. The WCC also provides for its own provincial symbols and honours. Other unique features of the WCC are the special constitutional institutions for which it makes provision, namely the cultural councils, and the Commissioners for the Environment and for Children. A law has been adopted pursuant to the WCC which provides for a Western Cape Cultural Commission and for the recognition of cultural councils within the Western Cape.

143. It is evident that although in principle the constitutional structures and processes in the provinces correspond to a large degree, there are a number of significant differences between the Western Cape, which has its own constitution, and the other provinces which operate under the NC.

§3. Traditional Authorities

144. Subject to the NC, traditional authorities and indigenous law are recognized in the NC. Traditional authorities existed in South Africa before the European occupation of the seventeenth century. These institutions never disappeared completely, and were not affected by the abolition of the self-governing territories and independent states in terms of the Interim NC. As a matter of fact, the NC gives recognition to traditional authorities and indigenous law and provides that traditional authorities which observe indigenous law may continue to function.[327] The courts must apply indigenous law, subject to the NC and any legislation dealing with indigenous law. This means that, in the long run, indigenous law will be recognized only insofar it is not inconsistent

327. Section 211(2). This gives effect to constitutional principle XIII –*Certification of the Constitution of the Republic of South Africa, 1996* 1996 10 BCLR 1253 (CC), 1996 4 SA 744 (CC) para. 189. Indigenous law is, however, subject to regulation by-law (s. 211(2)).

with the NC.[328] Subject to the provisions of the NC in this regard, traditional authorities and indigenous law are matters over which Parliament and the provincial legislatures have concurrent legislative powers.[329]

145. In terms of the Interim NC, attempts were made in different ways to link traditional authorities to the government institutions that were created by the NC.[330] Provision was made for the participation by traditional leaders in local government,[331] for the establishment of houses for traditional leaders in every province, and for a national council of traditional leaders.[332] The NC does not provide any particulars in this regard. It simply states that national legislation may provide for a role for traditional leaders as an institution at local level and for the establishment of houses and a council of traditional leaders.[333] The Local Government: Municipal Structures Act provides that traditional leaders may participate in the proceedings of a municipal council.[334] The number of traditional leaders that participate in this way may, however, not be more than 10% of the total number of councillors. The house of traditional leaders in the province in question must make a recommendation regarding the leaders who will

---

328. The extent to which indigenous law is inconsistent with the NC is the subject of an extensive debate. *See* e.g., J. Sinclair and V. Bronstein, *Family Law*, in *Constitutional Law of South Africa* 34–1 et seq. (M. Chaskalson et al. eds, Juta 1998); I. Currie, *Indigenous Law*, in *Constitutional Law of South Africa* 36–1 et seq. (Chaskalson et al. eds, Juta 1998); J. Sinclair, *Family Rights*, in *Rights and Constitutionalism: The New South African Legal Order* 502 et seq. (D.H. Van Wyk et al. eds, Juta 1994). *See also* T.W. Bennett, *The Equality Clause and Customary Law*, SAJHR 122 (1994); E. Bonthuys and L.M. Du Plessis, *Whither the Validity of Marriages Concluded Under a System of Religious Law Under the Transitional Constitution?* SA Public Law 200 (1995); A.J. Kerr, *The Bill of Rights in the New Constitution and Customary Law*, SALJ 346 (1997); I.P. Maithufi, *The Effect of the 1996 Constitution on the Customary Law of Succession and Marriage in South Africa: Some Observations*, De Jure 285 (1998). *See* in general T.W. Bennett, *Human Rights and African Customary Law* (Juta 1995). Similar problems are experienced in the case of Muslim law –*see* N. Moosa, *The Interim and Final Constitutions and Muslim Personal Law: Implications for South African Muslim Women*, Stell LR 196 (1998). *See* the solutions suggested by V. Bronstein, *Reconceptualizing the Customary Law Debate in South Africa*, SAJHR 388 (1998). *See also* the few reported cases like *Ryland v. Edros* 1997 1 BCLR 77 (C), 1997 2 SA 690 (C) and *Bangindawo v. Head of the Nyanda Regional Authority; Hlantlalala v. Head of the Western Tembuland Regional Authority* 1998 3 BCLR 314 (Tk), 1998 1 SA 262 (Tk).
329. Schedule 4 of the NC. The authority of the provinces in this regard was recognized in *In re: KwaZulu-Natal Amakhosi and Iziphakanyiswa Amendment Bill of 1995: In re: Payment of Salaries, Allowances and other Privileges to the Ingonyama Bill of 1995* 1996 7 BCLR 903 (CC), 1996 4 SA 653 (CC).
330. *See* on the background to these provisions Y. Mokgoro, *Traditional Authority and Democracy in the Interim South African Constitution*, Konrad Adenauer Stiftung, *Occasional Papers* (September 1994) 3–10.
331. In *African National Congress v. Minister of Local Government and Housing, Kwazulu-Natal* 1998 4 BCLR 399 (CC), 1998 1 SA 1 (CC) it was held that such membership applied also to the regional councils in that province, despite the fact that they were not fully elected bodies. *See also Premier of Kwazulu-Natal v. President of the Republic of South Africa* 1995 12 BCLR 1561 (CC), 1996 1 SA 769 (CC).
332. Sections 182–184 of the Interim NC. *See* Rautenbach (2012) (*supra*) 224–226.
333. Section 212.
334. Section 81 of Act 117 of 1998.

participate in the proceedings of the relevant municipality.[335] The National House of Traditional Leaders Act provides that the national house of traditional leaders consists of three members from each provincial house of traditional leaders that is in operation.[336] The national house continues for five years and aims to promote the role of traditional leadership within a democratic constitutional dispensation, enhance unity and understanding among traditional communities, and promote co-operation between the national and provincial houses. For this purpose, the national house may advise the national government on matters concerning traditional leadership and traditional leaders and indigenous law.[337] The Traditional Leadership and Governance Framework Act was adopted to regulate traditional leadership within the context of democratic governance in South Africa.[338] In the six provinces in which there are traditional leaders, provincial houses of traditional leaders have been established by-law.[339] They, too, only have advisory powers.

§4. Requirements for Adoption of Provincial Constitutions

146. The NC provides that every provincial legislature may adopt a constitution for that province. The NC provides for the procedures to be followed and the conditions that must be fulfilled, including provisions for national approval or certification that must be obtained before a provincial constitution may come into effect. These provisions are contained in sections 142–145 of the NC.

I. Sections 142–145 of the National Constitution

147. Every provincial legislature may adopt a constitution for its province which provides for its own institutions, but which must comply with certain constitutional requirements. The NC contains full particulars on the government institutions to be established in each province[340] and the provinces can function effectively without their own constitutions.[341] The Indian, Malaysian, Canadian, and Nigerian Constitutions also contain detailed provisions on regional structures and the regions do not even have any power to adopt their own constitutions. In contrast, the American, Australian,

335. Schedule 6 of Act 117 of 1998.
336. National House of Traditional Leaders Act 10 of 1997, as amended by Act 85 of 1998. (Act 10 of 1997 repealed the first Act in this regard, Act 31 of 1994.) The members are nominated by the provincial houses (s. 4).
337. Section 7 of Act 10 of 1997.
338. Act 41 of 2003.
339. The provinces are Eastern Cape, Free State, Kwazulu-Natal, Mpumalanga, Northern Province, and North West.
340. *See* Ch. 6 (particularly ss 104–141). *See also* K. Shubane, *Provincial institutions*, in *Birth of a Constitution* 230 et seq. (B. De Villiers ed., Juta 1994) with regard to similar structures that existed in terms of the Interim NC.
341. In *In re: Certification of the Constitution of the Western Cape, 1997* 1997 9 BCLR 1167 (CC), 1997 4 SA 795 (CC) para. 15 the Constitutional Court has stated that Ch. 6 provides a complete blueprint and that it is not necessary for any province to enact a constitution.

and German Constitutions do not contain such provisions on regional structures and every state of the federation must have its own constitution in order to function effectively.[342] Notwithstanding the detailed provisions of Chapter 6 of the NC, any provincial legislature in South Africa may, however, with a two-thirds majority, adopt a constitution for that province.[343] A provincial constitution may not be inconsistent with the NC and will have force and effect only if the Constitutional Court certifies that it has been adopted in accordance with the NC and that it complies with the requirements of the NC.[344] A provincial constitution must comply with Chapter 3 of the NC (the principle of co-operative government) and with the values contained in section 1[345] and may not confer on the province more powers than those conferred on it by the NC.[346] A provincial constitution may nonetheless provide for provincial legislative and executive structures and procedures that differ from those provided for in the NC. In addition, a provincial constitution may provide for the institution, role, authority, and status of a traditional monarch.[347]

148. So far, two provinces have adopted constitutions. This may appear surprising, given the fact that constitution-making was in vogue in South Africa during the 1990s. However, as explained in the General Introduction, the ANC was manifestly unenthusiastic about separate provincial constitutions, and this probably inhibited most provinces from embarking on this road. It is significant, therefore, that both provinces which have adopted constitutions, the Western Cape and KwaZulu-Natal, were initially governed by opposition parties while the Western Cape is governed by the DA since 2009. The attempt by the province of KwaZulu-Natal to make a constitution, which is discussed below in more detail, failed dismally. The Constitutional Court held that the KZN Constitution usurped more powers for the province than allowed by the interim NC and refused to certify the constitution.[348] The KZN Constitution contained, *inter alia*, a list of exclusive powers for which the interim NC did not make any provision. The Court also stated that there could be no objection in principle against the inclusion of a Bill of Rights in a provincial constitution.[349] However, a provincial

342. *See* in general R. Watts, *Provinces, States,* Länder *and Cantons: Content and Variations Among Sub-National Constitutions of the World*, Konrad Adenauer Stiftung, *Seminar Report: Sub-national Constitutional Governance* (1999) 11 et seq. On Australia, *see* C. Saunders, *The Relationship between National and Sub-National Constitutions*, Konrad Adenauer Stiftung, *Seminar Report: Sub-national Constitutional Governance* (1999) 23 et seq., and on the constitutions of the German states, C. Starck, *The Constitutions of the New German* Länder *and Their Origin: A Comparative Analysis*' Konrad Adenauer Stiftung, *Occasional Papers* (June 1995).
343. Section 104(1)(a), read with ss 142 and 143.
344. Section 144(2). *See* the discussion below.
345. *See* Part I, Ch. 2, §2.III.
346. Section 143(2). A provincial constitution that has been adopted before the commencement of the NC, must also comply with these requirements – item 13 Sch. 6.
347. Section 143(1). In terms of the Interim NC, it was mandatory for the provincial constitution of KwaZulu-Natal to provide for a traditional monarch (s. 160(3)(*b*)).
348. *In re: Certification of the Constitution of the Province of Kwazulu-Natal, 1996* 1996 11 BCLR 1419 (CC), 1996 4 SA 1098 (CC). The Court stated *inter alia* that the KZN Constitution was 'fatally flawed' (para. 47).
349. Paragraphs 17–24.

Bill of Rights may, firstly, only contain provisions on matters within the ambit of the powers of the province. Secondly, no provisions may be included in a provincial Bill of Rights that are inconsistent with the national Bill of Rights. Presumably, a provincial Bill of Rights may therefore provide for more rights or may impose stricter requirements for the limitation of rights,[350] but may not take away rights or make it easier to limit rights. This matter has not been explored further, as the only operative provincial constitution, the Western Cape Constitution, does not provide for a Bill of Rights.

149. The only other province that adopted its own provincial constitution was the Western Cape. The Constitution (WCC) has come into effect in 1998.[351] Initially, the Constitutional Court refused to certify the Constitution, *inter alia* on the ground that it provided for a proportional electoral system based in part on constituencies. The Court held that the authorization to include in the provincial constitution 'provincial legislative and executive structures and procedures' that differ from those in the Constitution, did not include the electoral system, despite the fact that the Court itself explained that 'structures' referred to the form, composition and organization of the provincial legislative and executive institutions.[352] Pursuant to the judgment of the Court, the provincial legislature nevertheless adopted the necessary amendments, after which the Constitution was certified[353] and came into effect.[354] The judgment is discussed and evaluated in Chapter 2 of this Part.

II. The Failed KwaZulu-Natal Constitution

A. Background

150. The WCC is discussed in depth in Chapter 2 of this Part, and in this part a fuller discussion of the failed KwaZulu-Natal Constitution is warranted.

151. The KwaZulu-Natal Constitutional Text (KNC) was preceded by extensive constitutional negotiations in that province and was eventually adopted unanimously by the provincial legislature.[355] At that time, between 1995 and 1996, widespread political violence ripped through the province and threatened to disrupt the democratic process and derail any attempt at the normalization of political development in the

350. *See* Starck (*supra*) 13; R. Williams, *The New Judicial Federalism in the United States: Expansive State Constitutional Rights Decisions*, Konrad Adenauer Stiftung, *Seminar Report: Sub-national Constitutional Governance* (1999) 67 et seq.

351. Western Cape Constitution, 1997, which came into effect on 16 Jan. 1998. *See* D.J. Brand, *The Western Cape Provincial Constitution: Comments, Text and Judgements*, Konrad Adenauer Stiftung, *Occasional Papers* (1999).

352. *In re: Certification of the Constitution of the Western Cape, 1997* 1997 9 BCLR 1167 (CC), 1997 4 SA 795 (CC) paras 48, 49 and 17.

353. *In re: Certification of the Amended Text of the Constitution of the Western Cape, 1997* 1997 12 BCLR 1653 (CC), 1998 2 SA 655 (CC).

354. On 16 Jan. 1998 – Proc 1/1998 16/1/98 (*Western Cape Provincial Gazette* 16/1/98).

355. For a full discussion *see* G.E. Devenish, *The Making and Significance of the Draft Kwazulu-Natal Constitution*, Jahrbuch des öffentlichen Rechts der Gegenwart Band 47 (1999). *See also* the discussion of the judgment by E.F.J. Malherbe, *Provinsiale grondwette: barometer van provinsiale outonomie?* TSAR 344 (1998).

province. The strongest party in KwaZulu-Natal, and senior partner in the provincial government, the Inkatha Freedom Party (IFP), which strongly favoured a federal solution, was so dissatisfied with the powers of the provinces in terms of the interim NC, that it initially refused to take part in the first democratic elections of 1994. It entered the campaign only two weeks before the elections after some superficial concessions were made by the other parties and the interim NC was amended slightly. It remained very much opposed to the direction the negotiations on the final NC took in respect of provincial autonomy, and threatened to withdraw from the national government and the negotiation process on the final NC. At times it did boycott the negotiations, and for a while there was even talk of seceding from South Africa.

152. The adoption of a provincial constitution was, on the one hand, aimed at the formation of a viable provincial government among a few parties, of which the IFP was the strongest, that excluded the African National Congress (ANC). It was also an attempt to keep the IFP in the national negotiation process by making a provincial constitution that would allow the province sufficient autonomy to appease the IFP. The IFP left no doubt as to its dissatisfaction with the lack, in its view, of provincial autonomy provided for in the various drafts of the NC, and remains one of the strongest protagonists of a federal system for South Africa. Eventually, the KwaZulu-Natal constitutional process also became something of an attempt to patch up the disruptive differences particularly between the IFP and the ANC in the province.

B. The Constitutional Court Judgment

153. This is the background against which the text adopted by the provincial legislature must be evaluated. Of course, despite being the product of negotiations and notwithstanding the fact that it was adopted unanimously, the KNC was a fatally flawed document. The brief discussion that follows under a few headings is based on the judgment which the Constitutional Court handed down when the text of the KNC was submitted for certification and on published discussions of the judgment.[356]

1. Provincial Powers

154. The KNC conferred more powers on the province than the interim NC (which was still in force at the time of certification by the Court). The Court, as a matter of fact, referred to this phenomenon as the 'usurpation of national powers.'[357] The background to this is exactly the political framework referred to above, particularly the IFP's determined quest for more powers for KwaZulu-Natal than those provided for in the interim NC and in the drafts of the final NC as they became available. However, conferring more powers on the province was inconsistent with the interim NC, and was contrary to an important federal principle that the distribution of powers in the national, or federal, Constitution cannot be amended unilaterally either by the federal government or a state. The KNC conferred more powers on the province than the interim NC in the following respects:

356. *In re: Certification of the Constitution of the Province of KwaZulu-Natal, 1996* 1996 11 BCLR 1419 (CC). *See* Malherbe (*supra*).

357. Paragraph 13.

(i) Clause 1 of Chapter 1 stated that KwaZulu-Natal was a self-governing province within the Republic, whereas clause 1(8) provided that the provincial Constitution would form the foundation for the relationship between the province and the Republic. According to the Court these kinds of provisions regulated the status of the province, which could only be done in the national Constitution.

(ii) In conflict with the interim NC, clause 1(6) conferred on the province autonomous powers over local government.

(iii) Although there was no objection in principle to the inclusion of a Bill of Rights in a provincial constitution, the Court felt that that power was restricted in some respects. First, a provincial Bill of Rights could not contain provisions on matters falling outside the field of competency of the province. Secondly, the provincial Bill of Rights could not contain provisions that were inconsistent with the national Bill of Rights.[358] Inconsistency would mean that they could not stand at the same time or together, or could not be obeyed at the same time. The Court held that the KNC indeed contained rights on matters outside the powers of the province (e.g., on a fair trial and labour relations). Further, the Court held that the national Bill of Rights is subjected to the provincial Bill of Rights by clause 30(3) which provided that the provincial Bill of Rights recognized other rights in the national Bill of Rights, provided that the rights in the latter Bill of Rights were consistent with the provincial Bill of Rights. For these and other reasons, the Court held that 'the Bill of Rights in the provincial Constitution is deeply flawed in many respects □ and will have to be thoroughly redrafted.'[359] (iv) Clause 1(5) of Chapter 5 conferred exclusive powers on the province, something which was directly in conflict with the interim NC, which did not provide for exclusive provincial powers.

(iv) The establishment of a provincial constitutional court also amounted to a usurpation of national powers, as the provinces did not have the power to create courts of law.

2. The Consistency Clauses

155. Clause 1(9) of Chapter 1 of the KNC provided that the KNC would be the supreme law of the province, insofar as it was not inconsistent with the interim NC. Clause 1(1) of Chapter 4 provided that any provision of the KNC inconsistent with the interim NC would have no force or effect. According to the Court these provisions had the effect to immunize the KNC against certification, because inconsistent provisions would have no force and effect and the Court would be unable to pronounce on them. What the Court meant, in effect, was that such provisions made it unnecessary to certify them (they were of no force and effect), and that the Court could not under such circumstances perform its certification function. In addition, such provisions would nevertheless remain part of the KNC and could come into effect later. In short, the consistency clauses created confusion and uncertainty and could not be certified.

358. Paragraphs 17–22.
359. Paragraph 31.

3. The Suspensive Provisions

156. In various so-called sunrise clauses the coming into operation of parts of the KNC had been made subject to provisions of the not yet adopted 1996 (final) NC, insofar as they would not be inconsistent with the 1996 NC. The objective was to finalize the KNC and have it certified in anticipation of the content of the final NC. The Court held that a suspensive mechanism could not save provisions that were inconsistent with the interim NC.[360] The coming into operation of the relevant provisions was indeed suspended because they were inconsistent with the interim NC. The Court could also have taken the view that the suspensive mechanism had the effect to exclude the relevant provisions from the certification procedure: as they would not come into effect under the interim NC, the Court actually had to refrain from pronouncing on them. The effect of such a mechanism was therefore that any sort of inconsistent provision could be included in a provincial constitution and simply be suspended in order to ensure the certification of the constitution. Again, that could only create uncertainty.

4 The Consequences

157. In view of these considerations, the Constitutional Court declared the KNC to be 'fatally flawed' and it had no option but to refuse to certify the text. Although the product of extensive negotiations, the fact that the KNC was so blatantly unconstitutional and uncertifiable paid a disservice to the adoption of provincial constitutions and to the development of the South African sub-national constitutional law.

158. Since the judgment of the Court and the coming into effect of the final NC, the politics of KwaZulu-Natal have changed. The IFP and the ANC made peace, and formed a coalition government in the province. They also worked together in the national sphere and a few IFP members have served in President Mbeki's Cabinet after the 1999 elections. For these and other reasons, the impetus for the adoption of a provincial constitution had been lost unfortunately and has not been regained since. Overall, the KwaZulu-Natal constitutional exercise has been a disappointment from the point of view of stable and evolutionary democratic sub-national constitutional development. Since 2004 the ANC formed the provincial government.

§5. Future Development

159. The question could be asked, Where do the provinces go from here regarding their own constitutional development? Is it feasible to expect all of them, or even a few, to adopt their own constitutions soon?[361] Of course, there is much to say for provincial constitutions. It would enable provinces, which differ in many respects quite significantly from one another, to put their own stamp on their constitutional arrangements. It would allow for innovation which perhaps was not encouraged during

360. Paragraph 41.

361. *See* also the remarks in §4 *supra* and Ch. 2 §3.

the 1990s when constitution-making was an urgent and intense process. It could also set in motion in the provinces new processes of getting together, getting to know each other, co-operation and reconciliation, which remain essential in the diverse South African society. It would most definitely serve the quest for lasting democratic solutions, as it would increase public awareness and involvement, assist in bringing government closer to the people, and extend and strengthen the democratic values underlying the NC.

160. There is a down side, however. Apart from the persisting reluctance on the side of the majority party to encourage sub-national constitutional development, it is simply a fact that most provinces experience too many financial and administrative problems, simply do not have the capacity and know-how, and are pre-occupied with too many other pressing problems to pay proper attention to the making of their own constitutions. It is probably regarded as a luxury they cannot afford. Beyond doubt most provincial governments have not so far succeeded in convincing the people of their effectiveness when it comes to the providing of services, and they may even regard it as politically unwise to initiate any constitution-making processes before they have gained or restored the confidence of their voters.

161. This means that in the short run the WCC will probably remain the only provincial constitution, and that South Africa has to wait for time to pass, for new situations, needs and power relationships to evolve, and new enthusiasm for constitutional solutions to develop before it can realistically expect more provincial constitutions to see the light of day.

162. Although the adoption of their own constitutions would be the ideal way to encourage meaningful constitutional development in the majority of provinces, that is by no means the only form which further sub-national constitutional development can or should take in the short term. A second possibility, therefore, relates to the development of an asymmetric provincial system, in which the different provinces are really allowed by the national government, and the NC amended if necessary to encourage such a possibility, to develop along different lines with regard to their respective powers and functions.[362] Not only will such a development confirm what is already happening in practice, but while it will recognize the capacity of the stronger provinces to look after themselves, it may well encourage the weaker provinces to get their house in order, especially in respect of their poor administrative performances, and catch up with the others.

163. Thirdly, the current debate on a new electoral system providing for constituencies within a system of proportional representation will most definitely affect the provinces, and it can be expected that many if not all provinces will seriously consider such a mixed system if allowed to do so. Fourthly, it is possible that the provinces may experiment with different ways to realize the constitutional values of accountable, responsible and open democratic government. It has been mentioned that this could lead to slower and more open legislative procedures, enhanced public participation, and different procedures for ensuring executive accountability.[363] Fifthly, provincial legislatures and executives need to take a good look at their functioning.

362. *See* Part I, Ch. 3, §1.II.

363. C. Murray, *Provincial Constitution-Making in South Africa: The (Non)Example of the Western Cape* (to be published).

Many provincial legislatures consist of so few members (six legislatures have less than fifty members each, and three of them have only 30 members each) that they are unable to cope with all the elaborate substructures and procedures traditionally put up in legislatures for the purposes of debate and decision-making. Much more flexible and simple procedures need to be devised and the number of substructures and office-holders need to be strictly limited. Although this is probably more a matter of administrative concern, the creation of substructures within provincial executives should undergo similar scrutiny.

164. Lastly, the further development of intergovernmental relations need to be given further thought. Apart from the constitutional obligation in terms of which legislation must be adopted to provide structures and institutions regulating and facilitating intergovernmental relations,[364] many other issues in this regard need to be resolved. Examples are the rationalization of existing structures, the enhanced involvement of local government, legislation to give further effect to the monitoring role of national government *vis-à-vis* provincial and local government and of provincial government *vis-à-vis* local government, the evolvement and adaptation of the NCOP into a more effective instrument for intergovernmental relations (which may require constitutional amendment), and possible adaptations to intergovernmental fiscal relations.[365]

165. In respect of intergovernmental relations, the provinces should take the initiative to develop their own unique relationships with local government, in particular. The focus in intergovernmental relations have so far been on the relationship between the national and provincial spheres of government, but each province needs to explore ways in which to foster closer, more constructive and more dynamic relations with local government.[366] This could also affect provisions of the NC, as local government is presently organized and governed to a large extent in terms of national legislation that gives effect to provisions of the NC.[367]

364. Section 41(2).

365. *See* e.g., Department of Provincial and Local Government, *The Intergovernmental Relations Audit: Towards a Culture of Co-operative Government* (December 1999) 188–206.

366. On various possibilities that can be considered, *see* B. De Villiers, *Local-Provincial Intergovernmental Relations: A Comparative Analysis*, Konrad Adenauer Stiftung, *Occasional Papers* (May 1997).

367. *See* Part III.

Chapter 2. The Western Cape Constitution

166. As explained in the previous Chapter, the Western Cape is the only province which has so far successfully adopted and implemented a provincial constitution.[368] As a matter of fact, the Western Cape Constitution (WCC) can be regarded as the first non-racial and democratic sub-national constitution in the history of South Africa. A few former homelands that became independent under South African law during the 1970s and 1980s also had their own constitutions, but they cannot be regarded as democratic constitutions and as legitimate attempts in the democratic constitutional development of South Africa. As the only sub-national constitution in South Africa, the WCC therefore deserves fuller attention and this Chapter is devoted to a discussion of the provisions of the WCC.

§1. Background

I. Introduction

167. In view of the fact that the nine provinces of South Africa were products of the constitutional negotiating process at Kempton Park and did not exist in this form previously, the possibility of provincial constitutions also originated during those negotiations. In fact, one of the elements of the political compromise reached on this issue was the power conferred on provinces to draft provincial constitutions.[369]

168. Of the nine provinces that were created in terms of the Interim NC, it was only Western Cape and Kwazulu-Natal which advocated the adoption of their own constitutions. Both provincial governments had firm intentions of designing their own constitutions, but the attempt made by Kwazulu-Natal to make its own constitution failed when the Constitutional Court refused to certify the constitutional text adopted by the KwaZulu-Natal legislature.[370] It was thus a significant constitutional milestone when the Western Cape became the first of the nine provinces to successfully put into effect a provincial constitution under the NC.

---

368. *See* the discussion in §4.II of the preceding Chapter of the unsuccessful attempt by KwaZulu-Natal to make a constitution.
369. It was largely due to the insistence of the Inkatha Freedom Party that the provisions on provincial constitutions were amended to allow for different constitutional structures than those provided for in the Interim NC. *See* D.H. Van Wyk et al., *Rights and Constitutionalism – The New South African Legal Order* 167 (Juta 1994).
370. *See* the discussion in Ch. 1 §4.II; *see also* G.E. Devenish, *The Making and Significance of the Draft Kwazulu-Natal Constitution*, Jahrbuch des öffentlichen Rechts der Gegenwart Band 47 (1999).

II. Historical Overview

169. The first constitution in the history of the Cape was developed during the nineteenth century when the Cape Colony was still part of the British Empire. The Cape of Good Hope Constitutional Ordinance of 1853 laid the foundation for a parliamentary system of government in South Africa by creating the first form of representative government in the Western Cape. It provided for a two-chamber Parliament in the Westminster mould, consisting of a Legislative Council and a House of Assembly, whose members were elected in multi-member constituencies.[371] The Governor, in whom the executive authority was vested, was appointed by the British government. The Cape Colony, and its constitution, which operated successfully for half a century, ceased to exist when it became part of the Union of South Africa in 1910 and was renamed the Cape Province. The four provinces of the Union of South Africa functioned in terms of the national Constitution, the South Africa Act of 1909, and until the democratic transformation of 1994, they never had their own constitutions.

170. It is significant that the Cape, which saw the creation of the first parliamentary system of government in South Africa, was also the place where the first provincial constitution was successfully developed. The last decade of the twentieth century, which produced dramatic constitutional and political developments in South Africa, also provided the opportunity for the Western Cape, one of the newly created provinces of South Africa, and one of three provinces into which the former Cape Province was divided, to develop its own constitution. Although during the negotiations on the Interim NC in 1993 the constitutional scope was created for provinces who wish to do so to develop their own provincial constitutions, it still requires a political decision to adopt a provincial constitution.[372]

171. The idea of a provincial constitution for the Western Cape was already raised at the negotiations of 1993, but was not given serious attention until the end of the negotiation process for the NC in 1996. In July 1996 the Premier of the Western Cape initiated the development of a provincial constitution when he requested the Speaker of the provincial legislature to launch a process whereby the Legislature would develop and adopt a provincial constitution. This took place against the backdrop of a significant milestone in South Africa's constitutional history, namely the adoption of the NC by the Constitutional Assembly on 8 May 1996 and the certification proceedings in the Constitutional Court during the first two weeks of July. On 23 July 1996, the Speaker of the Western Cape provincial legislature referred the matter to the Standing Committee on Constitutional Affairs, Local Government and Housing for its attention.[373] One of the first achievements of the Committee was to agree on a

371. It is interesting to note that the franchise was non-racial but had a financial qualification, viz. anybody who earned at least GPP 50 per year, paid rent, or occupied a property worth at least GBP 25 could vote. *See* H.J. Van Aswegen, *Geskiedenis van Suid-Afrika tot 1854* 185 (Academica 1989).

372. *See* the General Introduction for an overview of the development of the current provinces.

373. This Standing Committee, which was chaired by Mr Hennie Bester (DP), was a multi-party committee composed of representatives of the National Party, African National Congress, Democratic Party, African Christian Democratic Party and the Freedom Front, i.e., all the parties represented in the provincial legislature.

process for the development of a provincial constitution. It also appointed a team of five technical advisors who had the task of advising the Committee and drafting the actual text.[374]

172. The Committee decided to have an open process and accordingly invited the public to submit written or oral representations to it. This participatory process included five public hearings in towns throughout the Western Cape as well as a number of sessions in Cape Town.[375] Nine volumes of written submissions as well as various oral submissions were received during the drafting process. At the end of 1996, after four months of debating submissions and conducting negotiations in the Committee, a draft text was published for public comment. The final round of political negotiations took place during January and early February 1997 whereafter a bill on a provincial constitution was agreed to in the Committee. On 21 February 1997, the provincial legislature unanimously passed the Bill on the Western Cape Constitution.[376]

III. Certification

A. Process

173. Due to the particular requirements for provincial constitutions contained in sections 142–145 of the NC, the development of a provincial constitution entails a two-phase process. First, there is a political stage, which comprises the drafting and adoption of a text by the provincial legislature, followed by the judicial stage, which entails the certification of the text by the Constitutional Court. The role of the Constitutional Court in the certification of a provincial constitution is slightly different from its certification function in the case of the NC.[377] As far as the certification of a provincial constitution is concerned, the Constitutional Court fulfils the role of an independent umpire who is required to measure the text judicially against the requirements contained in sections 142–145 of the NC. In the case of the national certification process the duty of the Court was unique in the sense that it was part of the negotiated settlement that an independent Constitutional Court would have the final say and would test the constitutional text adopted by the elected constitutional assembly against the 34 constitutional principles agreed to during the negotiations on the Interim NC. The challenge for the drafters of a provincial constitution is thus not only to create a meaningful and workable constitution, but to creatively draft a provincial constitution within the framework of the NC that will pass the scrutiny of the Constitutional Court.

374. This team of advisors consisted of Prof Gerhard Erasmus (University of Stellenbosch), Prof Nico Steytler (University of the Western Cape), Adv Andrew Breitenbach (Cape Bar), Mr Steve Swart (Attorney) and Adv Dirk Brand (Office of the Premier) (co-ordinator).

375. Public hearings in the rural areas took place in Worcester, Beaufort West, Oudtshoorn, Vredendal and Vredenburg.

376. Section 142 of the NC requires a two-thirds majority of all the members to adopt a provincial constitution. *See* Hansard for the Western Cape Provincial Legislature on 18–21 Feb. 1997 for the record of the debate on the adoption of the WCC by the provincial legislature.

377. *See* General Introduction, §2.I for a discussion of the certification function applicable to the NC.

174. The WCC was presented to the Constitutional Court for certification. The certification proceedings entailed that the constitutional text had to be presented to the Court by a legal team representing the Speaker of the provincial legislature. By direction of the President of the Constitutional Court, any other interested party could also make submissions either in support or against the text being certified.[378] The duty of the Court was solely to measure the text against the requirements in the NC and to make its judgment accordingly. On 2 September 1997, the Court referred the bill back to the legislature for certain corrections.[379] The Standing Committee of the Provincial Legislature considered the corrections and on 11 September 1997, the amended text was again adopted by the legislature with the required two-thirds majority.[380] The new text satisfied the Court and it was thus certified on 18 November 1997 to be in compliance with all the requirements stipulated in the NC.[381] The WCC came into effect on 16 January 1998.[382]

B. The Judgment

175. In the first judgment on the certification of the WCC[383] the Court ruled that the following provisions of the text did not comply with the requirements of section 143 of the NC, namely:

- Clauses 14(a) and (d), 15(4) and Schedule 3, items 4(3) and 9(3) – electoral system.
- Clauses 16, 19(3), 20(2), 38(2), 39, 41(3) and 45, read with Schedule 1 – administration of oaths of office.
- Clause 46(3) – cabinet ministers undertaking 'paid work.'[384]

176. The main issue that was rejected by the Court, the provisions on an own electoral system for the Western Cape, was a highly contentious one. The other two

378. In addition to the Speaker of the Western Cape Provincial Legislature, the other parties represented at the hearing were the national government and the African National Congress.
379. *Ex parte Speaker of the Western Cape Provincial Legislature: In re Certification of the Constitution of the Western Cape, 1997* 1997 9 BCLR 1167 (CC); 1997 4 SA 795 (CC). The Constitutional Court refused certification on limited grounds of inconsistency, which related to the following issues, viz. an electoral system, references to functions of the Judge President of the Cape High Court, and the definition of 'paid work' undertaken by cabinet ministers. *See* the discussion below.
380. It is interesting to note that in this second debate in the provincial legislature the text was passed by a mere two-thirds of the members as required by the national Constitution, and not by a unanimous vote as was the case in the first round.
381. *Ex parte Speaker of the Western Cape Provincial Legislature: In re Certification of the Amended Text of the Constitution of the Western Cape, 1997* 1997 12 BCLR 1653 (CC); 1998 1 SA 655 (CC).
382. Proc 1/98 16/1/98 (*Western Cape Provincial Gazette* 16/1/98).
383. *Ex parte Speaker of the Western Cape Provincial Legislature: In re Certification of the Constitution of the Western Cape, 1997* 1997 9 BCLR 1167 (CC); 1997 4 SA 795 (CC).
384. Paragraph 86 of the judgment.

issues are relatively insignificant compared to the first, and did not form a major element of the text. Briefly, the rejected provisions entailed the following:

(a) The provisions dealing with oaths of office stipulated that the Judge President of the Western Cape High Court would perform the duties contained in these provisions, whereas the corresponding provisions in the NC placed such duty on the President of the Constitutional Court. The Court held that a province does not have authority over the President of the Constitutional Court or a Judge President, and it accordingly refused to certify these provisions.[385]
(b) The NC stipulates in section 136 that members of executive councils may not undertake any other paid work. Clause 46(2)(a) of the WCC provided that a provincial Act must define paid work for the purpose of the clause. The Court held that the ethical conduct of a provincial MEC is neither an executive structure nor an executive procedure; therefore the provincial Constitution could not contain provisions of that kind.[386]
(c) Clause 14(d) of the original text of the WCC provided for a so-called mixed electoral system as in Germany, which provided for proportional representation, but included constituencies. It stipulated that the Western Cape would have an electoral system that 'is based predominantly on the representation of geographic multi-member constituencies.'[387] Such electoral system must have generally resulted in proportional representation, as required by section 143(1)(a) of the NC. This provision was actually based on an interpretation of section 143(1)(a) that legislative structures and procedures that are different than those provided for in Chapter 6 of the NC include the provision of an own provincial electoral system.

177. In its judgment the Court explained that certification of a provincial constitutional text consists of two phases. In the first phase, the Court determines whether a province has been authorized to deal with a particular issue in the constitutional text, followed by an inquiry into the question whether the text contains impermissible inconsistencies compared to the NC.[388] On this, the Court held that its duty was to withhold certification unless the whole text complied with section 143. The Court also held that the constitution-making powers of a provincial legislature had to be viewed in the broader context of the provisions of the NC on provincial powers. The legislature may not confer on a province powers, functions, or attributes in conflict with the overall constitutional framework established by the NC. The provinces cannot alter their character or their relationship with the other spheres of government. The Court nevertheless regarded the constitution-making power of a province as significant, enabling a province to regulate its governance in its own fashion, subject to section 143. It includes organizing the provincial government, regulating, distributing and circumscribing the functions of its different departments, and prescribing the manner in which the powers derived from the NC are to be exercised. Finally, a provincial

385. Paragraphs 52–57.
386. Paragraphs 64–66.
387. WCC text clause 14(d).
388. Paragraph 7.

constitution may deal with powers incidental to such competences and may provide for or regulate other powers of the type normally found in a constitution.[389]

178. Regarding the electoral system, it was argued on behalf of the Speaker of the Western Cape provincial legislature that an electoral system was an integral part of the legislative structure of the province because it determined the way in which votes were translated into seats in the legislature. From an analysis of the phrase 'legislative or executive structures and procedures' in section 143, the Constitutional Court was however of the view that providing for an own electoral system for the Western Cape was not permitted by the wording of section 143(1)(a) of the NC. The Court held that the quoted phrase 'is concerned only with the form, composition and organization of a province's institutions ("structures") and the manner in which they exercise their powers ("procedures").'[390] The Court then analysed the term 'structure' and held that it referred to the elements or component parts which make up the legislature or executive (which interpretation even creates the possibility that a province may establish a bicameral legislature). On this basis, the Court found in an unconvincing manner that an electoral system was not an element constituting a legislative structure[391] and, therefore, that the provincial Constitution could not provide for the province's own electoral system. In terms of the Court's own explanation of the phrase 'legislative or executive structures and procedures' as referring to the 'form, composition and organization' of a province's institutions, this is, first, an extremely narrow interpretation. An electoral system is more or less the main element of the *composition* of a legislature, and it does not make sense that a province may provide for everything related to the composition of its legislature, except the electoral system. Secondly, the Court's view may lead to inconsistencies. As suggested, a province may, for example, go so far as to provide for a bicameral legislature, including the membership of each house, but it may not deal itself with the *way* in which the members of those houses are to be elected. Why matters such as the number of houses and the number of members in each house form part of the structure of the legislature, but not the electoral system, is not explained by the Court.

179. Regarding the provisions dealing with the duties of judges presiding at the taking of oaths of office by members of the provincial legislature and executive, the Court's view should be regarded as equally narrow and legalistic. The Court argued that a province does not have any authority to impose a duty on the Judge President, or to relieve the President of the Constitutional Court of duties imposed on him or her by the NC, and that those provisions could accordingly not be certified. These provisions did not in any way affect the status, independence, or powers of the judiciary, as they dealt with matters that cannot be regarded as anything more than ceremonial powers of judges and not affecting their substantive judicial authority. By including such provisions in its constitution, it cannot, therefore, by any stretch of the imagination be contended that the Western Cape usurped for itself judicial powers which the NC did not confer on it. Ironically, the President of the Constitutional Court in any case

389. Paragraph 8.
390. Paragraph 16.
391. Paragraphs 47–50 of the judgment. This part of the judgment was severely criticized by E.F.J. Malherbe, in an article on the certification of provincial constitutions, viz. *Provinsiale grondwette: 'n barometer van provinsiale outonomie?* TSAR 344 (1998).

designates local judges to preside at these oath-taking ceremonies in the various provinces.[392]

180. Regarding the other provision not certified, namely that a provincial law had to define the term 'paid work' in the provision prohibiting members of the executive to perform such work, the Court held, probably correctly, that the NC has a uniform definition of paid work in mind, and that it could not be left to each province to provide its own definition.[393] Various other provisions of the constitutional text were challenged, for example, the repetition of certain provisions of the NC, the recognition of the Almighty God in the Preamble, the recognition of the provincial Constitution as the supreme law of the province, subject to the NC, the names given to the provincial legislative and executive structures (Parliament, Cabinet and Ministers), the size of the provincial cabinet (four more than provided for in the NC), the establishment of cultural councils, and the directive principles contained in the text. These challenges were all rejected as insignificant, unfounded or within the powers of the province.

181. As mentioned, the provincial legislature amended the constitutional text in accordance with the judgment of the Constitutional Court, after which the text was certified. A few months later, on 16 January 1998, the Western Cape Constitution took effect.

§2. The Constitution

I. Constituent or Founding Provisions

182. The WCC affirms in its preamble that the Western Cape is founded on democratic values; the recognition of human rights; the recognition of the family; responsible and accountable government; the rule of law; the principles of mutual trust and co-operation; and loyalty to the NC. Reference to these fundamental values does not only indicate the frame of mind of the drafters of the WCC, but it clearly shows the close relationship between the NC and any provincial constitution.

183. The Western Cape is a province established by the NC and its boundaries are determined by the NC.[394] As part of the founding provisions, the WCC contains provisions on the hierarchy of laws applicable in the Western Cape and the interpretation of the WCC.[395] The Constitutional Court held that the objections to these provisions were unfounded and that the text indeed reflected the true position. It is clearly stipulated that the WCC applies to the Western Cape and that it is the supreme law of the Western

392. Malherbe (*supra*) 353.
393. Paragraph 66.
394. Sections 1 and 2 of the WCC.
395. Section 3 of the WCC.

Cape, subject to the NC.[396] Thus, these founding provisions were held to be in order.[397] These provisions of the WCC stand in stark contrast to the corresponding provisions in the failed KwaZulu-Natal constitutional text which expressly usurped extensive powers for the KwaZulu-Natal Province.[398]

184. Any duties and obligations contained in the WCC must be performed diligently and without delay.[399]

185. Two innovations in the WCC are the provisions relating to the official languages of the province and provincial symbols and honours.[400] A basic framework for the recognition of official languages is contained in the NC, but it also places duties on the national and provincial governments to develop legislative and other measures to give effect to these provisions.[401] Afrikaans is by far the dominant language in the Western Cape as far as mother tongue speakers are concerned, with English and isiXhosa as the two other important languages used in the province. In a multilingual province such as the Western Cape it is thus essential that constitutional provision be made for the use of different official languages. The Standing Committee debated this sensitive issue at length and eventually agreed to lay the basis for the recognition of official languages for the purposes of provincial government in the WCC, and to amplify it in more practical detail in provincial legislation. The WCC thus provides that Afrikaans, English and isiXhosa are the official languages for the purposes of government and that these languages enjoy equal status. Further legislation had to be developed to monitor the use of these official languages by the provincial government and to develop those indigenous languages of the people of the Western Cape the status and use of which have previously been diminished. In order to give effect to this constitutional requirement, the Western Cape Provincial Languages Act was passed by the Provincial Parliament.[402] It was the first language legislation in South Africa, although a draft national law has been considered during 2000.

---

396. The relevant parts of s. 3 provide as follows:

(1) This Constitution is adopted for the Western Cape in terms of the national Constitution, the supreme law of the Republic.
(2) The legislative and executive powers and functions of the Western Cape recorded in this Constitution emanate exclusively from the national Constitution.
(3) The provisions of this Constitution must not be interpreted as conferring any legislative or executive authority on the Western Cape which is inconsistent with the national Constitution.

Section 4 provides: 'This Constitution applies to the Western Cape. Subject to the national Constitution, it is the highest law in the Western Cape, and the obligations imposed by it must be performed diligently and without delay.'

397. Paragraphs 29–34.
398. *See* Part II, Ch. 1, §4.II.
399. Section 4 of the WCC.
400. Sections 5, 6 of the WCC.
401. Section 6 of the NC.
402. Act 13 of 1998. A Western Cape Language Committee has been established in terms of this Act and it has been in operation since May 1999.

186. The last founding provision of the WCC stipulates that provincial legislation may provide for provincial symbols and the conferral of provincial honours.[403] Effect was given to this provision through the Western Cape Provincial Coat of Arms Act,[404] in terms of which a provincial coat of arms has been adopted, and the Western Cape Provincial Honours Act.[405]

II. The Provincial Parliament

A. Composition

187. Provincial legislative authority in the Western Cape is vested in the Provincial Parliament, as it is now called in terms of the WCC. Although the NC allows alternative provincial legislative structures to be developed in a provincial constitution, the WCC contains the same kind of provincial legislative structure that has been established in terms of the NC. It, however, fixes the size of the Provincial Parliament at 42 members.[406] In the case of all the other provincial legislatures without their own provincial constitutions the number of members must be determined in terms of a formula prescribed by national legislation.[407]

188. As part of its preparations for the June 1999 general election, the Electoral Commission determined that the Western Cape Provincial Parliament should consist of 39 members. This was clearly inconsistent with the provisions of the WCC. The matter was thus argued before the Constitutional Court shortly before the election. The Court, in a unanimous judgment, found that the Electoral Commission could not make a determination of seats for the Western Cape Provincial Parliament due to the fact that such provision was already validly made in the WCC.[408] Section 143(1) of the NC permits provincial constitutions to provide for different legislative structures and procedures than those provided in Chapter 6 of the NC. The scope of this permissible difference includes the authority to determine the number of seats of a provincial legislature. It was thus beyond the scope of authority of the Electoral Commission to validly make any determination for the Western Cape Provincial Parliament in view of the particular provisions contained in the WCC. Any other province that wishes to have a different number of seats in its legislature is currently bound by the determination of the Electoral Commission, unless it adopts a provincial constitution and makes an own determination in such constitution.

189. The members of the Provincial Parliament must be elected in terms of an electoral system prescribed by national legislation and which is based on the province's

403. Section 6 of the WCC.
404. Act 7 of 1998.
405. Act 9 of 1999.
406. Sections 9 and 13 of the WCC.
407. Section 105(2) of the NC. The national Electoral Act 73 of 1998, which constitutes such national legislation, prescribes a formula in terms of which the Electoral Commission has determined the seats of the legislatures in all the provinces, including the Western Cape.
408. *The Premier of the Province of the Western Cape v. The Electoral Commission* 1999 11 BCLR 1209 (CC).

segment of the national voters' roll.[409] An election in terms of this electoral system must furthermore result, in general, in proportional representation. In view of the failed attempt by the Western Cape to provide for a particular provincial electoral system,[410] the proponents of a mixed electoral system that is partly based on constituencies and partly based on proportional representation will have to wait and see what the national legislation envisaged in terms of both the WCC and the NC may provide.

190. Elections must be held every five years, unless the Provincial Parliament is dissolved under certain circumstances before the end of its normal five-year term. The Premier must dissolve the Provincial Parliament and call new elections if a decision to that effect is taken by a majority of all the members of the Provincial Parliament and three years have passed since the previous election. If there is a vacancy in the office of Premier and the Provincial Parliament fails to elect a new Premier within thirty days after the vacancy has occurred, the Acting Premier must also dissolve the Provincial Parliament.[411]

191. Every citizen over the age of 18 and who is qualified to vote for the National Assembly is eligible to be elected as a member of the Provincial Parliament, except:

- anyone in the paid service of the state;
- members of the National Assembly, permanent delegates to the NCOP or members of a municipal council;
- unrehabilitated insolvents;
- anyone legally declared to be of unsound mind; or
- a specified category of people serving jail sentences for criminal offences.[412]

192. A person who does not qualify may nevertheless be a candidate for the Provincial Parliament, implying that the person must qualify upon his or her election. Before assuming office, each member must swear or affirm faithfulness to the Republic and the province, and obedience to the NC and the WCC. A code of conduct for members of the Provincial Parliament must be provided by provincial legislation. A member of the Provincial Parliament loses membership if the person ceases to be eligible, resigns as a member, or is absent from the Provincial Parliament without permission in circumstances for which the rules of the Parliament prescribe loss of membership.[413] A vacancy must be filled in terms of provincial legislation.

193. The seat of the Provincial Parliament is Cape Town, which is also the seat of the Parliament of South Africa.[414] Provision is made that the Provincial Parliament or any of its committees may sit elsewhere in the Western Cape when necessary.

409. Section 14 of the WCC.
410. *See* para. 178 above.
411. Sections 17 and 18 of the WCC. This provision is obviously aimed at the event when for political reasons the Provincial Parliament is unable to muster a majority vote for a particular candidate, but in this unqualified form it may also have the unfair result that the Provincial Parliament is dissolved for a reason totally beyond the control of the Provincial Parliament (*see* Rautenbach (2012) (*supra*) 212–213).
412. Section 15 of the WCC.
413. Section 15(3).
414. Section 19 of the WCC. *See* iro the national Parliament, s. 42(6) of the NC.

194. In order to establish a close link between the Provincial Parliament and the NCOP it is provided that permanent delegates to the NCOP may voluntarily attend and speak in the Provincial Parliament and any of its committees, and may be required to attend such meetings. These permanent delegates do not have any voting rights in the Provincial Parliament.[415]

B. Powers

195. The powers of provincial legislatures have been discussed in Part I above and the WCC does not affect that. The Provincial Parliament has the authority to pass legislation in terms of both the NC and the WCC, which *inter alia* include matters falling within Schedules 4 and 5 of the NC, to pass legislation with regard to matters assigned to the Western Cape by national legislation, to replace, amend or repeal the WCC, and to assign to a municipal council any of its ordinary legislative powers.[416] In *DVB Behuising (Pty) Ltd v. North West Provincial Government*[417] the Constitutional Court provided a clear interpretation of the complex issue of the assignment of national legislation to provinces and the consequences thereof, when it held that provinces had the legislative authority to amend or repeal national legislation assigned to it to the extent that it became provincial legislation. The constitutional scope of provincial legislative authority was given a boost when the Court further found that the functional areas of provincial legislative authority 'must be purposively interpreted in a manner which will enable the national Parliament and the provincial legislatures to exercise their respective legislative powers fully and effectively.'[418]

196. In addition to these powers the Provincial Parliament may, on the strength of a two-thirds supporting vote, request Parliament to change its name. It may also recommend to the national Parliament the adoption of legislation concerning a matter outside the Provincial Parliament's authority, or a matter in respect of which an Act of the national Parliament prevails over provincial legislation. In addition, it may recommend to the NCOP the adoption of legislation on any other matter. The Provincial Parliament has other important duties, including the monitoring of the executive authority and any provincial organ of state. In particular, the Provincial Parliament must provide for mechanisms to oversee the exercise of provincial executive authority, and to oversee and ensure that all provincial organs of state are accountable to it.[419]

C. Functioning

197. At its first sitting after an election, the Provincial Parliament must elect a Speaker and may elect a Deputy Speaker and any other presiding officers from amongst

415. Section 22 of the WCC.
416. Section 9 of the WCC. Section 23(1) further provides that in the exercise of its legislative authority, the Provincial Parliament may consider, pass, amend or reject any bill before it, and may initiate or prepare legislation, except money bills, which may only be initiated by the executive –*see* s. 30.
417. 2000 4 BCLR 347 (CC).
418. Paragraph 17.
419. Section 23 of the WCC.

its members. There is currently both a Speaker and a Deputy Speaker.[420] Any of these office holders may be removed from office by a resolution of the Provincial Parliament supported by a majority of its members.

198. The Provincial Parliament has a continuous session commencing on the date of its first sitting after its election and ending on the day before the election of the next Provincial Parliament. The Provincial Parliament has fewer plenary meetings than the national Parliament. By far the bulk of the legislature's work is done in various multi-party standing committees that are appointed mainly to discuss new legislation and to exercise oversight of the executive and the provincial organs of state.[421] The standing committees are mainly established for different functional areas of provincial government.[422]

199. The procedures of the Provincial Parliament are not dissimilar to those of other provincial legislatures. The Provincial Parliament may determine its own internal arrangements, proceedings and procedures and may make rules concerning its business, with due regard to representative and participatory democracy, accountability, transparency and public participation.[423] The rules must provide for a number of matters, including the establishment, composition, powers and procedures of committees; the recognition of the leader of the opposition; the participation in all proceedings of minority parties represented in the Provincial Parliament in a manner consistent with democracy; financial and administrative assistance to parties represented in the Provincial Parliament; the participation of representatives of local government in committee deliberations on bills affecting local government; co-ordination between the Provincial Parliament and the NCOP; and the receipt of petitions, representations and submissions. In particular, a standing committee must be established to monitor socio-economic conditions in the Western Cape.[424] The Rules of the Western Cape Provincial Parliament have been adopted to provide for these matters.[425]

In terms of the WCC, the Provincial Parliament and its members enjoy certain privileges.[426] Members have freedom of speech in the Provincial Parliament and its committees, and are not liable to civil or criminal proceedings, arrest, imprisonment, or damages on account of anything said in, produced before or submitted to the Provincial Parliament or any committee. The Provincial Parliament and any committee may summon any person or provincial organ of state to appear before it to give evidence or to produce documents.

200. The WCC deals expressly with public involvement and participation in the activities of the Provincial Parliament and provides that the proceedings of the

420. Section 20 of the WCC.
421. Section 23 of the WCC.
422. The following standing committees are in existence, viz: Budget, Community Development, Community Safety. Conduct Committee, Parliamentary Oversight, Cultural Affairs and Sport, Finance, Environmental Affairs and Development Planning; Economic Opportunities, Tourism and Agriculture, Human Settlements, Local Government, Standing Committee on the Premier; Education, Public Accounts; Petitions, Transport and Public Works, and Rules.
423. Section 23(4).
424. Section 23(4)(d).
425. *See* www.wcpp.gov.za/standing-rules.
426. Sections 25–26.

Provincial Parliament and its committees take place in public.[427] Reasonable steps may be taken, however, to regulate access. The public, including the media, may not be excluded from any proceedings unless it is reasonable and justifiable in an open and democratic society. The Provincial Parliament must also facilitate public participation in its activities.

201. The legislative procedures in the Provincial Parliament are similar to those of the National Assembly. Only a provincial minister, a committee or a member of the Provincial Parliament may introduce a bill in the Provincial Parliament. Money bills may be introduced only by the Provincial Minister of Finance.[428] In terms of the Rules of the Provincial Parliament, a bill, upon introduction, is referred to the appropriate standing committee, which deliberates on the bill, amends it as it deems fit, and reports on it to the Provincial Parliament. The Provincial Parliament debates the bill as reported by the standing committee, and may refer it back to the committee for further amendments. On its return, the Provincial Parliament decides to pass or reject the bill. Decisions in the Provincial Parliament are taken mostly by way of a majority of the votes cast, but a majority of members must be present when a vote is taken on a bill or an amendment to a bill and one-third of the members must be present when a vote is taken on any other question before the House.[429] Within forty-five days of its adoption by the Provincial Parliament, the Premier must assent to a bill. A bill assented to and signed by the Premier becomes an Act of the Provincial Parliament.[430] However, should the Premier have reservations as to the constitutionality of a bill presented to him or her, he or she may refer it back to the Provincial Parliament for reconsideration. If, on its resubmission by the Provincial Parliament, the Premier still has reservations, he or she must assent to the bill, or must refer it to the Constitutional Court for a decision.[431] Members of the Provincial Parliament may apply to the Constitutional Court for an order declaring a provincial Act unconstitutional. The application must be supported by at least 20% of the members of the Provincial Parliament, and must be made within thirty days of the date on which the Premier assented to and signed the Act.[432]

202. Constitutional legislation is dealt with in a special way. A bill amending, replacing, or repealing the WCC must be passed with a supporting vote of at least two-thirds of the total number of members of the Provincial Parliament and may not contain any other but constitutional provisions.[433] At least thirty days before its introduction, the bill must be published for comment in the Provincial Gazette and in at least three newspapers circulating in the province, and must be submitted to municipalities in the province. Any written comments received must be tabled at the introduction of the bill. A bill amending or replacing the WCC must, upon its adoption, be submitted to the Constitutional Court for certification in accordance with section

427. Section 28.
428. A money bill is a bill that appropriates money or imposes taxes, levies or duties and may not deal with any other matter (s. 30(1)).
429. Section 21 of the WCC.
430. Section 33.
431. Section 31.
432. Section 32.
433. Section 10(1).

144 of the NC. The Premier must assent to and sign a certified text or amendment, upon which the text or amendment must be published in the Provincial Gazette.

III. The Executive

A. Executive Authority

203. The executive authority of the Western Cape is vested in the Premier, who exercises the authority together with the other members of the Provincial Cabinet.[434] This they do by implementing provincial legislation, as well as national legislation within the functional areas listed in Schedules 4 and 5 of the NC and in respect of which the province has the administrative capacity to assume effective responsibility, and national legislation outside those areas that has been assigned to the province.[435] In addition, the Premier and Cabinet develops and implements provincial policy, prepare and initiate provincial legislation, and co-ordinate the functions of the provincial administration.[436] Exercising the executive authority together with the other members of the Provincial Cabinet means that the Premier requires their consent for decisions, but that the degree of their consent depends on the procedures followed in the Cabinet of which the Premier is, of course, the chairperson, and on the Premier's political standing within the Provincial Parliament.[437]

B. The Premier

204. At its first meeting after its election the Provincial Parliament must elect a Premier from amongst its members.[438] The Premier must swear or affirm faithfulness to the Republic of South Africa and the Western Cape before assuming office, which must be done within five days after his or her election.[439] The Premier has a five-year term of office and may not serve more than two terms. The Premier appoints the other members of the Provincial Cabinet. Unlike the national President, the Premier remains a member of the Provincial Parliament and is normally the leader of the majority party in the Provincial Parliament. Currently a somewhat different situation prevails, because the Premier is the leader of the second largest party in the Provincial Parliament which had to form a coalition with one of the other minority parties in order to muster a majority with which to govern.[440]

434. Section 35 of the WCC.
435. Section 35(2).
436. They also perform any other function assigned to the Provincial Cabinet in terms of the NC or an Act of Parliament (s. 35(2)(g)).
437. *See* the explanation by Rautenbach (2012) (*supra*) 212–214.
438. Section 38 of the WCC.
439. Section 39 and Sch. 1 of the WCC.
440. After the 1999 elections, in which no party obtained a clear majority of seats, a coalition government led by the Premier, Mr Gerald Morkel, and consisting of members of both the New National Party and the Democratic Party, has been formed.

The Premier may be removed from office on the grounds of a serious violation of the NC, the WCC or the law, serious misconduct or the inability to perform the functions of the office. A decision to this effect must be taken by a two-thirds majority of the members of the Provincial Parliament.[441] A motion of no-confidence in the Premier, supported by a majority of the members of the Provincial Parliament, will also cause the removal of the Premier, because on that account the Premier must resign. If, however, a majority of the members of the Provincial Parliament passes a motion of no-confidence only in the Provincial Cabinet, excluding the Premier, the Premier must appoint a new Provincial Cabinet.[442] The WCC provides for an Acting Premier when the Premier is absent or otherwise unable to fulfil his or her duties.[443]

The following office-holders in the order below may act as Premier:

- a provincial minister designated by the Premier;
- a provincial minister designated by the other provincial ministers; or
- the Speaker, until the Provincial Parliament designates one of its members.

An Acting Premier must take an oath or affirmation before assuming office and has the responsibilities, powers, and functions of the Premier.

205. The Premier has the powers entrusted to that office by the NC, the WCC and any legislation. These powers include assenting to and signing of bills, referring bills back to the Provincial Parliament or to the Constitutional Court, chairing the Provincial Cabinet, summoning the Provincial Parliament for an extraordinary sitting, appointing commissions of inquiry, e.g., the Khayelitsha Commission appointed by the Premier in 2012,[444] and calling a referendum in the province.[445] Any executive decision of the Premier must be in writing if it is taken in terms of a law or if it has legal consequences, and such a written decision must be countersigned by a provincial minister if the decision concerns a function assigned to that minister.[446]

C. The Provincial Cabinet

206. The Provincial Cabinet consists of the Premier as its head and a number of provincial ministers, as they are called in terms of the WCC, appointed by the Premier. The constitutional mandate of the Premier to appoint his or her Cabinet and to assign functions to the members thereof was confirmed by the Constitutional Court.[447] The composition of the Western Cape Provincial Cabinet differs slightly from the

441. Section 40 of the WCC.
442. Section 51 of the WCC.
443. Section 41.
444. Section 206 of the NC. A Commission of Inquiry into policing in Khayelitsha was appointed by Premier Helen Zille after receiving various complaints from the community – media statement on 21 Aug. 2012 (www.westerncape.gov.za/news/appointment-commission-inquiry-policing-khayelitsha).
445. Sections 35 and 37 of the WCC.
446. Section 50(1) and (2).
447. *Premier of the Province of the Western Cape v. President of the RSA* 1999 4 BCLR 382 CC paras 91–92.

standard provisions relating to provincial executives found in the NC. Provision is made for two categories of provincial ministers, namely a group of between five and ten provincial ministers drawn from members of the Provincial Parliament, and a second category made up of a maximum of two persons who are not members of the Provincial Parliament. The ratio behind the inclusion of this provision, which only applies until the second election of the Provincial Parliament under the WCC, is to enable the Premier to bring into the Provincial Cabinet specific expertise that is not available in the Provincial Parliament.[448]

207. Provincial ministers perform the functions assigned to them by the Premier.[449] The Premier may transfer to a minister the functions of another minister, and may temporarily assign to a minister the functions or powers of another minister who is absent or unable to perform those functions or exercise those powers.[450] A provincial minister may also assign any power that he or she may have in terms of a law to a municipality.[451] Provincial ministers must perform their functions diligently and are collectively and individually accountable to the Provincial Parliament for the performance of their functions. Ministers must report regularly to the Provincial Parliament on their performance and they must furthermore act in accordance with a code of ethics prescribed by national legislation.[452] They may not undertake any other paid work, act in any way inconsistent with their office or use their position as provincial minister to enrich themselves or to improperly benefit any other person.[453]

208. In addition to its other functions in terms of the NC, the WCC and legislation, the Provincial Cabinet has an important supervisory role in respect of local government within the Western Cape. It must support and strengthen the capacity of municipalities in the Western Cape and has the authority to intervene when a municipality cannot or does not fulfil an executive obligation in terms of legislation.[454]

209. An innovation in the WCC is the inclusion of a set of directive principles of provincial policy, which is not legally enforceable, but is supposed to guide the

448. Section 42 read with Item 8 Sch. 3 of the WCC. After the June 1999 elections the Western Cape Provincial Cabinet initially consisted of the Premier plus twelve members – eight of the New National Party and four of the Democratic Party. Two of these members were appointed from outside the Provincial Parliament. Actually, during 2000, the two parties entered into a national alliance called the Democratic Alliance (DA), which governed the Western Cape since 2009. The NNP does not exist anymore.
449. Section 43.
450. Sections 47 and 48.
451. Section 36. The assignment must be made in terms of an agreement between the provincial minister and the municipal council, must be consistent with the law in question, and must be promulgated by the Premier in the Provincial Gazette.
452. Sections 42, 43 and 46 of the WCC; the Executive Members' Ethics Act 82 of 1998.
453. Section 46 of the WCC. *See also* para. 180 *supra* regarding the Constitutional Court's findings iro 'paid work.'
454. Sections 49, 52 and 54 of the WCC.

provincial government in its adoption and implementation of policies and legislation.[455] The current coalition government of the Western Cape used these directive principles as a point of reference to determine their policy objectives and priorities for the current term of office.[456] The directive principles cover a wide field of subjects, and include references to safety and security, promotion of non-racialism, advancement of persons disadvantaged by unfair discrimination, protection of the rights of cultural, religious and linguistic communities, creation of job opportunities, promotion of a work ethic, promotion of a market-oriented economy, realizing the right of access to adequate housing, health care services, sufficient food and water, and social security, special care for children, development of rural communities, a fair taxation system, special care for frail and elderly persons, protection of the environment, conservation of the historical heritage of the Western Cape, and development of the youth. It remains to be seen to which extent these directive principles indeed determine, or at least influence, the policies of the Western Cape government.

IV. Administration and Finance

210. Public administration throughout South Africa is governed by the democratic values and principles contained in the NC, including the principles listed in section 195 thereof. Although in terms of the NC there is one public service in South Africa, provincial governments are responsible for the recruitment, appointment, promotion, transfer and dismissal of members of the public service within their administrations.[457] In an application by the Premier of the Western Cape to the Constitutional Court, the

455. Section 81 of the WCC. Three other constitutions which contain directive policy principles were considered as examples when the WCC was drafted, namely those of Ireland, India and Namibia. *See* Arts 36–51 of the Constitution of India; Dube, *Role of the Supreme Court in Indian Constitution* (1988) 154. The relationship between fundamental rights and directive principles in India is discussed by Chinappa Reddy J in *Akhil Bharatiya Soshit Karamchari Sangh v. Union of India* [1981] 1 SCC 246 and Hegde J in *Chandra Bhawan Boarding v. State of Mysore* AIR 1970 SC 2042. Article 45 of the Constitution of Ireland contains 'principles of social policy.' The status and development of these principles in Irish jurisprudence are discussed in depth by Kelly *The Irish Constitution* (1994).

456. The Provincial Cabinet formed after the June 1999 election adopted the following policy objectives:

- To contribute to the creation of a safer environment for our people;
- To create an enabling environment for economic growth; – To prepare the people of the Western Cape for the knowledge economy of the 21st century;
- To contain the spread of HIV/AIDS and Tuberculosis;
- To empower the poor people of our Province through the provision of basic services;
- To improve the quality and accessibility of services provided by the Provincial Government;
- To protect, enhance and promote the total environment for the optimal development of our people;
- To maintain and improve the physical infrastructure required for the development of this Province; and
- To bind the Province, as the gateway to Africa, ever stronger to the country and the continent.

457. Sections 55 and 56 of the WCC; s. 197 of the NC.

constitutional validity of certain amendments to the national Public Service Act 103 of 1994 was questioned. The Court confirmed that provincial powers in the field of public administration included the authority to determine which departments should be established within the provincial government and that the Premier could allocate functions to the respective provincial departments.[458]

211. Good administration includes sound financial administration, including budgetary processes and financial management. This is confirmed by the inclusion of a legislative framework for South Africa's financial intergovernmental relations system in Chapter 13 of the NC. The provisions applicable to provinces are reiterated in Chapter 7 of the WCC. These provisions must, in view of the fact that they only provide a framework, be complemented by additional legislation.

212. In terms of the particular financial intergovernmental relations system established by the NC, provinces have limited possibilities to raise taxes.[459] The revenue of the Western Cape consists mainly of the equitable share of revenue raised nationally and allocated to the province. The right to an equitable share of nationally raised revenue is a way of compensating provinces for their own limited revenue sources which are insufficient to fund their constitutionally allocated responsibilities.[460] Other sources of revenue are additional allocations from the national government, revenue raised by the Western Cape provincial government and other money or assets which it receives.[461] The limited potential sources of provincial taxes in the Western Cape are taxes, levies, and duties, *other* than personal and corporate income tax, value-added tax, general sales tax, rates on property or customs duties, or flat-rate surcharges on the tax base of nationally imposed taxes excluding corporate income tax, value-added tax, rates on property, or customs duty.[462] Provision is further made that provincial legislation may provide for user charges. This source of provincial revenue was mentioned by the Constitutional Court when it heard the application for the certification of the NC.

213. All the money received by the Western Cape provincial government must by paid into the Provincial Revenue Fund and can only be withdrawn either by way of an appropriation act or as a direct charge against the Provincial Revenue Fund.[463] This provision is in line with the principle that the provincial budget and budgetary process must promote transparency, accountability, and effective financial management.[464]

214. The provincial budget process is a comprehensive exercise that lies on two levels, namely, first, an internal process of determining fundamental budget allocation principles and determining the actual division of funds. Secondly, this process fits into the national budgetary process in terms of which the Budget Council, composed of

458. *Premier of the Province of the Western Cape v. President of the RSA* 1999 4 BCLR 382 CC para. 91.

459. *See* Part I, Ch. 3, §2.

460. For a discussion of the provincial equitable share and the latest division of funds *see* RSA National Treasury, *Budget Review 2016*, 75 et seq.; Division of Revenue Act 3 of 2016.

461. Section 57 of the WCC; s. 214 of the NC.

462. These are still potential sources and is a right not yet exercised due to political pressure and an informal arrangement among the members of the Budget Council to delay its implementation.

463. Section 58 of the WCC.

464. Section 60 of the WCC.

the national Minister of Finance and the nine provincial executive members responsible for finance, undertakes a collective multi-year financial planning exercise (MTEF) with a significant input from the Financial and Fiscal Commission.[465]

215. A basis for a proper legislative framework for the management of provincial assets has been established in section 65 of the WCC. The Provincial Parliament adopted the Western Cape Land Administration Act 6 of 1998 in terms of this provision, which in turn led to the appointment of a provincial minister and the establishment of a dedicated component to manage the Western Cape's fixed assets portfolio.

V. Other Constitutional Institutions

216. In this area the drafters of the WCC attempted to provide for institutions that reflect the particular needs and circumstances of the Western Cape. The WCC accordingly provides the basic legislative framework for three specific constitutional institutions, namely cultural councils,[466] a Commissioner for the Environment[467] and a Commissioner for Children.[468] Further legislation had to be developed to give full effect to these provisions. The Provincial Parliament accordingly passed the Western Cape Cultural Commission and Cultural Councils Act,[469] in terms of which the Western Cape Cultural Commission was established during May 1999. This Act also provides for the recognition and reasonable funding of cultural councils within the Western Cape. Legislation to establish a Commissioner for the Environment and a Commissioner for Children is still under consideration. The legislative environment in the field of environmental affairs has changed since the adoption of the WCC and could have an impact on whether or not a Commissioner for the Environment is still required.

217. In view of the importance and sensitivity surrounding the official use of languages, the Western Cape Language Committee was established in 1999 in terms of the Western Cape Provincial Languages Act.[470] The Act was passed by the Provincial Parliament in order to give effect to the constitutional requirement to regulate for the purposes of provincial government the use of the official languages of the province, Afrikaans, English, and isiXhosa.[471] The Western Cape Language Committee fulfils the important function not only to monitor the use of official languages by the provincial government, but also to provide practical and positive measures for the development of the indigenous languages of the people of the Western Cape of which the status and use have been historically diminished and for the elevation of their status.[472]

465. *See* the discussion of financial intergovernmental relations in Part I, Ch. 3, §2.1; the Intergovernmental Fiscal Relations Act 97 of 1997. For a discussion of the Western Cape budget and budgetary process *see* Western Cape Provincial Government Department of Finance, *Budget Review 1999*.
466. Section 70 of the WCC.
467. Sections 71–77 of the WCC.
468. Sections 78–80 of the WCC.
469. Act 14 of 1998.
470. Act 13 of 1998.
471. *See* s. 5 of the WCC.
472. Section 5(3) of the WCC.

VI. Miscellaneous

218. Various other matters provided for in the WCC deserve to be mentioned. First, the importance of intergovernmental relations in the South African constitutional system is reflected in the WCC by the inclusion of two sections that deal specifically with this matter. First, the adherence of the Western Cape provincial government to the principles of co-operative government and intergovernmental relations set out in the NC is reiterated.[473] Secondly, the delegates of the Western Cape to the NCOP are required to promote the interests of the Western Cape and of the country as a whole in accordance with these principles.[474]

219. The term 'intergovernmental relations' is used in practice within the Western Cape provincial government in a related but slightly amended form as a functional area, which includes the Western Cape province's relations with the national government, other provinces and local government, as well as the province's international relations. These international relations or relations with other regions in the world cover one or more of the areas of provincial government as established by the NC.[475] The conclusion of co-operation agreements between the Western Cape and other regional governments is not regulated by international law, but falls within the field of constitutional law.

220. Policing functions in the provinces is a highly contentious issue and the drafting of the NC was accompanied by much debate on the extent of the policing functions to be allocated to the provinces. Eventually, limited powers regarding the police were conferred on the provinces.[476] The WCC accordingly contains a chapter on police, in which it is confirmed that the Western Cape government is entitled to oversee and assess the effectiveness and efficiency of the police service and visible policing in the province, monitor police conduct, promote good relations between the police and the community, and liaise with the national Minister responsible for police services in respect of crime and policing in the province.[477] The Western Cape government may appoint commissions of inquiry for these purposes, and the Provincial Parliament may pass any legislation necessary to carry out these functions. The Provincial Cabinet is involved in the appointment of the commissioner of police in the Western Cape, and the commissioner must report annually to the Provincial Parliament. The Provincial Cabinet must determine the policing needs and priorities of the Western Cape and must convey them to the national minister, and is responsible for any policing functions conferred on it by national legislation.

---

473. Section 7.
474. Sections 7 and 8 of the WCC; s. 41 of the NC.
475. Currently the Western Cape has active co-operation agreements with the following other regions in the world, viz. with Bavaria (Germany), Upper Austria (Austria), Burgundy (France), Georgia (USA), Shandong (People's Republic of China), Monaco and Pusan (South-Korea), as well as multi-lateral co-operative relations.
476. Sections 205–208 of the NC.
477. Chapter 8 of the WCC. *See* n 444 regarding the Commission of Inquiry into policing in Khayelitsha.

221. Lastly, the WCC contains a chapter on local government,[478] but it simply reiterates to a large extent the most important provisions relating to local government in the NC. This matter is discussed below in Part III.

§3. Conclusion

222. It may well be argued that the WCC reiterates to a large extent the provisions dealing with provincial structures and procedures in the NC, and that it has not succeeded to any significant degree in putting its own stamp on its constitutional system.[479] However, a number of arguments may be raised against such a harsh and unsympathetic view of the Western Cape's contribution to sub-national constitutional development in South Africa. First, the WCC still remains the only provincial constitution in operation, which in itself must be regarded as no mean feat, given the fact that in its endeavours to develop its own constitution the province has enjoyed only the half-hearted support of the ANC, the majority party in South Africa, which presently does not really exert itself to encourage sub-national constitutional development. Secondly, the WCC does contain some unique features, as mentioned above, such as the cultural councils, the Commissioners for the Environment and for Children, and the directive principles. Thirdly, the development of a unique constitutional culture in the province does not only depend on the uniqueness of its constitutional provisions themselves, but equally on the practices, customs and traditions that may develop in terms of the constitution and around the structures provided in the constitution. There is ample evidence that this is beginning to happen. Lastly, the contribution of the Western Cape lies not so much in the uniqueness of its constitution as in the proof it has provided that there is scope for sub-national constitutional development in South Africa and that provincial constitutions are indeed feasible.

223. For the moment, the challenge for sub-national constitutional law in South Africa is not in the first place to draft unique provincial constitutions, as exciting as that may be from a constitutional point of view, but to produce any other provincial constitutions at all. It remains for the other provinces to become convinced that, despite various obstacles such as limited resources and the struggle to achieve and maintain effective administration, the making of their own constitutions can provide an impetus for confidence, stability, growth, and development in many respects in their provinces. The Western Cape is providing an example in this regard that can be emulated.

478. Chapter 5.

479. *See* e.g., C. Murray, *Provincial Constitution-Making in South Africa: The (Non)Example of the Western Cape*, Neue Folge Band 49 Jahrbuch des öffentlichen Rechts 481–512 (2001).

Part III. Local Government

§1. Background

224. Traditionally, local government had been regarded as the third level of government in South Africa, but constitutionally a hierarchical relationship had always existed between the different levels of government and, accordingly, local government had always been subject to the other levels of government, particularly provincial government. Previous constitutions made no significant mention of local government and simply referred to local government as one of the matters on which provincial governments could legislate. In addition, being a unitary state, the provinces had always exercised their powers regarding local government subject to and within the framework of parliamentary legislation relating to local government. This enabled Parliament, as a matter of fact, to impose apartheid laws and systems on local government level, and thereby reducing the authority of the provinces to nothing more than the regulation of local government within the apartheid framework created by national legislation. On this basis, more than 1,200 racially segregated local governments of various types, sizes and shapes came into existence over the years.[480]

225. The so-called white local governments were mostly affluent and generally had the capacity to administer their local communities and render the necessary services fairly effectively. In most cases, the Coloured and Indian townships formed adjuncts of the white local governments, but the black townships, which were mostly very poor, had their own local governments created in terms of national legislation specifically aimed at regulating the affairs of the black communities. The provinces had almost

480. *See generally* on the development of local government in South Africa J. De Beer and L. Lourens, *Plaaslike Regering: Die Pad na Demokrasie* (Van Schaik: Pretoria 1995); A. Van Rooyen, *A History of Local Government in South Africa* (Rhodes University Institute for Social and Economic Research 1991). *See* regarding local government arrangements relating to the black townships e.g., the Black Local Authority Act 102 of 1982, the Local Authority Ordinance 17 of 1939 (Transvaal), the Municipal Ordinance 20 of 1974 (Cape Province), the Local Authorities Ordinance 25 of 1974 (Natal) and the Local Authority Ordinance 8 of 1962 (OFS).

no local government powers relating to the black townships apart from those they exercised under delegation by national legislation.[481]

226. With the advent of majority government in the 1990s, it proved to be wholly impractical to abolish the existing system overnight and its dismantling commenced in terms of a three phase-process provided by the Local Government Transition Act of 1993.[482] First, the various racially segregated townships in every town and city were brought together to manage their local affairs together on an interim basis while they negotiated on new, non-racial local governments for their towns and cities. Secondly, local elections were held to create interim non-racial local governments in terms of existing local government legislation and, thirdly, legislation had to be put in place for a new non-racial local government system.[483] This third phase of the transition process has now been completed and various laws are in place to provide the detail legislative framework for local government.[484]

§2. Constitutional Status of Local Government

I. Constitutional Status

227. Although, as explained, the actual transformation of local government eventually followed different procedures from that of the national and provincial spheres of government, local government was part and parcel of the constitutional negotiations of the 1990s. It was the intention from the start to include certain key provisions on local government in the constitution. Eventually, a whole chapter of the NC, Chapter 7, was dedicated to local government. Not only was local government recognized as a fully fledged sphere of government; its existence and status was also constitutionally entrenched. Section 40(1) of the NC provides that government in the Republic is constituted as national, provincial and local spheres of government which are distinctive, interdependent and interrelated. Section 151(1) then provides that the local sphere of government consists of municipalities which must be established for the whole of the Republic. In the case of the Western Cape, the WCC reiterates certain key provisions of the NC relating to local government and does not affect the status of local government in that province. The exact status of local government and its relationship with the other spheres of government as determined by various other provisions of the NC are discussed further below.

228. It should be mentioned that some commentators seem to suggest that the reference in section 40 of the NC to 'spheres' instead of 'levels' of government indicates something significant regarding the status of local government in relation to the other

481. *See* e.g., W. Zybrands, *Local Government*, in *Government and Politics in the New South Africa* 193, 195 (A. Venter ed., Van Schaik 1998).
482. Act 209 of 1993.
483. *See* I.M. Rautenbach (2012) (*supra*) 229–244.
484. Some of the important Acts are the Municipal Systems Act 32 of 2000, Municipal Structures Act 117 of 1998 and the Municipal Finance Management Act 56 of 2003.

spheres.[485] The mere use of the concept 'sphere of government' is, however, in itself insufficient and, as explained below, one needs to analyse all relevant provisions of the NC in order to determine the constitutional status of local government.

II. Relationship with Other Spheres of Government

229. The relationship between local government and governments in other spheres is also determined by the principle of co-operative government. However, governments in the other spheres have wide constitutional powers with regard to local government matters. The relationship between local government and governments in the other spheres determines the status of local government. In terms of section 85 of the South Africa Act, and section 84 of the 1961 Constitution, local government was one of the subjects under the jurisdiction of the provinces and, accordingly, local government was subject to laws of both the provinces and Parliament. In this way, Parliament and the provinces exercised extensive control over local government.[486] Constitutionally, the position has changed in several ways:

- It has been mentioned that now for the first time, local government enjoys constitutional recognition as a fully fledged sphere of government. It means, at the least, that the other spheres of government may not abolish local government, or otherwise disregard the provisions of the NC on local government.[487] However, as mentioned, the exact status of local government can be determined properly only by taking into account all relevant provisions of the NC, and does not in the first place depend on the fact that local government, like national and provincial government, is described as a sphere of government.[488]
- The principle of co-operative government also applies to the relationship between local government and the other spheres of government.[489] Therefore, mutual respect for the constitutional status, institutions, powers, and functions of governments in the various spheres and the prohibition not to encroach on one another's geographical, functional, and institutional integrity also apply here.[490] The national and provincial governments, by legislative and other measures, must also support and strengthen the capacity of municipalities to manage their own affairs, exercise their powers, and perform their functions.[491] In addition, structures

485. *See* J. Meyer, *Local Government Law 1997* 6 (Butterworths 1998).

486. De Beer and Lourens (*supra*) 7.

487. It was stated in *Executive Council of the Western Cape v. Minister of Provincial Affairs and Constitutional Development; Executive Council of KwaZulu-Natal v. President of the RSA* 1999 12 BCLR 1360 (CC) para. 29: 'The Constitution therefore protects the role of local government, and places certain constraints upon the powers of Parliament to interfere with local government decisions.'

488. Meyer (*supra*) 6.

489. Chapter 3 of the NC. *See* the remarks by G. Pimstone, *local Government*, in *Constitutional Law of South Africa* 5A.25 et seq (M. Chaskalson et al. eds, Juta 1998).

490. Section 41(1)(*e*) and (*g*).

491. Section 154(1).

and processes for intergovernmental relations involving local government need to be developed by the provinces.

- Local government enjoys representation in the National Council of Provinces (NCOP). Section 67 of the NC provides that organized local government may designate not more than ten part-time representatives to represent different categories of municipalities in the NCOP. They participate in the proceedings of the NCOP whenever necessary, but may not vote. The Organized Local Government Act provides for the recognition of national and provincial organizations that represent municipalities and for procedures in terms of which such organizations may designate representatives in the NCOP.[492]
- Local government is closely involved in some of the structures that have been established to promote intergovernmental relations, and is represented in the national sphere mainly by the South African Local Government Association (SALGA).[493] Local government is also represented in the Financial and Fiscal Commission (FFC).[494] Much more still needs to be done, however, to develop intergovernmental relations structurally and otherwise, and to fully accommodate local government in such structures within provinces.[495]

230. Despite these constitutional changes, local government remains subject to the other spheres of government and under their control.[496] The NC expressly makes municipal by-laws (legislation) subject to national and provincial legislation and provides that a municipal by-law that conflicts with national or provincial legislation is invalid.[497] Furthermore, governments in the other spheres have wide, albeit not limitless, powers with regard to local government affairs.

231. (a)*The autonomy of local governments is limited by the provision that municipalities have the right to govern their communities 'subject to national and provincial legislation.'*[498] This means that local autonomy may be limited by-laws adopted by Parliament and the provinces. The NC itself envisages such laws:

- The NC authorizes or prescribes the adoption of specific laws. National legislation must be adopted to define the types of municipalities that may be established in

492. Act 52 of 1997, adopted pursuant to s. 163 of the NC.
493. The Association has been recognized in terms of the Organized Local Government Act 52 of 1997. *See* on the role of the Association Pimstone (*supra*) 5A.32.
494. *See* s. 5(c) of the Financial and Fiscal Commission Act 99 of 1997 as amended, which gives effect to s. 163(*b*)(iii) of the NC.
495. *See* the ideas of B. De Villiers, *Local-Provincial Intergovernmental Relations: A Comparative Analysis*, SA Public Law 469 (1997); G. Pimstone, *The Constitutional Basis of Local Government in South Africa*' Konrad Adenauer Stiftung, *Occasional Papers* (March 1998) 8–10.
496. *See* in general the remarks by Pimstone (*supra*) 5A.25–35. *See also* Pimstone, *The Constitutional Basis of Local Government in South Africa*, Konrad Adenauer Stiftung, *Occasional Papers* (March 1998) 2–5.
497. Section 156(3). If the municipal by-law conflicts with a national or provincial law that is inoperative because it is itself in conflict with another national or provincial law, as the case may be (*see* s. 149), the municipal by-law is regarded as valid as long as that national or provincial law is inoperative.
498. Section 151(3).

the various categories of municipalities, establish criteria for the demarcation and establishment of municipalities and provide for the division of their powers and functions.[499] The particulars of the electoral system for local government,[500] certain aspects relating to membership of municipal councils,[501] the terms of municipal councils,[502] the participation of members in proceedings[503] and the recognition of organized local government[504] must also be regulated by national legislation. National legislation may provide for the size of municipalities and for their committee systems.[505] Most of these matters are regulated in the Local Government: Municipal Structures Act of 1998.[506] Provincial legislation must determine the types of municipalities to be established in every province,[507] and may provide for the establishment, monitoring, support, and development of municipalities.[508]

– Parliament and the provinces are generally empowered to make laws on all local government matters that are not dealt with by the NC.[509] These powers of Parliament and the provinces are limited, however, because they may not be exercised in conflict with the provisions of the NC. Such laws may not, for example, compromise or impede the ability or right of municipalities to exercise their powers or perform their functions.[510] Parliament and the provinces may, therefore, limit the autonomy of local governments through legislation, as long as such limitation does not affect the essence of local government.[511] Any national or provincial bill that affects local government must also be published in a way that enables municipalities to make representations.[512]

232. (b) *All traditional local functional areas are included in the lists of exclusive and concurrent provincial functional areas which are contained in schedules 4 and 5*

499. Section 155(2) en (3).
500. Section 157(2) and (6). *See* below.
501. Section 158(1)(*a*) and (*b*) and (2).
502. Section 159.
503. Sections 160(3) and 161.
504. Section 163. *See* the Organized Local Government Act 52 of 1997.
505. Section 160(6).
506. Act 117 of 1998. A few provisions of this Act was struck down in *Executive Council of the Western Cape v. Minister of Provincial Affairs and Constitutional Development; Executive Council of KwaZulu-Natal v. President of the RSA* 1999 12 BCLR 1360 (CC). *See* below.
507. Section 155(5). *See* for example the Western Cape Determination of Types of Municipalities Act 9 of 2000.
508. Section 155(6).
509. Section 164. In *Executive Council of the Western Cape v. Minister of Provincial Affairs and Constitutional Development; Executive Council of KwaZulu-Natal v. President of the RSA* 1999 12 BCLR 1360 (CC) it was held that on the basis of s. 164, it could not be contended that Parliament had concurrent, and, consequently, full residual legislative powers on all local government matters referred to in the NC.
510. Section 151(4).
511. This is also the position in Germany – H.D. Jarass and B. Pieroth, *Grundgesetz für die Bundesrepublik Deutschland* 507–513 (C.H. Beck 1995).
512. Organized local government and other interested persons must also be able to react (s. 154(2)).

of the NC.[513] On the one hand, this means that the powers of local governments are entrenched in the NC. On the other hand, the implication is that local governments do not have exclusive powers and that they share their authority over the relevant functional areas with Parliament and the provinces. Consequently, the provinces and, under certain circumstances, Parliament may make laws over local government matters – subject to the provisions and restrictions of the NC.[514] Whenever a local by-law on such a matter is inconsistent with a provincial or national law, the by-law is simply invalid. However, national and provincial laws on local matters may not be inconsistent with the provisions of the NC on local government. While local government are, therefore, still under the control of Parliament and the provinces, the position has changed because these authorities cannot exercise control according to their own discretion. They must specifically act in accordance with the provisions of the NC on local government.

233. (c) *Provincial governments have legislative and executive authority to monitor the local government matters which are mentioned in schedules 4 and 5 and to see to it that municipalities administer them effectively.*[515] The provinces exercise this power subject to the qualifications that Parliament may also adopt laws on those matters, that the autonomy of municipalities may not be compromised or impeded, and that the national and provincial governments must support and strengthen the capacity of municipalities to govern their own affairs.[516] The Western Cape has adopted a law in 2014 to regulate its monitoring and support of municipalities in the province.[517]

234. (d) *When a municipality does not fulfil an executive obligation, the relevant provincial government may intervene through any appropriate steps to ensure that the obligation is fulfilled.*[518] This may include a directive to fulfil the obligation, or the provincial government may itself assume responsibility for it to the extent that it is necessary to maintain or establish essential national standards, maintain economic unity, or prevent the municipality from taking unreasonable steps that are prejudicial to the interests of another municipality or the province. The intervention must end unless it is approved by the national minister responsible for local government within fourteen days.[519] A notice of the intervention must be tabled in the provincial legislature and the NCOP.[520] The intervention must end unless it is approved by the NCOP within thirty days and the NCOP must also review the intervention regularly.

513. Although the NC does not provide, unlike previous Constitutions, that local government is one of the functional areas over which the provinces have legislative authority. *See* e.g., Sch. 6 of the Interim NC.
514. *Executive Council of the Western Cape v. Minister of Provincial Affairs and Constitutional Development; Executive Council of KwaZulu-Natal v. President of the RSA* 1999 12 BCLR 1360 (CC) para. 27.
515. *See* e.g., on the appointment of a commission of enquiry into the affairs of a local government *Van der Merwe v. Slabbert NO* 1998 6 BCLR 697 (N), 1998 3 SA 613 (N).
516. Section 155(6).
517. Western Cape Monitoring and Support of Municipalities Act 4 of 2014.
518. Section 139(1). *Cf.* the national government's power to intervene in respect of the provinces – s. 100.
519. Section 139(2)(*a*).
520. This must take place within fourteen days from their first sittings after the intervention (s. 139(2)(*b*)).

235. (e) *A provincial executive must intervene if a municipality fails to approve a budget or any revenue-raising measures necessary to give effect to the budget.*[521] The provincial executive must take appropriate steps to ensure that the budget or those revenue-raising measures are approved. What constitutes appropriate measures depends on the situation, but include dissolving a municipal council, appointing an administrator, and approving a budget.[522]

§3. Local Government Structures

I. Background

236. Despite considerable provincial differences in respect of both designations and particulars, autonomous local governments in South Africa in the past had displayed certain common features. They exercised legislative powers through directly elected councils and executive authority in each local government was vested either in the council sitting as a committee, in an executive committee elected from among the members of the council, or in several committees of the council. Each council had its own sources of revenue, of which property taxes and user charges were the most important. They also depended to a large degree on subsidies and allocations from the national and provincial governments.

237. Although these general characteristics have been retained to a large extent in the transformation of local government, the provisions of the NC, the Local Government Transition Act and the Local Government: Municipal Structures Act have profoundly affected the composition, powers and functioning of existing local governments.

II. Composition, Powers and Functioning

A. Establishment

238. Local governments (municipalities) must be established for the whole Republic.[523] The NC provides for different categories of municipalities and the Local Government: Municipal Structures Act defines the different types of municipalities that may be established in each category.[524] National legislation also determines the criteria for the demarcation of municipal boundaries by an independent demarcation

521. Section 139(4).
522. *See* De Vos & Freedman 301–303; *Premier of the Western Cape v. Overberg District Municipality* 2011 (4) SA 441 (SCA).
523. Section 151(1).
524. Act 117 of 1998, adopted in terms of s. 155(2) of the NC.

board.[525] Each province determines the type of municipalities to be established in the province and deals with their actual establishment.[526]

B. Composition

239. Every municipality has a directly elected council. Under the Interim NC, this did not mean that every member had to be elected, allowing for membership of traditional leaders.[527] The NC leaves open the question of their membership and the Local Government: Municipal Structures Act merely provides for the participation of traditional leaders in the proceedings of a municipal council.[528] The council must be elected democratically for a term not exceeding four years.[529] The municipal electoral system is determined by the Local Government: Municipal Structures Act and may entail a proportional system according to the list system, or a proportional system combined with ward representation.[530] Proportionality is the overriding principle applicable to the composition of a municipal council and must be maintained throughout.[531] The relevant municipality's segment of the national common voters roll must be used

525. Local Government: Municipal Demarcation Act 27 of 1998, adopted in terms of s. 155(3)(*b*) of the NC. Section 174(2) of the Interim NC provided that provision could be made for metropolitan, urban and rural local governments with differentiated powers, functions and structures in accordance with different demographic, economic, physical and environmental conditions. Section 11 of the Local Government Transition Act already provides for a demarcation board in every province. Provisions in the Local Government: Municipal Structures Act which empowered the national minister to determine and apply criteria for the establishment of metropolitan councils were struck down on the basis that the NC intended for the independent demarcation board to perform that function –*Executive Council of the Western Cape v. Minister of Provincial Affairs and Constitutional Development; Executive Council of KwaZulu-Natal v. President of the RSA* 1999 12 BCLR 1360 (CC).
526. Section 155(5) and (6). *See* s. 12 of Act 117 of 1998.
527. *African National Congress v. Minister of Local Government and Housing, Kwazulu-Natal* 1998 4 BCLR 399 (CC), 1998 2 SA 1 (CC).
528. Section 81 provides that the number of traditional leaders who may so participate may not exceed 10% of the total number of members.
529. Section 159. In *Executive Council of the Western Cape v. Minister of Provincial Affairs and Constitutional Development; Executive Council of KwaZulu-Natal v. President of the RSA* 1999 12 BCLR 1360 (CC) a provision in the Local Government: Municipal Structures Act 117 of 1998 which empowered the national minister to determine the terms of councils was struck down on the ground that the NC did not allow the delegation of this power to the minister.
530. Schedule 1 of Act 117 of 1998. *See also* s. 157(2) of the NC. If the electoral system provides for ward representation, the wards must be demarcated by an independent body (s. 157(4)). The Demarcation Board has been designated to perform this function – item 2 of Sch. 1 to Act 117 of 1998.
531. Section 157(3). *See* on the principle |J.R. De Ville and F. Chohan-Khota, *Local Government Elections: An Exercise in Proportional Representation*, SA Public Law 30 (1996). In *Democratic Party v. Miller NO* 1997 2 BCLR 223 (D), 1997 1 SA 758 (D) it was held that a particular regulation was inconsistent with the principle and accordingly invalid. The regulation provided that if a party's candidate list contained fewer names than the party is entitled to pursuant to the results of the election, the number of members of the party in the council is reduced accordingly.

for the election, and only persons who are registered on that segment of the national voters roll may participate in the local election. Juristic persons and persons who own property in the municipal area, but who are not registered there on the national voters roll, therefore have no right to vote.[532] Everybody who is qualified to vote may be elected as a member of the municipal council, but certain persons are not eligible.[533] A person who is in the service of the municipality or the state,[534] a member of Parliament, a provincial legislature, or another municipal council, and a person who does not qualify for membership of the National Assembly, may not be elected as a member of the municipal council. Somebody who does not qualify to be a member may, however, be a candidate.[535] That person must thus qualify before he or she is elected. The validity of election regulations providing that a person whose municipal debt is in arrears for more than three months does not qualify for membership of the council, has not been decided finally.[536] A councillor vacates the office when he or she ceases to be a member of the party on whose list he or she was elected.[537]

240. Other arrangements regarding the determination of the number of members of each municipal council, proportional and ward elections, terms of office, by-elections, and a code of conduct for councillors are made in the Local Government: Municipal Structures Act.[538]

C. Powers

241. The legislative and executive authority of a municipality is vested in the municipal council.[539] This authority must be exercised to realize the objects of local government[540] and is constitutionally protected as explained before.[541] A municipal council may make by-laws[542] on the local government matters which are listed in Schedules 4 and 5 of the NC.[543]

---

532. Section 157(5).
533. Section 158. *See also* s. 21 of Act 117 of 1998.
534. National legislation may exempt such a person (s. 158(1)(*a*) and (*b*)).
535. Section 158(2).
536. *O'Meara NO v. Padayachi; O'Meara NO v. Govender* 1997 2 BCLR 258 (D); *Frans v. Munisipaliteit van Groot Brakrivier* 1997 3 BCLR 346 (C), 1998 2 SA 770 (C). In the former case, the constitutionality of the regulation had been referred to the Constitutional Court for a decision, but in the latter case, the validity of the regulation was not in contention and the court accepted its validity.
537. Section 27(c) of Act 117 of 1998. In *De Villiers v. Munisipaliteit van Beaufort-Wes* 1998 9 BCLR 1060 (C) it was held that a party could not terminate a councillor's membership of the council without terminating his or her membership of the party.
538. *See* on the latter Sch. 5 to Act 117 of 1998.
539. Section 151(2). The so-called predominant administrative role for local government allegedly envisaged in s. 156 (Pimstone (*supra*) 5A.34) is off-set by this express provision.
540. Section 152.
541. Section 151(3) and (4).
542. They must be published in the official gazette of the province and must be accessible to the public (s. 162).
543. Section 156(1) and (2). *See* part B of each schedule to the NC. As mentioned, a municipal by-law is subject to national and provincial legislation (s. 156(3)).

242. These matters include the following subjects: air pollution, building regulations, child care facilities, electricity and gas reticulation, fire-fighting services, local tourism, airports, planning, health services, public transport, public works, pontoons, ferries, jetties, piers and harbours (excluding international and national shipping), storm-water management systems, trading regulations, water and sanitation services, beaches and amusement facilities, billboards and advertisements in public places, cemeteries, funeral parlours and crematoriums, cleansing, control of public nuisances, control of undertakings that sell liquor, facilities for the accommodation, care and burial of animals, fencing and fences, licensing of dogs, licensing and control of undertakings that sell food, local amenities, sport facilities, markets, abattoirs, parks and recreation, roads, noise pollution, pounds, public places, refuse removal, refuse dumps and solid waste disposal, street trading, street lighting, and traffic and parking.

243. A municipal council may also make by-laws on any matter assigned to it by national or provincial legislation. A municipal council has executive authority over, and the right to administer, all these matters and may implement by-laws on these matters for the effective management and administration of the city or town.[544] The national and provincial governments must, by agreement, assign to a municipality the administration of the local government matters mentioned in the schedules to the NC. The condition is that the specific matter will be administered most effectively at local level, and that the municipality has the capacity to administer it.[545] The obligation of provincial and national authorities to support and strengthen the capacity of municipalities to exercise their powers is particularly relevant in this regard.[546] A municipal council may also exercise any power that is reasonably necessary for, or incidental to, the effective performance of its functions.[547]

244. With regard to finance, a municipality's powers are constitutionally entrenched.[548] It may impose rates on property, surcharges on service fees and, if authorized by national legislation, may impose other taxes, levies or duties, but not income tax, value-added tax, general sales tax, or customs duty.[549] This power may not be exercised in a way that materially and unreasonably prejudices national economic policies, economic activities across municipal boundaries, or the national mobility of goods, services, capital, or labour.[550] National legislation must ensure that municipalities raise taxes commensurate with their fiscal capacity and the capacity of their residents.[551]

544. Sections 151(3) and 156(2).
545. Section 156(4).
546. Section 154(1).
547. Section 156(5).
548. *Executive Council of the Western Cape v. Minister of Provincial Affairs and Constitutional Development; Executive Council of KwaZulu-Natal v. President of the RSA* 1999 12 BCLR 1360 (CC) para. 26.
549. Section 229(1). The initial text included excise taxes, but in *In re: Certification of the Constitution of the Republic of South Africa, 1996* 1996 10 BCLR 1253 (CC), 1996 4 SA 744 (CC) the Constitutional Court regarded it as an inappropriate tax for municipalities to impose: 'Suffice it to say that the expression [municipal excise taxes] includes taxes that are inappropriate for municipalities to impose' (para. 305).
550. Section 229(2)(*a*).
551. Section 229(3). The High Court confirmed that 'service fees' include user charges for electricity and water – *see Geyser v. Mzunduzi Municipality* 2003 (3) BCLR 235 (N).

In addition, a relationship of trust exists between a local government and its ratepayers, which gives the latter *locus standi* to question the validity of decisions regarding rates and the spending of the income derived from it.[552]

245. The requirement in the Interim NC that the rates, levies and tariffs imposed by a municipality had to be based on a uniform structure for its whole area of jurisdiction[553] caused problems and in a number of cases different aspects of this matter came before the courts.[554] The Constitutional Court finally held that a uniform structure does not necessarily imply uniform tariffs.[555] Without deciding the case on this basis,[556] the Court gave the impression that, in view of the vast differences in prosperity between the traditional white and black residential areas, a municipality would be entitled, *inter alia* for the purposes of cross-subsidization, to impose as a temporary measure in the former residential areas tariffs based on consumption, and in the latter tariffs based on a flat rate.[557] In other words, there was justification for the differentiation in tariffs and this did not discriminate unfairly against the residents of white residential areas. *In casu*, however, the Court held that the selective enforcement of the system in that only residents of white areas were prosecuted for outstanding debt, amounted to unfair discrimination.[558] In *Fedsure Life Assurance Ltd v. Greater Johannesburg Transitional Metropolitan Council* a uniform rates tariff was imposed on all substructures of the Metro Council.[559] This created in some substructures a surplus which was used to finance the deficit in other substructures. Apart from section 178(2) of the Interim Constitution, the provision in the proclamation in terms of which the Metro Council had been established, that the Metro Council was entitled to claim from every substructure an equitable contribution based on its gross or rates income was contended. The Constitutional Court was equally divided on the question whether or not the uniform

552. *Fedsure Life Assurance Ltd v. Greater Johannesburg Transitional Metropolitan Council* 1998 6 BCLR 671 (SCA) 676G-H, 1998 2 SA 1115 (SCA).
553. Section 178(2) of the Interim NC.
554. *Beukes v. Krugersdorp Transitional Local Council* 1996 3 SA 467 (W); *Municipality of the City of Port Elizabeth v. Prut NO* 1997 6 BCLR 828 (SE);*East London Transitional Local Council v. Tax Payers Action Organisation* 1998 10 BCLR 1221 (E);*Lotus River, Ottery, Grassy Park Residents Association v. South Peninsula Municipality* 1999 4 BCLR 440 (C).
555. *City Council of Pretoria v. Walker* 1998 3 BCLR 257 (CC) para. 85:

Section 187(2) does not stipulate that a uniform tariff be established but that it be based on a 'uniform structure.' It should not be interpreted therefore to mean that the tariff must provide for identical rates to be charged to all consumers regardless of the quality of service or the type or circumstances of the user. That could produce a highly inequitable result.

556. The case was fought and decided on the basis of the equality principle (s. 9).
557. *See* paras 49 et seq.
558. Paragraphs 69–81.
559. *Fedsure Life Assurance Ltd v. Greater Johannesburg Transitional Metropolitan Council* 1998 12 BCLR 1458 (CC).

tariff was based on the gross or rates income, and whether the Metro Council acted *ultra vires* by imposing it.[560]

246. Where two municipalities exercise financial powers in the same area (e.g., in the case of a metropolitan council and its substructures), their powers must be divided in terms of the Local Government: Municipal Structures Act, taking into account certain financial considerations.[561] This provision is aimed at the division of powers between a district council and its constituent local municipalities. Like the provinces, local governments are in addition entitled to an equitable share of the national income to enable them to provide basic services and perform the functions allocated to them.[562] Additional income that a municipality raises by itself may not be deducted in the determination of that municipality's share, but the national government has no obligation to compensate a municipality that does not raise income commensurate to its capacity. A municipality may, under certain conditions, raise loans for capital or current expenditure.[563] Municipal finances and budgets are subject to national directives and control.[564]

D. Functioning

247. A municipal council may make rules with regard to the internal arrangements, business, and proceedings of the council, and the establishment, composition, powers, and functioning of committees of the council.[565] Unlike the Interim NC, the NC does not prescribe the establishment of an executive committee,[566] but subject to national legislation a municipality may choose to function according to the executive committee system.[567] The particulars regarding which municipalities may establish executive committees, and the composition, powers, and functioning of executive committees appear in the Local Government: Municipal Structures Act.[568] Every municipality must elect a speaker and a mayor, but the Act provides that only certain types of municipalities may elect executive mayors.[569] Like municipal councils, an executive committee must

560. In effect, this caused the appeal against the decision of the Court *a quo* (*Fedsure Life Assurance Ltd v. Greater Johannesburg Transitional Metropolitan Council* 1997 5 BCLR 657 (W)) to be dismissed and the tariff to remain in force.
561. Section 229(3). *See* s. 84 of Act 117 of 1998. (The Act could be adopted only after consultation with organized local government and the FFC (s. 229(6)).
562. Section 227(1). *See also* s. 214(1); annual division of revenue Act, e.g., Division of Revenue Act 3 of 2016.
563. Section 230.
564. Sections 215 and 216.
565. Section 160(6). *See also* Act 117 of 1998.
566. Section 177 of Act 200 of 1993.
567. Section 160(1)(*c*). National legislation may provide criteria for the establishment of committees (s. 160(5)).
568. Section 42–47 of Act 117 of 1998.
569. Section 54 of Act 117 of 1998. *See* ss 55 et seq. on their election, powers, terms of office, etc. (*See* s. 48 on a ceremonial mayor.)

also be composed on a proportional basis.[570] If there is, however, an executive mayor, the mayoral committee supports the mayor and does not have to be based on proportional representation.[571] A municipal council must function in an open manner and may close sittings of the council or its committees only when it is reasonable to do so having regard to the nature of the business to be transacted. Members of the council must be able to participate in all proceedings in a way that allows parties fair representation and that is consistent with democracy.[572] A majority of the members must be present before a vote is taken and a decision is taken by a majority of votes cast. Decisions regarding the approval of by-laws, the budget, tariffs and loans must, however, be supported by a majority of the total number of members.[573] No by-law may be passed unless all members have received reasonable notice and it has been published for comment.[574] Provincial legislation must provide for the privileges of council members.[575]

248. The provisions of the NC form the framework on which the Local Government: Municipal Structures Act and all future laws and measures relating to local government must be based.[576]

§4. The Western Cape Constitution

249. One of the points of departure when drafting the WCC was to have a comprehensive document that includes appropriate references to the other spheres of government and that inevitably had to repeat a number of provisions of the NC in this regard. Chapter 5 of the WCC on local government was accordingly included in order to ensure that the WCC was a complete and comprehensible piece of constitutional

570. Section 43(2) of Act 117 of 1998. This was also the position in terms of the Interim NC (s. 177), but often led to litigation –*see Louw v. Matjila* 1995 11 BCLR 1476 (W);*Crowther v. Plaaslike Oorgangsraad vir Bethlehem* 1997 8 BCLR 1010 (O); *Nasionale Party in die OosKaap v. Port Elizabeth Oorgangsraad* 1998 2 BCLR 141 (SE). The same interpretation has been given to s. 160(8)(a) of the 1996 NC –*Democratic Party v. Brakpan Transitional Local Council* 1999 6 BCLR 657 (W).
571. *See* Rautenbach (2012) (*supra*) 240; *Democratic Alliance v. Masondo NO* 2003 (2) BCLR 128 (CC).
572. Such participation can be regulated by national legislation (s. 160(3)(*c*)).
573. Section 160(3). Decisions about these matters may not be delegated (s. 160(2)). Many of these particulars were added after the Constitutional Court had held in *In re: Certification of the Constitution of the Republic of South Africa, 1996* 1996 10 BCLR 1253 (CC), 1996 4 SA 744 (CC) that the procedures of municipalities needed to be explained in more detail (para. 305). *See* also s. 30 of Act 117 of 1998. In *Member of the Executive Council for Development Planning and Local Government in the Provincial Government of Gauteng v. Democratic Party* 1998 7 BCLR 855 (CC) the approval of a budget by a majority of councillors was declared invalid because a majority of two-thirds, as prescribed by the Local Government Transition Act 209 of 1993 (which remained in force until 30 Apr. 1999 in terms of item 26 of Sch. 6 of the 1996 NC) was not obtained. (*See* the comments by Pimstone (*supra*) 5A.25.)
574. Section 160(4).
575. *See Waters v. Khayalami Metropolitan Council* 1997 3 SA 476 (W) on the privileges of councillors and their discipline. *See also* s. 28 of Act 117 of 1998.
576. Constitutional principle XXIV. *See In re: Certification of the Constitution of the Republic of South Africa, 1996* 1996 10 BCLR 1253 (CC), 1996 4 SA 744 (CC) paras 299–305.

legislation.[577] It does not contain any innovations, but is rather a collection of key provisions found in Chapter 7 of the NC that stipulate the basic constitutional framework for local government in the Western Cape.

250. In the evolutionary process of the development of local government the final phase of establishing the new local government structures as envisaged in Chapter 7 of the NC and Chapter 5 of the WCC took place at the end of 2000 when elections were held for the new municipalities. The Western Cape provincial government had, as part of its constitutional obligations, adopted a provincial Act to determine the various types of municipalities that were established in the Western Cape. Various transformation structures, within which municipalities as well as the provincial government co-operated, had been formed in order to provide a smooth transition from the current system of local government to the new system. In order to give effect to the constitutional requirement that provincial legislation had to determine the different types of municipality to be established in a province, the Provincial Parliament passed the Western Cape Determination of Types of Municipality Act 9 of 2000.

§5. Conclusion

251. Local government is in many ways the backbone of a democratic system of government. The services provided at this level make the real difference to people's lives. In many ways, accordingly, the success of a democracy is measured in terms of its performance at local level. Local government in South Africa has suffered much under apartheid and under the traditional neglect of this sphere of government in a system of parliamentary sovereignty. A new system of local government is now being erected. Although there is a distinct possibility of over-regulation, it is under present circumstances understandable. However, exciting possibilities for future developments are being opened up and, in co-operation with the national and provincial governments; local government should at the same time be allowed the scope to fulfil its unique role as the sphere of government closest to the people.

577. *In re: Certification of the Constitution of the Western Cape, 1997* 1997 9 BCLR 1167 (CC), 1997 4 SA 795 (CC) para. 23.

Part IV. Miscellaneous

252. There are a number of issues mainly of a national character not addressed elsewhere in this volume, but which also impact on sub-national government. They include the acquisition and loss of South African citizenship and the position and treatment of aliens, the protection of fundamental human rights and liberties in the Bill of Rights, and the protection of minorities or, as they are more accurately called in South Africa, cultural, religious and linguistic communities. These issues are discussed in concise terms in this Part, and the extent to which they relate to sub-national government will be explained whenever applicable.

Chapter 1. Citizenship and Aliens

§1. Citizenship

253. The NC provides for a common South African citizenship.[578] There is no express provision in the NC for citizenship of a province or other sub-national structure. In addition, the Bill of Rights provides for a right not to be deprived of one's citizenship.[579] Any provision dealing with the deprivation of citizenship must, therefore, comply with the general limitation clause in the Bill of Rights, section 36.[580] Like Article 7 of the Convention on the Rights of the Child, the Bill of Rights provides that every child has the right to a nationality from birth.[581] This right has certain implications.[582] First, the right means that no child with South African citizenship may be made stateless. Second, the provision implies that South Africa has a duty to grant South African citizenship to stateless children residing in South Africa. Of course, like all other rights, the right may be limited provided that the limitation complies with section 36.

254. The NC provides that the acquisition, loss, and restoration of citizenship must be regulated in other legislation. These matters are accordingly dealt with in the South African Citizenship Act.[583]

I. Acquisition of Citizenship

255. The Act provides that citizenship can be acquired in the three generally recognized ways, namely birth, descent, and naturalization.

256. The general rule is that every person born on South African soil is a South African citizen by birth.[584] In addition, any person not born in South African territory is still a South African citizen by birth, if any parent, or the mother if the child was born out of wedlock, is in the service of the South African government, a South African employer, or an international organization of which South Africa is a member. On the other hand, a person born in South African territory is not a South African citizen by birth, if any parent was a diplomat or representative of a foreign country, or an employee or member of the household of such a diplomat or representative, and the other parent was not a South African citizen; or any parent was not lawfully admitted into the Republic for permanent residence and the other parent was not a South African citizen.

578. Section 3(1).
579. Section 20.
580. *See* the discussion in the following Chapter, §2.II.
581. Section 28(1)(a).
582. Rautenbach (2012) (*supra*) 42.
583. Act 88 of 1995.
584. Section 2.

257. A person born outside the Republic can become a citizen by descent.[585] That may only happen if the birth is registered in South Africa, and one parent is a South African citizen, or one parent has resumed South African citizenship and the person applying has entered the Republic to take up permanent residence, or the person has been adopted by a South African citizen.

258. Aliens who settle permanently in the Republic may acquire South African citizenship by naturalization.[586] Applicable qualifications include a minimum period of ordinary residence in South Africa, good character, ability to communicate in an official language, and adequate knowledge of the rights and duties of citizenship.

259. Note that marriage does not automatically affect the citizenship of a person. One does not automatically acquire South African citizenship by marrying a South African citizen, nor does one lose South African citizenship by marrying an alien.

II. Loss of Citizenship

260. One may lose South African citizenship under certain circumstances.[587] First, one may voluntary renounce one's South African citizenship, or acquire the citizenship of another country, or serve in the armed forces of another country which is at war with South Africa. Second, the minister may deprive one's citizenship under certain circumstances. In the case of citizenship by naturalization, the minister may deprive a person of citizenship if the citizenship was acquired fraudulently or unlawfully. The minister may deprive any citizen who also has the citizenship of another country of citizenship if the person was convicted of certain offences, if the minister is satisfied that it is in the public interest, or if the person has made use of the citizenship of that other country.

§2. Aliens

261. Aliens have less constitutional rights than citizens. The rights of citizens to enter, remain in, and reside in the Republic, and the right of a citizen to a passport as provided by the South African Passports and Travel Documents Act[588] do not apply to aliens. The so-called political rights to vote, to form a political party, to participate in its activities, and to recruit members and campaign for a political party, as well as the right to stand for public office, also do not apply to aliens.[589] Finally, the right to choose a trade, occupation, or profession applies only to citizens. As explained in the following Chapter (§2.I), that does not necessarily mean that aliens have none of these rights. In terms of ordinary laws they may be, and have been, granted rights such as these, but those rights are not constitutionally protected.

585. Section 3.
586. Section 5.
587. Sections 6–9.
588. Act 4 of 1994.
589. Section 19.

262. The position of aliens, or non-citizens, regarding their entry and sojourn in and departure from the Republic is further regulated by the Immigration Act.[590] The Act provides among other things for different kinds of applications by aliens, including temporary residence permits and permanent residence permits for the purposes of immigration to the Republic.

263. The Refugees Act[591] gives effect to various international instruments regarding the status and treatment of refugees, *inter alia* the Convention relating to the Status of Refugees of 1951 and the Protocol relating to the Status of Refugees of 1967.

590. Act 13 of 2002.
591. Act 130 of 1998.

Chapter 2. Fundamental Rights and Liberties

§1. The Bill of Rights

264. In Part I (*supra*) the view is taken that the Bill of Rights (Chapter 2 of the NC) is a modern, comprehensive, and entrenched instrument for the effective protection of fundamental human rights and liberties in South Africa. In terms of section 7 of the NC, the Bill of Rights is a cornerstone of democracy in South Africa. It enshrines the rights of all people in the country and affirms the democratic values of human dignity, equality, and freedom, on which the Republic is founded. Although the Constitutional Court did not exclude the possibility that provinces could adopt their own bills of rights as part of their provincial constitutions,[592] the national Bill of Rights remains the only instrument of this kind and applies in all spheres of government.

265. The state has the obligation to respect, protect, promote, and fulfil the rights in the Bill of Rights.[593] The Bill of Rights applies to all law, and binds the legislature, the executive, the judiciary, and all organs of state in all their actions.[594] This refers to all law and all government bodies in all spheres of government. A provision of the Bill also binds a natural or juristic person if, and to the extent that, it is applicable, taking into account the nature of the right and the nature of the duty imposed by the right.[595] In addition to natural persons, juristic persons are entitled to the rights in the Bill to the extent required by the nature of the rights and the nature of the juristic person in question.[596] The rights in the Bill of Rights may be limited only in accordance with the general and specific limitation provisions in the Bill. In the interpretation of the Bill of Rights, a court must promote the values that underlie an open and democratic society based on human dignity, equality, and freedom. The interpretation of the Bill of Rights is discussed together with the interpretation of the NC in Part I above.

266. Also mentioned elsewhere is that any person may approach a court to enforce the rights in the Bill of Rights, either on his or her own behalf, or on behalf of another person or body.[597] In court proceedings the onus is on the applicant to establish (a) that he or she, or the person or body in question, is protected by the right the violation or threatened violation of which the applicant is complaining; (b) that the conduct or interest allegedly being violated or interfered with is protected by the right in question; and (c) that the person or body against whom the complaint is filed

592. *In re: Certification of the Constitution of the Province of KwaZulu-Natal, 1996* 1996 11 BCLR 1419 (CC), 1996 4 SA 1098 (CC) paras 17–24. *See* the discussion in Part II, Ch. 1, §4 above.

593. Section 7(2).

594. Section 8(1). It was held e.g., in *De Lille v. Speaker of the National Assembly* 1998 7 BCLR 916 (C); 1998 3 SA 430 (C) that Parliament was subject to the NC not only in respect of its law making function, but all its activities, including its internal proceedings.

595. Section 8(2) –*see* below.

596. Section 8(4) – *see* below.

597. Section 38.

is bound by the right. Once these questions have been settled, the onus shifts to the respondent to establish that the limitation imposed on the right complies with the requirements for lawful limitations set out in the Bill of Rights.[598]

267. The specific rights protected in the Bill of Rights cover a wide field. Briefly, the rights can be summarized as follows: the rights to equality, human dignity, life, freedom and security of the person, not to be subjected to slavery, servitude and forced labour, and the right to privacy, freedom of religion, belief and opinion, freedom of expression, the right to assemble and demonstrate, freedom of association, political and citizenship rights, freedom of movement, of trade and occupation, rights pertaining to labour relations, the right to a healthy environment, property rights, access to housing, health care, food, water and social security, the rights of children, educational rights, rights pertaining to language and culture, access to information, the right to just administrative action, access to courts, and the rights of arrested, detained and accused persons.

§2. Application of the Bill of Rights

268. Highlighted in the discussion that follows are, first, the protection the Bill of Rights affords natural as well as juristic persons, secondly, its horizontal application, in other words, the extent to which the Bill of Rights also binds natural and juristic persons in their private relationships and, thirdly, the provisions for the lawful limitation of the rights in the Bill of Rights.[599]

I. Who Is Protected?

269. In general, every natural person is a bearer of the rights in the Bill of Rights. However, certain rights apply only to certain categories of natural persons. Only citizens are the bearers of the political rights, like the right to vote, the right to free, fair and regular elections, the right to form political parties and to participate in their activities, and the right to stand for and hold public office when elected.[600] The right to enter into and remain and reside in the Republic, the right to a passport, and the right to choose a trade, profession, or occupation also apply only to citizens. Aliens are the bearers of all the other rights. Certain rights naturally apply only to children, workers and employers, or arrested, detained and accused persons. Previously, under South African law, the foetus has not been regarded as a person and as the Bill of Rights has not changed this common law position directly, the foetus is not a bearer of rights. On this basis the Court in *Christian Lawyers Association of South Africa v. Minister of Health* rejected the argument that the law allowing abortion on request

598. Currie & De Waal (*supra*) (2005) 27–28. *See generally* I.M. Rautenbach, *Introduction to the Bill of Rights*, in Butterworths editorial team *Bill of Rights Compendium* 1A-1 et seq (Butterworths 1996).

599. De Vos & Freedman (*supra*) 323–345.

600. Section 19.

was unconstitutional.[601] It remains to be seen whether it may be decided in future that the state has an interest in the protection of the unborn child *vis-à-vis* the right of the mother to her personal integrity, a question which will then have to be addressed in a more refined way.[602]

270. What is sometimes misunderstood is that the Bill of Rights confers rights and does not withdraw rights. Therefore, it changes the existing law only to the extent that the latter is inconsistent with the Bill of Rights. The effect of this is, first, that when a person is not the bearer of a particular right in the Bill of Rights, it does not necessarily mean that the person does not enjoy the right in terms of ordinary rules of law. For example, the fact that aliens do not enjoy the constitutional right to participate in the activities of a political party does not exclude aliens from participating in such activities in terms of ordinary rules of law. The difference is that the right is then conferred and withdrawn by ordinary law and does not enjoy the constitutional protection afforded by the Bill of Rights. Also, any restriction of the right need not comply with the limitation provisions in the Bill of Rights. Another example is the right to economic activity, which aliens may exercise in terms of the ordinary laws of the land, but which they cannot claim as a constitutional right in terms of the Bill of Rights.[603]

271. Secondly, the Bill of Rights does not deny the existence of other rights recognized or conferred by the common law or legislation, to the extent that they are consistent with the Bill of Rights.[604] There are many rights conferred by ordinary legislation or the common law which are not affected by the Bill of Rights and which continue to exist. Many rights one acquires in terms of one's competence as a legal subject to act are as real and enforceable as one's constitutional rights, with the difference that they do not enjoy the same measure of protection as the latter.[605]

272. The Bill of Rights also protects juristic persons to the extent required by the nature of the rights and the nature of that juristic person.[606] With regard to the former qualification, it is obvious that juristic persons cannot be bearers of rights that by their nature only apply to human beings, like the right to life, human dignity, and freedom and security of the person, but they can enjoy the right to equality, property, freedom of expression and association. Obviously, too, this applies to private juristic persons, but what about public juristic persons? To the extent that town councils, universities, and state enterprises exercise public authority, they are bound by the Bill of Rights and, in principle, they cannot simultaneously be bearers of those rights. However, certain public juristic persons are indeed in the unique position to be both bound by the Bill of Rights and be bearers of the rights in the Bill of Rights. A university is a good example. In terms of South African law a university is a public juristic person, or an organ of state, that is created by statute and performs a public function, the provision of higher education, in terms of that legislation.[607] However, it enjoys the

601. 1998 11 BCLR 1434 (T).
602. *Cf.* the German position – 88 BVerfGE 203. *See* the comments by T. Naudé, *The Value of Life: A Note on Christian Lawyers Association of SA v Minister of Health*, SAJHR 541 (1999).
603. Section 22 confers this right only on citizens.
604. Section 39(3).
605. Rautenbach (*supra*) 1A-31–32.
606. Section 8(4).
607. Section 239.

right to academic freedom, which includes the right to institutional autonomy,[608] and can enforce the right *vis-à-vis* the state. A university should also be able to claim against the state rights such as the right to equal protection of the law, the right to privacy, the right to freedom of expression, the right to freedom of economic activity, property rights, the right of access to the courts, the right of access to information, and the right to fair administrative action.[609]

II. Horizontality

273. As mentioned, the state is bound by the Bill of Rights (its so-called vertical application), but in addition it is directly applicable to private relationships (its so-called horizontal application). Section 8(2) provides: 'A provision of the Bill of Rights binds a natural or a juristic person if, and to the extent that, it is applicable, taking into account the nature of the right and the nature of any duty imposed by the right.' This provision has quite a history. The interim NC did not contain a corresponding provision, and considerable confusion existed on whether the Bill of Rights applied horizontally.[610] Eventually, in *Du Plessis v. De Klerk*, the Constitutional Court held that the Bill of Rights applied to private law.[611] However, the Court made a distinction between the 'direct' and 'indirect' application of the Bill of Rights and explained that to a large extent the Bill of Rights applied only indirectly in private relationships. (It should be borne in mind that the state action doctrine as applied in the United States of America does not apply in South Africa.)

274. This uncertainty has been resolved by section 8(2) of the final NC.[612] There can be no doubt that the Bill of Rights applies directly in private relationships. Regarding the extent to which it applies, the following observations may be made:

(a) The Bill of Rights applies to all law, including legislation made by any legislature in any sphere of government, subordinate legislation made by members of executives, common law, and customary law.[613] Naturally, this includes the rules of private law, in other words the statutory and common law rules applicable to private relationships. A rule of private law inconsistent with the Bill of Rights is unconstitutional to the extent of its inconsistency.

608. E.F.J. Malherbe, *Die regsbeskerming van akademiese vryheid en universiteitsoutonomie in 'n nuwe Suid-Afrika*, TSAR 359, 363–366 (1993).

609. *See* the examples mentioned by E.F.J. Malherbe, *Constitutional Perspectives on Higher Education in South Africa*, Stell LR 328 (1999).

610. *See* the accounts by Rautenbach (*supra*) 1A-46 et seq.; I.M. Rautenbach, *Die 'primaat van die privaatreg,' en die handves van regte*, in *Suprema Lex: Essays on the Constitution presented to Marinus Wiechers* 99 et seq. (G. Carpenter ed., Butterworths 1998). *See also* D. Davis et al., *Fundamental Rights in the Constitution: Commentary and Cases* 30 et seq. (Juta 1997); S. Woolman, *Application*, in *Constitutional Law of South Africa* 10–43 et seq. (M. Chaskalson et al. eds, Juta 1998).

611. 1996 5 BCLR 658 (CC).

612. *See* the excellent exposition of the current position by I.M. Rautenbach, *The Bill of Rights Applies to Private Law and Binds Private Persons*, TSAR 296 (2000).

613. Section 8(1).

(b) The Bill of Rights binds all legislative, executive, and judicial bodies in all spheres of government.[614] They are bound not only when they make or apply rules of law regulating the relationship between the state and its subjects. They remain bound also when they make or apply the rules of law applicable to private relationships.

(c) Section 8(2) means, first, that the nature of a particular right and the duty imposed by that right will determine whether that right binds a private person. There are rights that by their nature do not apply in private relationships, like the right to citizenship, or the right to a fair trial. Furthermore, the duty that may follow from a particular right may also determine whether the right applies to private relationships. The duty to provide courts which the right of access to the courts imposes, or the duty to hold elections that the right to vote imposes, will not become issues in private relationships and these rights clearly do not apply horizontally.

(d) Secondly, section 8(2) has a bearing on the nature of the relationship between private persons. Keeping in mind that bills of rights are primarily designed to apply in unequal relationships, in other words relationships in which one party exercises authority over the other, it follows that the Bill of Rights can easily find application in unequal private relationships. Examples are the relationship between an association and its members, a company and its shareholders, or a parent and a child.

(e) When private persons act in terms of rules of private law that are constitutionally valid, the Bill of Rights may still apply. Often, when one performs an act in terms of the rules of private law, conflicts arise in which a balancing of interests must take place. The Bill of Rights must be applied to this balancing process if and to the extent that it can be applied. Of course, private law has been developed over centuries exactly for the purpose of balancing the conflicting interests of private persons, and it remains to be seen to which extent there remains scope for the Bill of Rights to be applied in this context.

(f) Further recognition of the fact that the Bill of Rights applies horizontally is found in section 8(3) which provides that when the Bill of Rights is applied to a private person, a court must apply and, if necessary develop, the rules of private law (as contained in the common law and in legislation) to the extent that the common law or legislation does not give effect to the right in question.

III. The Limitation of Rights

275. As mentioned, the general limitation provision, section 36, is one of the most explicit and comprehensive in the world. Section 36(1) reads as follows:

> The rights in the Bill of Rights may be limited only in terms of law of general application to the extent that the limitation is reasonable and justifiable in an open and democratic society based on human dignity, equality and freedom, taking into account all relevant factors, including –

614. Section 8(1).

(a) the nature of the right;
(b) the importance of the purpose of the limitation;
(c) the nature and extent of the limitation;
(d) the relation between the limitation and its purpose; and
(e) less restrictive means to achieve the purpose.

276. Section 36 is obviously a pivotal provision in the Bill of Rights. It recognizes the simple fact that in principle constitutional rights may be limited, but then it provides in detail the requirements for such limitation.[615] Section 36 has to be applied every time the constitutionality of an alleged infringement of a right in the Bill of Rights has to be determined. This is a tremendous aid to the courts as it provides an explicit test that determines how far anyone may go in limiting the rights protected in the Bill of Rights.[616]

277. One should keep in mind that, in addition to section 36, the Bill of Rights contains several specific limitation provisions each applying to a particular right. A specific limitation provision contains one or more elements usually found in limitation provisions and may emphasize or qualify the body that may impose the limitation, the purpose for which or the conditions or circumstances under which the limitation may be imposed, or the balance that must exist between the limitation and its purpose.[617] Simply put, the relation between section 36 and a specific limitation provision is that the former applies to all rights in the Bill of Rights, but that the latter qualifies the application of section 36 in the case of the right in question.[618]

278. Returning to section 36, a brief word is required about the phrase 'in terms of law of general application.' This refers to all law, and means that any legislature in any sphere of government, acting within its sphere of competence, may limit the rights in the Bill of Rights. It further means that whereas legislative bodies may impose limitations on rights directly in the laws that they adopt, they may also, for the purposes of effective administration, authorize in those laws executive bodies and functionaries to limit rights. However, a legislature may not authorize the executive to ignore the Bill of Rights, or confer on the executive a limitless discretion to limit rights.[619] The legislature must, as the representative of the electorate, adopt the principle to limit rights or to allow the executive to limit rights. This impacts on the amount of particulars a law is required to contain in order for a discretion conferred on the executive to limit

615. Davis et al. (*supra*) 304–305 regards s. 36 as 'an express constitutional route to reconcile individual rights with a majoritarian imperative of a parliamentary legislative programme.'
616. S. Woolman, *Limitation*, in Chaskalson (*supra*) 12–1–2 calls it a reasonably precise guideline that alleviates the counter-majoritarian problem where a non-elected judiciary must review the actions of the elected government.
617. Rautenbach (2012) (*supra*) 302–314. On definitional and other problems in this regard *see* G. Carpenter, *Internal Modifiers and Other Qualifications in Bills of Rights – Some Problems of Interpretation*, SA Public Law 260 (1995).
618. Examples of specific limitation provisions are the affirmative action provision in s. 9 which protects the equality rights, the provision for the expropriation of property in s. 25 which guarantees property rights, and the qualification in ss 26 and 27 in terms of which the state must take reasonable measures within its available resources to realize the rights of access to adequate housing and health care.
619. This is also the established position in Germany –*BVerfGE* 8, 274/325.

rights to be valid. It can be accepted, firstly, that the legislature must take all material decisions regarding the authorized limitation itself and, secondly, that the more sensitive and far-reaching an authorized limitation is, the more particulars will have to be included in the enabling law.

279. As mentioned, the courts approach the application of section 36 in two stages.[620] Firstly, the applicant has to establish that a particular right has been infringed. She must show that her activity, conduct, or interest that has been violated falls within the ambit of the activities, conduct, or interests protected by the right in question. She must then establish that the right binds the respondent and that the actions of the respondent have indeed infringed the right. Secondly, once all this has been established, the onus shifts to the respondent to show that the infringement of the right, in other words, the limitation imposed on the right, complies with the provisions of section 36 and is thus constitutional.

280. Now the enquiry is squarely within the ambit of section 36. The requirement that a limitation must be reasonable and justifiable in an open and democratic society based on human dignity, equality and freedom means that a balance must be found between the limitation and its purpose in order for the limitation to be reasonable and justifiable. In the Canadian, German and several other legal systems this is called the proportionality test.[621] Furthermore, it must be a particular kind of balance, viz one found in an open and democratic society based on human dignity, equality, and freedom. To assist the court in this enquiry, section 36 mentions five factors that must be taken into account in establishing whether this balance exists. In other systems these factors have been developed by the courts, and the South African Constitution is the first to mention them explicitly. The factors referred to may not be the only factors to be taken into account in a particular case, but at least those mentioned must always be considered. The factors are also not criteria or tests and section 36 does not determine the weight to be attached to each.[622] They are simply aids in the determination of the main question whether the limitation is reasonable and justifiable in an open and democratic society based on human dignity, equality, and freedom. The five factors can be applied as follows.

A. The Nature of the Right

281. This factor allows the court to determine the importance of the violated right for the purposes of weighing it up against the purpose of the limitation imposed on that right. Formally, there is no hierarchy of rights in the South African Bill of

620. The courts adopted this approach developed by the Canadian courts even before the adoption of the final Constitution – *S v. Makwanyane* 1995 6 BCLR 665 (CC) para. 102. *See also* Davis et al. (*supra*) 305 et seq.; Currie & De Waal (*supra*) 165–168; Rautenbach, *The Right to Access to Sufficient Water and the Two-Stage Approach to the Application of the Bill of Rights*, (74) THRHR 107–119 (2011).

621. *See* e.g., P.W. Hogg, *Constitutional Law of Canada* 866 (Carswell 1992), with reference to *R v. Oakes* [1986] 1 SCR 103.

622. Rautenbach, *Introduction to the Bill of Rights*, in Butterworths editorial team *Bill of Rights Compendium* 1A-51 (Butterworths 1996); *see* De Vos & Freedman (*supra*) 349–379 for a detailed discussion on the limitation clause.

Rights, but this factor will enable courts to develop stricter tests for limitations in the case of certain rights. Rights that are regarded as important for the promotion of an open and democratic society based on human dignity, equality, and freedom, like the rights to life,[623] human dignity, equality,[624] personal freedom, freedom of expression, or the political rights, obviously carry more weight than others, and the purpose for which these rights are being limited should be scrutinized very closely.[625]

B. The Importance of the Purpose of the Limitation

282. The purpose of the limitation on the right and its importance in an open and democratic society must be determined in order to weigh it up against the nature of the right. First of all, the limitation must be directed at the promotion or protection of a permissible or lawful public interest, like state security, public order, public health, or the rights of others.[626] Having established the purpose of a limitation, its importance must be determined. For example, it is more important to limit the right of access to information for the purposes of protecting strategic national interests than for mere administrative effectiveness or convenience. This example also indicates that different tests may be developed with regard to different purposes for which a right may be limited. Both in *S v. Makwanyane* and *S v. Williams*, in which the death penalty and corporal punishment, respectively, were declared unconstitutional, the Constitutional Court discussed at length the purposes of punishment, namely prevention, retribution, deterrence, and rehabilitation.[627] The importance of the purpose of the limitation is not determined by whether the limitation is being imposed by a national or provincial law. Within its sphere of competence a provincial legislature may pursue as legitimate a purpose as Parliament.

C. The Nature and Extent of the Limitation

283. It must be determined how and to which extent the right in question is affected by the limitation. This is essential to determine the relation between the limitation and its purpose, whether less restrictive means should have been employed, and whether the limitation is disproportionate to its purpose. In *S v. Bhulwana; S v. Gwadiso* the Constitutional Court explained: 'The Court places the purpose, effects, and importance of the infringing legislation on one side of the scales and the nature and effect of the infringement caused by the legislation on the other. The more substantial the inroad into fundamental rights, the more persuasive the grounds of justification must be.'[628] In simple terms, this factor points to the proportionality test that must be applied eventually, viz whether the limitation of a right is not more extensive than is

623. In *S v. Makwanyane* (n 43) para. 144, Chaskalson P held that 'the rights to life and dignity are the most important of all human rights, and the source of all other personal rights.'
624. *Brink v. Kitshoff* 1996 6 BCLR 752 (CC) para. 33.
625. Currie & De Waal (*supra*) 178–179.
626. *See* e.g., *S v. Ntuli* 1996 1 BCLR 141 (CC).
627. *S v. Makwanyane* (n 43);*S v. Williams* 1995 7 BCLR 861 (CC).
628. 1995 12 BCLR 1579 (CC) para. 18.

warranted by the purpose which the limitation seeks to achieve.[629] Once again, too, it seems possible to set different requirements for different limitations.

D. The Relation between the Limitation and Its Purpose

284. Taking into account the nature and extent of the limitation as determined above, the court must now determine, firstly, whether the limitation is at all capable of promoting its purpose and, secondly, to which extent it succeeds in promoting its purpose. De Waal et al. states: 'This requires there to be a causal connection between the law [that imposes the limitation] and its purpose: the law must tend to serve the purpose that it is designed to serve.'[630] If a limitation does not promote its stated purpose, no rational connection or relation exists. Regarding the extent to which the limitation promotes its purpose, it may happen that a limitation does indeed promote its purpose, but only marginally. Then the relation between the limitation and its purpose may be too weak.[631]

285. The limitation may also either be under inclusive or over-inclusive. The limitation is under inclusive when it does not go far enough to promote the stated purpose effectively. In *Brink v. Kitshoff* the Constitutional Court struck down a provision of the Insurance Act 27 of 1943 which provided that a life insurance policy ceded by a husband to his wife within two years of his sequestration was deemed to belong to his estate. The Court held that this amounted to unfair discrimination against the wife – it limited her right to equality before the law. The Court further pointed out that the purpose of the provision was to protect creditors, but as they could also be prejudiced in the opposite situation where a wife had ceded a policy to her husband, the limitation was under inclusive and therefore invalid.[632] The opposite may also be true. The limitation may be over-inclusive in that it goes too far in its attempt to achieve the stated purpose. In *S v. Ntuli* the Constitutional Court held unconstitutional the provision in the Criminal Procedure Act that a prisoner could not in person appeal against his conviction unless a judge had certified that reasonable grounds for review existed. The stated purpose of this limitation on the right to a fair trial was to prevent frivolous appeals by prisoners, but the Court held that the limitation also affected meritorious appeals and that it was therefore over-inclusive and unconstitutional.[633]

E. Less Restrictive Means to Achieve the Purpose

286. The body or person imposing the limitation is compelled by this factor to consider alternative ways that can achieve the purpose more or less equally effective. If alternatives exist, the less restrictive, but more or less equally effective, alternative should be preferred. The state has a considerable margin of discretion here with which

---

629. De Waal et al. (*supra*) 125; Currie & De Waal (*supra*) 182; De Vos & Freedman (*supra*) 373–379.
630. *Supra* 125.
631. *S v. Williams* (*supra*) para. 86.
632. 1996 6 BCLR 752 (CC) paras 47–48.
633. 1996 1 BCLR 141 (CC) paras 22–24.

the courts will not interfere lightly. However, in *S v. Makwanyane* the Constitutional Court held with regard to the death penalty:

> The purposes of the death penalty are deterrence and prevention of violent crime. However, in the course of achieving these ends, the death penalty imposes considerable costs: grave and irreparable violations of the right to life, dignity, and freedom from cruel punishment. Where other methods of achieving these purposes exist that do not impose the same costs, it becomes difficult to claim that the method chosen is reasonable and justifiable.[634]

F. Conclusion

287. Section 36 has been of immeasurable assistance in the development of South Africa's human rights jurisprudence. Section 36 has gone a long way to systematize the enquiry into whether a limitation of a right is constitutional. Every enquiry in this regard should now follow more or less the same pattern, which facilitates the task of later courts and the analysis of court decisions. Section 36 has contributed tremendously to the understanding of a justiciable Bill of Rights and its application to real-life situations.

§3. Creating A Human Rights Culture

288. To a large extent the Bill of Rights was transplanted overnight onto a society most definitely longing for, but not really prepared for it. Various institutions and mechanisms have therefore been created to further the development of a human rights culture. As provided in the NC,[635] a Human Rights Commission was established to promote respect for human rights and the development of a culture of human rights. The Commission also promotes the protection of human rights and monitors and assesses the observance of human rights.[636] In addition, a Commission for Gender Equality has been put up,[637] and a Commission for the Promotion and Protection of the Rights of Cultural, Religious and Linguistic Communities is envisaged.[638] It is, furthermore, the overall responsibility of the state and all its organs to 'respect, protect, promote, and fulfil the rights in the Bill of Rights.'[639] This puts a particular obligation on the state to promote a human rights culture when it exercises its powers and performs its functions. This holds true for all legislatures when they make laws, all executive bodies, and administrative structures when they execute and administer those laws, and all courts when they apply the Bill of Rights. In the final analysis, every South African has the responsibility to become involved in the promotion of a culture of

634. 1995 6 BCLR 665 (CC) para. 123.
635. Chapter 9, ss 181–194.
636. *See* the Human Rights Commission Act 54 of 1995.
637. Section 187.
638. Section 185. *See* Ch. 3, §5 below.
639. Section 7(2).

human rights, and therefore civil society, academics, and the printed and electronic media should consider the various ways in which they can contribute in this regard.[640]

640. C.M.R. Dlamini, *The Relationship between Human Rights and Education*, in *Human Rights in South African Education: From the Constitutional Drawing Board to the Chalkboard* 39, 46–47 (J. De Groof and E.F.J. Malherbe eds, Acco 1997).

Chapter 3. Protection of Cultural, Religious, and Linguistic Communities

§1. Introduction

289. It is not without reason that President Mandela has coined the phrase 'rainbow nation.' South Africa remains a highly heterogeneous country and the racial, ethnic, cultural, religious, and linguistic diversity pervasive in society cannot be denied. As a matter of fact, much of the strife and turmoil experienced during the twentieth century stemmed directly from these differences and from the treatment of these differences by the apartheid government. Accordingly, while advocating in strong terms the elimination of the injustices of the past, the achievement of equality, the protection of everybody's dignity and the necessity of nation-building, the NC makes particular provision for the recognition and protection of cultural, religious and linguistic communities and related matters, as mentioned in Part I, Chapter 2 above.[641] However, although these differences in society correspond to some extent with provincial boundaries (some ethnic and cultural communities are concentrated in certain provinces), the provincial constitutional arrangements do not reflect this to any significant degree. The WCC contains a few provisions in this regard, and the failed KwaZulu-Natal Constitution made special provision for the Zulu monarch, but otherwise the formal recognition of cultural, religious, and linguistic communities is a matter which is confined to the NC.

290. The constitutional protection of cultural, religious, and linguistic communities was a fiercely fought bone of contention throughout the negotiations of the 1990s. The ANC was vehemently opposed to the entrenchment of any form of apartheid or privilege from the past, and fought any notion of constitutional protection for minorities with teeth and nails. Some parties such as the National Party and the Freedom Front were equally fearful of minority communities being overrun and dominated by the black majority. Several proposals for minority protection ranging from a so-called territorial solution (an Afrikaner state or *volkstaat*) to power-sharing at executive level between blacks and whites were continuously tabled and debated. There were also different proposals around the idea of self-determination for communities on a non-territorial basis, for example, community councils with decision-making powers analogous to the Flemish and French community councils in Belgium. Of course, none but the provisions now contained in the NC succeeded. They are discussed briefly below.

291. One major result, however, of the chequered background in this regard and particularly the racism, discrimination and injustice triggered over the years by the differences among the people of South Africa was the express commitment in the NC to eradicate these consequences of apartheid and to ensure that they never recur.

641. *See also* the exposition by F. Venter, *The Protection of Cultural, Linguistic and Religious Rights: The Framework Provided by the Constitution of the Republic of South Africa, 1996*, SA Public Law 438–459 (1998).

The Preamble to the NC, as well as section 1, which contain the underlying values of the new South Africa, provide for this in express terms. In addition, section 9, which guarantees the right to equality, also prohibits any form of unfair discrimination on the basis, *inter alia*, of race, ethnic, or social origin, colour, religion, belief, culture and language. The Constitutional Court held that the meaning of unfair discrimination in section 9 should be determined against the background of the past unequal treatment of people in which their inherent dignity was denied. The Court accordingly held that 'in our view unfair discrimination principally means treating persons differently in a way which impairs their fundamental dignity as human beings, who are inherently equal in dignity.'[642]

292. In addition, the NC provides that in the interpretation and application of the Bill of Rights, the values underlying an open and democratic society must be promoted.[643] The Constitutional Court held in this regard that the Constitution must be interpreted and applied against the background of past injustices and the disruptive and alienating effect of apartheid on almost every sphere of life.[644] The past is to inform the future, in order to avoid the mistakes made in the past. The challenge is therefore not only to protect cultural, religious and linguistic communities on a clean canvas; it is also a matter of correcting and avoiding past mistakes, of building new relationships of trust in a diverse society dispersed by gross injustice and mistrust, and of fostering a positive recognition of the differences that do exist and that have been abused in the past as the very pillars of the apartheid system, but which now form the building blocks of the new nation.

293. The discussion below is conducted against this backdrop and within the framework of these values embraced in the NC.

§2. Language

294. The NC recognizes the multilingual nature of the South African society and makes express provision with regard to language matters, first, in respect of the recognition of the official languages and, second, in respect of the right to use the language of one's choice in different contexts.[645]

I. Official Languages

295. With more than twenty significant languages used, South Africa is a multilingual country and the language provisions of the NC reflect this reality.[646] Accordingly, South Africa has eleven official languages and the NC determines their

642. *Prinsloo v. Van der Linde* 1997 6 BCLR 759 (CC) paras 31–33.
643. Section 39(1).
644. *S v. Mhlungu* 1995 3 BCLR 793 (CC) para. 111.
645. *See* the discussion by Rautenbach (2012) (*supra*), 79–80.
646. *See* constitutional principle XI: 'The diversity of language and culture shall be acknowledged and protected, and conditions for their promotion shall be encouraged.'

use by government bodies in all spheres and how all languages of the Republic must be developed.[647]

296. The official languages are Sepedi, Sesotho, Setswana, siSwati, Tshivenda, Xitsonga, Afrikaans, English, isiNdebele, isiXhosa, and isiZulu.[648] It is uncertain what exactly are the practical consequences of official status,[649] but at least it indicates which languages must be used for the purposes of official communication by governments in all spheres.[650] These are therefore the languages in which governments must make and promulgate laws, in which decisions and other government actions must be made known, and in which the public may communicate with those governments. All official languages enjoy parity of esteem and must be treated equitably. Parity of esteem does not necessarily mean equality, but it means, at least, that all official languages must receive recognition in government activities, that some may not dominate at the expense of others, and that some will not be neglected.[651]

297. The Constitution deals with the practical implications of eleven official languages in a flexible way and provides that the national and provincial governments may use any particular official languages as languages for government purposes.[652] A few remarks should be made about this provision:

- The term 'government purposes' refers to all activities of the national and provincial governments that require communication between the government, departments, administrations and officials, and with the public.[653] It thus refers at least to laws, bills, minutes, and other official documents of legislatures, and decisions, notices and official press statements by the executive.[654] It also refers to the administrative components of the governments in question which meet with the public on a daily basis. In addition, it can be accepted that it includes internal communication, in other words, within departments and other government bodies.
- The provision refers to the national and provincial governments and not to organs of state in general.[655] This does not mean that such other organs of state that exercise public powers and perform public functions in terms of legislation and

647. Concerning the official language provisions of the Interim Constitution, *see* I. Currie, 'Official languages,' in Chaskalson et al. (*supra*) para. 37.
648. Section 6(1).
649. *See* P.W. Hogg, *Constitutional Law of Canada* 53.6(a) (1992); Currie (*supra*) 37.3.
650. *See* E.F.J. Malherbe, *The Language Provisions of the 1993 Constitution as Applied in Gauteng,* TSAR 353, 357 (1995), who refers *inter alia* to s. 89(3)(a)(ii) of the Constitution of 1983 (Act 110 of 1983), in which it was expressly mentioned that the official languages must be used for official purposes; Rautenbach (2012) (*supra*) 79–82.
651. Currie (*supra*) 37.6 states: 'The parity of esteem requirement insists that, considerations of practicality aside, a sincere attempt must be made to ensure that particular languages do not dominate while others are neglected.'
652. Section 6(3).
653. Currie (*supra*) 37.8.
654. *See* *Lourens v. Speaker of the National Assembly of Parliament* [2016] ZASCA 11 for a discussion about the use of official languages by Parliament.
655. *See* on organs of state s. 239 and above on local governments. It may seem as if 'government' as used rather restrictively in the NC does not include the courts, but in e.g., *S v. Pienaar* 2000 7 BCLR 800 (NC) it was accepted as a matter of course that the judiciary was bound by s. 6.

are subject to the Constitution in all respects, may disregard the language provisions. They must also in their choice and use of languages respect the equality of esteem of the official languages and treat the languages equitably.

- The purpose of the provision is to facilitate the task of the relevant governments and they may not in making a choice violate the equality of esteem of any official language or treat any language inequitably. In order, therefore, to prevent the violation of the equality of esteem of any official language and for the purposes of equity, the relevant governments must, in making a choice, take into account usage, practicality, expense, regional circumstances, and the balance of the needs and preferences of the population as a whole or in the respective provinces. These factors strengthen the flexibility of the arrangement and allow, for example, for regional or provincial differences. They must nevertheless be considered together, and a choice must be made that is equitable in view of all relevant circumstances.
- No government body in the national or provincial spheres may use only one language and they are obliged to use two or more languages. This prevents preference for or domination by a single official language and strengthens the recognition of the multilingual nature of society. The recognition of eleven official languages has an inclusive intent, and the state should communicate in as many languages as possible. This is particularly true in the case of the promulgation of laws. The public must take cognizance of the rules of law that apply to them in a proper and meaningful way, but can do so only if governments communicate the laws to them in a language or languages that they properly understand.[656]
- The national and provincial governments, by legislation and other measures, must regulate and monitor their use of the official languages.[657]

298. The provincial government of the Western Cape has already given effect to this latter obligation to regulate and monitor the use of official languages in the province. Not only is a similar provision included in the WCC, but also detailed legislation gives effect to it. The Western Cape Provincial Languages Act 13 of 1998 provides for a Provincial Language Committee which fulfils both a watchdog and a developmental role.[658] Practical measures for the equal treatment of the three provincial official languages for the purposes of government in the Western Cape, such as a requirement that all notices and advertisements issued by the provincial government must be published in all three languages in the Provincial Gazette and in the daily newspapers in the language of that newspaper, are prescribed in the Western Cape Provincial Languages Act.[659]

299. Municipalities must take into account the language usage and preferences of their residents.[660] Unlike the national and provincial governments, they are therefore not compelled to select at least two official languages, but the provision is enforceable

656. *See* Currie (*supra*) 37.8. He argues in the same vein that the legislative process itself must be multilingual to enable members of parliament to participate fully.
657. Parliament passed a law in 2012 to regulate the use of official languages by the national government, namely the Use of Official Languages Act 12 of 2012.
658. *See* the discussion of the language provisions in WCC in Part II, Ch. 2, §2.I.
659. Section 3 of Act 13 of 1998.
660. Section 6(3)(b).

and they must be able to demonstrate that in their choice or use of languages the equality of esteem of no official language is violated, that they treat languages equitably, and that they take into account the language usage and preferences of their residents.[661] This requires a considered decision in which, among others, demographic statistics should be taken into account.[662]

300. Due to the historical handicap of indigenous languages, whose usage and status have been diminished over the years, the government must take steps to elevate their status and advance their use.[663] They must be developed in order for them to take their rightful place as official languages. In addition, the Pan South African Language Board[664] must promote the development and use of the official languages, the Khoi, Nama and San languages, and sign language, and must promote respect for various languages used by smaller language communities and for religious purposes.[665] According to the NC, these languages include German, Greek, Gujarati, Hindi, Portuguese, Tamil, Telugu, Urdu, Arabic, Hebrew, and Sanskrit.

II. Language Rights

301. Section 6 on the official languages must be considered together with the language rights in the Bill of Rights. As mentioned, section 9(3) prohibits unfair discrimination *inter alia* on the ground of language. Section 30 provides that everyone is entitled to use the language of their choice.[666] Significantly, section 29(2) provides that everyone has the right to education in the official language of their choice, where reasonably practicable.[667] In terms of section 31, anyone belonging to a linguistic community may not be denied the right, in association with other members of that

661. The decision in *Louw v. Transitional Local Council of Greater Germiston* 1997 8 BCLR 1062 (W) that the provision of the Interim Constitution on official languages did not apply to local governments does therefore not apply to the position in terms of the 1996 Constitution. The decision of the city council, taken without thorough investigation, to use only one language in a city in which there are four large language groups, will be hard to justify in terms of the 1996 Constitution. (The court was in any case wrong in finding that the Bill of Rights did not apply to decisions of a municipality.)
662. *See* Currie (*supra*) 37.12.
663. Section 6(2). Afrikaans is an indigenous language, but is not in a position that it can be said that its use and status has been historically diminished to the extent experienced by other indigenous languages. All official languages must nevertheless be developed in terms of s. 6(5)(a)(i).
664. *See* para. 303 below.
665. Section 6(5).
666. Section 31 provides *inter alia* that everyone has the right, with other members of the relevant language community, to use their language and form linguistic associations.
667. This provision has been discussed in depth elsewhere. *See* e.g., *Minister of Education (Western Cape) v. Mikro Primary School Governing Body* [2005] ZASCA 66; *Head of Department of Education: Mpumalanga v. Hoërskool Ermelo* [2009] ZACC 32; 2010 (2) SA 415 (CC); 2010 (3) BCLR 177 (CC); Currie & De Waal, *(supra)* 636–640; E.F.J. Malherbe, *Reflections on the Background and Contents of the Education Clause in the South African Bill of Rights*, TSAR 85 (1997); R.R. Kriel, *Education*, in Chaskalson et al. (*supra*) 38; I. Currie, *Culture, Language and Education*, in Currie and Erasmus (De Waal ed.) (*supra*) 349; Davis et al. (*supra*) 294.

community, to use their language and to form, join and maintain linguistic associations. This provision has been described as an individual right that can be exercised collectively.[668] Section 35(3)(k) provides that every accused person has the right to be tried in a language that he or she understands, or, if that is not practicable, to have the proceedings interpreted in that language.[669] All information that must be provided to arrested, detained, and accused persons in terms of the Bill of Rights must be provided in a language that the person understands.[670]

302. These provisions qualify in some respects the powers that the national and provincial governments have with regard to the use of the official languages in terms of section 6. While these governments may choose to use certain official languages, they must take into account the fact that a member of the public may choose to communicate with them in a particular official or other language, or to receive education in a particular official language, and that an accused person has the language rights as mentioned above. These provisions of the Bill of Rights give further expression to the multilingual nature of the South African community, and any limitation that a government imposes on these rights must be justified in terms of the limitation provisions.

III. The Pan South African Language Board

303. The interim Constitution envisaged a Pan South African Language Board to be established in terms of national legislation. Such legislation, the Pan South African Language Board Act 59 of 1995, had indeed been adopted and the Board was established soon afterwards.[671] The Board must *inter alia* promote the equal use and enjoyment of all official languages, extend the use and status of languages restricted to certain regions, promote multilingualism, promote respect for other languages, and prevent the use of any language for the purposes of exploitation, domination, or division.[672] The Board is empowered to investigate complaints, assist persons or communities in asserting or enforcing their language rights, and recommend to state organs possible action to rectify matters. The Board must also report annually to Parliament. Initially, the complaint against the Board has been that it lacks real powers to enforce the language provisions of the NC effectively. Recently, however, the Board has taken a strong stand against government departments and organs of state that do not give meaningful effect to the provisions of section 6.

304. In the Western Cape the Provincial Language Committee created by the Western Cape Provincial Languages Act 13 of 1998 performs a similar function for that province.

668. *See* Currie & De Waal (*supra*) 623.

669. *See* e.g., *Mthethwa v. De Bruin NO* 1998 3 BCLR 336 (N);*S v. Matomela* 1998 3 BCLR 339 (Ck) and the reaction to them by K. Malan, 'Oor die hofnotuleringstaal in die lig van die Grondwet en na aanleiding van onlangse regspraak,' 1998 THRHR 696.

670. Section 35(4).

671. In terms of item 20 of Sch. 6 of the NC, the Board has continued to exist after the commencement of the NC.

672. Section 3 of Act 59 of 1995.

§3. Religion

305. There is complete religious freedom in South Africa. Section 15 of the NC guarantees the right to freedom of conscience, religion, thought, belief, and opinion. According to the Constitutional Court, section 15 does not include an establishment clause and, accordingly, there does not exist in South Africa the same strict 'wall of separation' between church and state as, for example, in the United States of America. In other words, section 15 does not expect from the state total abstinence from religious matters nor does it prohibit the state from any involvement in such matters.[673] This corresponds with the traditional South African approach to religious freedom in terms of which the state has always been actively involved in the creation of favourable circumstances for the exercise of religious freedom.[674] In this respect, the traditional legal position in South Africa has been compared to the German Constitution, which imposes a positive duty on the state to provide religious instruction and to further religious observances in schools.[675]

306. This position is reinforced by section 15(2), which provides that religious observances may be conducted at state or state-aided institutions, provided that rules made by the appropriate authorities are followed, and the observances are conducted on an equitable basis and attendance is free and voluntarily. Section 15(2) acknowledges the traditional prominence of religion in and religious observances in South African public institutions, like schools, hospitals, prisons, and state departments. 'Religious observances' refers to individual and collective Scripture reading, prayers, moments of silence for personal devotion or meditation and, possibly, the exhibition of religious symbols. It seems as if this does not include religious instruction, which often forms part of the official curricula in schools, and on which there are official policies issued by education departments, but which is seemingly not recognized by section 15(2) as a constitutional right.[676] The conditions for the conducting of the observances are significant. First, it must be conducted in terms of rules made by the appropriate authorities – in the case of schools, the governing bodies. Second, it must be conducted on an equitable basis, in other words, no religion should be treated with favour or prejudice. Third, attendance must be free and voluntarily, which means that nobody may be coerced in attending, either directly or indirectly. Obviously, questions may be asked regarding the practical application of the provision, but at least the right is guaranteed and the conditions under which it may be exercised are provided as guidance.

307. For the purposes of this discussion, section 15(3) is important. It provides that section 15 does not prevent legislation recognizing systems or personal and family law under any tradition or adhered to by persons professing a particular religion. It

673. *S v. Lawrence; S v. Negal; S v. Solberg* 1997 10 BCLR 1348 (CC) paras 100–101.

674. *See* the discussion by E.F.J. Malherbe, 'Die grondwetlike beskerming van godsdiensvryheid,' 1998 TSAR 673–701. The legal position has also been summarized in W.F. Foster, R. Malherbe and W.J. Smith, 'Religion, language and education: contrasting constitutional approaches,' 1999 *Education and Law Journal* 211 at 216–222.

675. *See* e.g., H.D. Jarass and B. Pieroth, *Gründgesetz für die Bundesrepublik Deutschland* (1995) 232. *See* , however, the more recent *Classroom Crucifix* case, in which the court expected a greater measure of neutrality from the state (93 *BVerfGE* 1).

676. Foster, Malherbe and Smith (*supra*) 221.

also authorizes legislation recognizing marriages concluded under any tradition, or a system of religious, personal, or family law. However, this recognition must be consistent with the NC. Section 15(3) accommodates indigenous and Muslim law, both of which are inconsistent with the NC in important respects, such as the status of women, but which are nevertheless adhered to by millions of people in South Africa. The idea is that these systems of law must gradually be brought into line with the NC.[677] In the meantime, section 15(3) must be regarded as yet another way in which the rights and interests of cultural and religious communities are recognized by the NC.

§4. CULTURE

308. In terms of section 30 of the NC every person has the right to participate in the cultural life of their choice. According to some commentators, the reference to 'cultural life' indicates a wider meaning than mere culture, and refers to a way of life. This is a broad term which may also include the institutional aspects of culture, such as schools, publications, broadcasting services, libraries, museums, monuments, etc.[678] Persons belonging to a cultural community may also not be denied the right, in association with other members of that community, to enjoy their culture, and to form, join and maintain cultural associations and other organs of civil society.[679] Section 185, dealing with the Commission for the Promotion and Protection of the Rights of Cultural, Religious and Linguistic Communities,[680] in fact refers to the establishment of cultural or other councils for communities on the recommendation of the Commission. Read together, these provisions give rise to the question to which extent cultural and other communities may rightfully claim some form of autonomous decision-making powers over identifiable cultural matters such as these mentioned above.

309. In this regard it is also important to note that 'cultural matters' are listed in Schedule 4 of the NC as a functional area on which the national and provincial governments share concurrent powers, whereas 'provincial cultural matters' are listed in Schedule 5 as an exclusive provincial affair. This constitutional distribution of powers on cultural matters could impact on the way in which cultural communities are being treated or accommodated nationally and in the various provinces. In fact, the WCC provides in section 70 for the establishment and reasonable funding of a cultural council or councils for a community or communities in the Western Cape that share a common language and cultural heritage. This has led to the establishment of the Western Cape Cultural Commission which aims to preserve, promote, and develop

677. Much has been written in this regard –*see* the extensive references by Rautenbach (2012) (*supra*) 364 n 32. *See* also E.F.J. Malherbe 'Enkele kwelvrae oor die grondwetlike beskerming van die reg op godsdiensvryheid' 2006 TSAR 636–641; *Prince v. President of the Law Society of the Cape of Good Hope* 2002 3 BCLR 231 (CC); *Amod v. Multilateral Motor Vehicle Accidents Fund* 1999 4 SA 1319 (SCA).

678. *See* e.g., Currie & De Waal (*supra*) 636.

679. Section 31. This provision is based on Art. 27 of the International Covenant on Civil and Political Rights. *See* the remark above on the nature of the provision as providing for an individual right which can be exercised collectively.

680. *See* §5 below.

culture in the Western Cape.[681] Cultural councils, which are voluntary associations of persons, may thus apply for registration with the Cultural Commission and may apply to the Commission for financial support for culturally related projects.[682] Whereas cultural councils will have the interests of their respective communities at heart, the task of the Cultural Commission is much wider since it has to preserve, promote and develop culture in general and not only for a specific community. This purpose is supported by the wording of the Preamble to the Western Cape Cultural Commission and Cultural Councils Act 14 of 1998 where it is *inter alia* stated that 'the rich cultural diversity in the Western Cape should be protected and promoted in such a way that it will lead to a better understanding and mutual respect for various cultures in the Western Cape.'

310. Lastly, the impact of the constitutional recognition of traditional authorities on the preservation and promotion of culture as a dominant feature of life in South Africa should not be underestimated.[683] These tribal and other traditional authorities are formidable bearers and guardians of the cultural heritage of many black communities, particularly in the rural areas.

§5. Commission for the Promotion and Protection of the Rights of Cultural, Religious and Linguistic Communities

311. Section 185 of the NC provides for a Commission for the Promotion and Protection of the Rights of Cultural, Religious and Linguistic Communities to be established in terms of national legislation. The fact that it took a long time since the NC has come into effect to adopt the legislation probably attests to the sensitivity and complexity of the matter in the South African context. A law was eventually adopted in 2002, namely the Commission for the Promotion and Protection of the Rights of Cultural, Religious and Linguistic Communities Act 19 of 2002. Although the official viewpoint is that the Commission will be an instrument of nation-building in the multi-cultural South Africa, there are others who regard any recognition of cultural differences as inconsistent with the notion of nation-building. Still others believe that nation-building will remain an illusion if it is not founded on those very differences, or if it does not at least take the diversity into account. Some also feel that their loyalty to the new South Africa depends on the extent to which their culture is afforded some form of official recognition and, if at all possible, they obtain some limited form of self-determination. There are even sceptic observers who believe that the Commission will serve no purpose other than to be a political instrument of the government.

312. The Commission, which must be broadly representative of the main cultural, religious, and linguistic communities in South Africa, and must broadly reflect the gender composition of South Africa, must promote respect for the rights of such communities.[684] It must promote and develop peace, friendship, humanity, tolerance, and national unity among such communities, on the basis of equality, non-discrimination,

681. Section 3 of the Western Cape Cultural Commission and Cultural Councils Act 14 of 1998.
682. Section 16 of Act 14 of 1998.
683. The institutional aspects of traditional authorities are discussed in Part II, Ch. 1, §3 above.
684. Sections 185 and 186.

and free association, and its object is also to recommend the establishment or recognition, in accordance with national legislation, of a cultural or other council or councils for a community or communities. The Commission must have the powers necessary to achieve these objects and may monitor, investigate, research educate, lobby, advise and report on relevant issues. Despite the underlying difficulties regarding the establishment of the Commission, it is evident from section 185 of the NC that the focus of the Commission will be wider than that of the Cultural Commission of the Western Cape referred to above. The first Commission was appointed by the President during 2003. It will make practical sense to establish a good working relationship between the Commission and the Western Cape Cultural Commission, at least as far as cultural matters in the Western Cape are concerned.

§6. Self-determination

313. Section 235 of the NC, an obvious product of last-minute negotiations to get certain parties on board,[685] provides as follows:

The right of the South African people as a whole to self-determination, as manifested in this Constitution, does not preclude, within the framework of this right, recognition of the notion of the right of self-determination of any community sharing a common cultural and language heritage, within a territorial entity in the Republic or in any other way, determined by national legislation.

314. As mentioned, the notion of territorial self-determination for certain communities has in fact been regarded as apartheid in disguise and therefore unacceptable. In the end, this provision was nevertheless included in the NC to appease certain communities and ensure their support for the NC. What it really means, in other words, whether it has any practical significance and, more importantly, whether any community would be able to convince Parliament to adopt a law providing for such a form of self-determination, is of course anybody's guess. At least, the notion has been recognized constitutionally and for some communities that has been enough to secure their support for the NC. The significance of the provision is therefore that it serves to postpone the issue so that, some time in the future, a particular community that desires self-determination will have to take up their aspirations with the government of the day.

§7. Conclusion

315. The provisions in the NC for the protection of cultural, religious, and linguistic communities are neither dramatic nor far-reaching by any standards, but they are real. They do signify the awareness of South Africans of the realities of their diverse country and they do contain possibilities for further development. South Africans should, however, also be aware of international developments in this regard and the extent to which various recent instruments of international law provide for the

685. *See* H. Ebrahim, *The Soul of a Nation – Constitution-making in South Africa* 198 (Oxford University Press 1998).

effective protection of minorities.[686] These developments should be allowed to inform and enrich the South African debate on the effective recognition and accommodation of the cultural, religious, and linguistic diversity of the South African society.[687]

686. *See* e.g., the Declaration on the Rights of Persons belonging to National or Ethnic, Religious and Linguistic Minorities (1992); European Charter for Regional or Minority Languages (1992); Framework Convention for the Protection of National Minorities (1995).

687. *See* the discussion of international developments and their possible application to South Africa by H.A. Strydom, *South African Constitutionalism between Unity and Diversity: Lessons from the New Europe*, SA Public Law 373–403 (1997); *Minority Rights Protection: Implementing International Standards*, SAJHR 373–387 (1998); *Rehabilitering van die reg op selfbeskikking*, TSAR 346 (2000). *See also* G.N. Barrie, *Ubuntu ungamntu ngabanye abantu: the recognition of minority rights in the South African constitution*, TSAR 271 (2000).

Part V. Representative Texts

Chapter 1 Excerpts from the South African Constitution

as adopted on 8 May 1996, amended on 11 October 1996 and coming into effect on 4 February 1997

Chapter 3 Co-operative Government

Section 40. Government of the Republic

(1) In the Republic, government is constituted as national, provincial, and local spheres of government which are distinctive, interdependent, and interrelated.
(2) All spheres of government must observe and adhere to the principles in this Chapter and must conduct their activities within the parameters that the chapter provides.

Section 41. Principles of co-operative government and intergovernmental relations

(1) All spheres of government and all organs of state within each sphere must –

(a) preserve the peace, the national unity, and the indivisibility of the Republic;
(b) secure the well-being of the people of the Republic;
(c) provide effective, transparent, accountable, and coherent government for the Republic as a whole;
(d) be loyal to the Constitution, the Republic and its people;
(e) respect the constitutional status, institutions, powers and functions of government in the other spheres;
(f) not assume any power or function except those conferred on them in terms of the Constitution;
(g) exercise their powers and perform their functions in a manner that does not encroach on the geographical, functional or institutional integrity of government in another sphere; and
(h) co-operate with one another in mutual trust and good faith by –
(i) fostering friendly relations;
(ii) assisting and supporting one another;
(iii) informing one another of, and consulting one another on, matters of common interest;
(iv) co-ordinating their actions and legislation with one another;
(v) adhering to agreed procedures; and
(vi) avoiding legal proceedings against one another.

(2) An Act of Parliament must –

(a) establish or provide for structures and institutions to promote and facilitate intergovernmental relations; and
(b) provide for appropriate mechanisms and procedures to facilitate settlement of intergovernmental disputes.

(3) An organ of state involved in an intergovernmental dispute must make every reasonable effort to settle the dispute by way of mechanisms and procedures provided for that purpose, and must exhaust all other remedies before it approaches a court to resolve the dispute.
(4) If a court is not satisfied that the requirements of subsection (3) have been met, it may refer a dispute back to the organs of state involved.

Chapter 6 Provinces

Section 103. Provinces

(1) The Republic has the following provinces:

(a) Eastern Cape
(b) Free State
(c) Gauteng
(d) KwaZulu-Natal
(e) Limpopo
(f) Mpumalanga
(g) Northern Cape
(h) North West
(i) Western Cape

(2) The geographical areas of the respective provinces comprise the sum of the indicated geographical areas reflected in the various maps referred to in the Notice listed in Schedule 1A.
(3) (a) Whenever the geographical area of a province is re-determined by an amendment to the Constitution, an Act of Parliament may provide for measures to regulate, within a reasonable time, the legal, practical, and any other consequences of the re-determination.

(b) An Act of Parliament envisaged in paragraph (a) may be enacted and implemented before such amendment to the Constitution takes effect, but any provincial functions, assets, rights, obligations, duties or liabilities may only be transferred in terms of that Act after that amendment to the Constitution takes effect.

Provincial Legislatures

Section 104. Legislative authority of provinces

(1) The legislative authority of a province is vested in its provincial legislature, and confers on the provincial legislature the power –

(a) to pass a constitution for its province or to amend any constitution passed by it in terms of sections 142 and 143;
(b) to pass legislation for its province with regard to –
(i) any matter within a functional area listed in Schedule 4;
(ii) any matter within a functional area listed in Schedule 5;
(iii) any matter outside those functional areas, and that is expressly assigned to the province by national legislation; and
(iv) any matter for which a provision of the Constitution envisages the enactment of provincial legislation; and
(c) to assign any of its legislative powers to a Municipal Council in that province.

(2) The legislature of a province, by a resolution adopted with a supporting vote of at least two thirds of its members, may request Parliament to change the name of that province.
(3) A provincial legislature is bound only by the Constitution and, if it has passed a constitution for its province, also by that constitution, and must act in accordance with, and within the limits of, the Constitution and that provincial constitution.
(4) Provincial legislation with regard to a matter that is reasonable necessary for, or incidental to, the effective exercise of a power concerning any matter listed in Schedule 4, is for all purposes legislation with regard to a matter listed in Schedule 4.
(5) A provincial legislature may recommend to the National Assembly legislation concerning any matter outside the authority of that legislature, or in respect of which an Act of Parliament prevails over a provincial law.

Section 105. Composition and election of provincial legislatures

(1) A provincial legislature consists of women and men elected as members in terms of an electoral system that –

(a) is prescribed by national legislation;
(b) is based on that province's segment of the national common voters roll;
(c) provides for a minimum voting age of 18 years; and
(d) results, in general, in proportional representation.

(2) A provincial legislature consists of between 30 and 80 members. The number of members, which may differ among the provinces, must be determined in terms of a formula prescribed by national legislation.

Section 106. Membership

(1) Every citizen who is qualified to vote for the National Assembly is eligible to be a member of a provincial legislature, except –

(a) anyone who is appointed by, or is in the service of, the state and receives remuneration for that appointment or service, other than –
(i) the Premier and other members of the Executive Council of a province; and
(ii) other office-bearers whose functions are compatible with the functions of a members of a provincial legislature, and have been declared compatible with those functions by national legislation;
(b) members of the National Assembly, permanent delegates to the National Council of Provinces or members of a Municipal Council;
(c) unrehabilitated insolvents;
(d) anyone declared to be of unsound mind by a court of the Republic; or
(e) anyone who, after this section took effect, is convicted of an offence and sentences to more than 12 months' imprisonment without the option of a fine, either in the Republic, or outside the Republic if the conduct constituting the offence would have been an offence in the Republic, but no one may be regarded as having been sentenced until an appeal against the conviction or sentence has been determined, or until the time for an appeal has expired. A disqualification under this paragraph ends five years after the sentence has been completed.

(2) A person who is not eligible to be a member of a provincial legislature in terms of subsection (1)(a) or (b) may be a candidate for the legislature, subject to any limits or conditions established by national legislation.
(3) A person loses membership of a provincial legislature if that person –

(a) ceases to be eligible;
(b) is absent from the legislature without permission in circumstances for which the rules and orders of the legislature prescribe loss of membership; or
(c) Ceases to be a member of the party that nominated that person as a member of the legislature.

(4) Vacancies in a provincial legislature must be filled in terms of national legislation.

Section 107. Oath or affirmation

Before members of a provincial legislature begin to perform their functions in the legislature, they must swear or affirm faithfulness to the Republic and obedience to the Constitution, in accordance with Schedule 2.

Section 108. Duration of provincial legislatures

(1) A provincial legislature is elected for a term of five years.
(2) If a provincial legislature is dissolved in terms of section 109, or when its term expires, the Premier of the province, by proclamation, must call and set dates for an election, which must be held within 90 days of the date the legislature was dissolved or its term expired. A proclamation calling and setting dates for an

election may be issued before or after the expiry of the term of a provincial legislature.

(3) If the result of an election of a provincial legislature is not declared within the period referred to in section 190, or if an election is set aside by a court, the President, by proclamation, must call and set dates for another election, which must be held within 90 days of the expiry of that period or of the date on which the election was set aside.

(4) A provincial legislature remains competent to function from the time it is dissolved or its term expires, until the day before the first day of polling for the next legislature.

Section 109. Dissolution of provincial legislatures before expiry of term

(1) The Premier of a province must dissolve the provincial legislature if –

(a) the legislature has adopted a resolution to dissolve with a supporting vote of a majority of its members; and
(b) three years have passed since the legislature was elected.

(2) An Acting Premier must dissolve the provincial legislature if –

(a) there is a vacancy in the office of Premier; and
(b) the legislature fails to elect a new Premier within 30 days after the vacancy occurred.

Section 110. Sittings and recess periods

(1) After an election, the first sitting of a provincial legislature must take place at a time and on a date determined by a judge designated by the Chief Justice, but not more than 14 days after the election result has been declared. A provincial legislature may determine the time and duration of its other sittings and recess periods.

(2) The Premier of a province may summon the provincial legislature to an extraordinary sitting at any time to conduct special business.

(3) A provincial legislature may determine where it ordinarily will sit.

Section 111. Speakers and Deputy Speakers

(1) At the first sitting after its election, or when necessary to fill a vacancy, a provincial legislature must elect a Speaker and a Deputy Speaker from among its members.

(2) A judge designated by the Chief Justice must preside over the election of a Speaker. The Speaker presides over the election of a Deputy Speaker.

(3) The procedure set out in Part A of Schedule 3 applies to the election of Speakers and Deputy Speakers.

(4) A provincial legislature may remove its Speaker or Deputy Speaker from office by resolution. A majority of the members of the legislature must be present when the resolution in adopted.
(5) In terms of its rules and orders, a provincial legislature may elect from among its members other presiding officers to assist the Speaker and the Deputy Speaker.

Section 112. Decisions

(1) Except where the Constitution provides otherwise –

(a) a majority of the members of a provincial legislature must be present before a vote may be taken on a Bill or an amendment to a Bill;
(b) at least one third of the members must be present before a vote may be taken on any other question before the legislature; and
(c) all questions before a provincial legislature are decided by a majority of the votes cast.

(2) The member presiding at a meeting of a provincial legislature has no deliberative vote, but –

(a) must cast a deciding vote when there is an equal number of votes on each side of a question; and
(b) may cast a deliberative vote when a question must be decided with a supporting vote of at least two thirds of the members of the legislature.

Section 113. Permanent delegates' rights in provincial legislatures

A province's permanent delegates to the National Council of Provinces may attend, and may speak in, their provincial legislature and its committees, but may not vote. The legislature may require a permanent delegate to attend the legislature or its committees.

Section 114. Powers of provincial legislatures

(1) In exercising its legislative power, a provincial legislature may –

(a) consider, pass, amend or reject any Bill before the legislature; and
(b) initiate or prepare legislation, except money Bills.

(2) A provincial legislature must provide for mechanisms –

(a) to ensure that all provincial executive organs of state in the province are accountable to it; and
(b) to maintain oversight of –
(i) the exercise of provincial executive authority in the province, including the implementation of legislation; and
(ii) any provincial organ of state.

Section 115. Evidence or information before provincial legislatures

A provincial legislature or any of its committees may –

(a) summon any person to appear before it to give evidence on oath or affirmation, or to produce documents;
(b) require any person or provincial institution to report to it;
(c) compel, in terms of provincial legislation or the rules and orders, any person or institution to comply with a summons or requirement in terms of paragraph (a) or (b); and
(d) receive petitions, representations or submissions from any interested persons or institutions.

Section 116. Internal arrangements, proceedings and procedures of provincial legislatures

(1) A provincial legislature may –

(a) determine and control its internal arrangements, proceedings and procedures; and
(b) make rules and orders concerning its business, with due regard to representative and participatory democracy, accountability, transparency and public involvement.

(2) The rules and orders of a provincial legislature must provide for –

(a) the establishment, composition, powers, functions, procedures and duration of its committees;
(b) the participation in the proceedings of the legislature and its committees of minority parties represented in the legislature, in a manner consistent with democracy;
(c) financial and administrative assistance to each party represented in the legislature, in proportion to its representation, to enable the party and its leader to perform their functions in the legislature effectively; and
(d) the recognition of the leader of the largest opposition party in the legislature, as the Leader of the Opposition.

Section 117. Privilege

(1) Members of a provincial legislature and the province's permanent delegates to the National Council of Provinces –

(a) have freedom of speech in the legislature and in its committees, subject to its rules and orders; and
(b) are not liable to civil or criminal proceedings, arrest, imprisonment or damages for –
(i) anything that they have said in, produced before or submitted to the legislature or any of its committees; or

(ii) anything revealed as a result of anything that they have said in, produced before or submitted to the legislature or any of its committees.

(2) Other privileges and immunities of a provincial legislature and its members may be prescribed by national legislation.
(3) Salaries, allowances and benefits payable to members of a provincial legislature are a direct charge against the Provincial Revenue Fund.

Section 118. Public access to and involvement in provincial legislatures

(1) A provincial legislature must –

(a) facilitate public involvement in the legislative and other processes of the legislature and its committees; and
(b) conduct its business in an open manner, and hold its sittings, and those of its committees, in public, but reasonable measures may be taken –
(i) to regulate public access, including access of the media, to the legislature and its committees; and
(ii) to provide for the searching of any person and, where appropriate, the refusal of entry to, or the removal of, any person.

(2) A provincial legislature may not exclude the public, including the media, from a sitting of a committee unless it is reasonable and justifiable to do so in an open and democratic society.

Section 119. Introduction of Bills

Only members of the Executive Council of a province or a committee or a member of a provincial legislature may introduce a Bill in the legislature, but only the member of the Executive Council who is responsible for financial matters in the province may introduce a money Bill in the legislature.
Section 120. Money Bills

(1) A Bill is a money Bill if it-

(a) appropriates money;
(b) imposes provincial taxes, levies, duties or surcharges;
(c) abolishes or reduces, or grants exemptions from, any provincial taxes, levies, duties or surcharges; or
(d) authorises direct charges against a Provincial Revenue Fund.

(2) A money Bill may not deal with any other matter except-

(a) a subordinate matter incidental to the appropriation of money;
(b) the imposition, abolition or reduction of provincial taxes, levies, duties or surcharges;

(c) the granting of exemption from provincial taxes, levies, duties or surcharges; or
(d) the authorisation of direct charges against a Provincial Revenue Fund.
(e) A provincial Act must provide for a procedure by which the province's legislature may amend a money Bill.

Section 121. Assent to Bills

(1) The Premier of a province must either assent to and sign a Bill passed by the provincial legislature in terms of this chapter or, if the Premier has reservations about the constitutionality of the Bill, refer it back to the legislature for reconsideration.
(2) If, after reconsideration, a Bill fully accommodates the Premier's reservations, the Premier must assent to and sign the Bill; if not, the Premier must either –

(a) assent to and sign the Bill; or
(b) refer it to the Constitutional Court for a decision on its constitutionality.

(3) If the Constitutional Court decides that the Bill is constitutional, the Premier must assent to and sign it.

Section 122. Application by members to Constitutional Court

(1) Members of a provincial legislature may apply to the Constitutional Court for an order declaring that all or part of a provincial Act is unconstitutional.
(2) An application –

(a) must be supported by at least 20 percent of the members of the legislature; and
(b) must be made within 30 days of the date on which the Premier assented to and signed the Act.

(3) The Constitutional Court may order that all or part of an Act that is the subject of an application in terms of subsection (1) has no force until the Court has decided the application if –

(a) the interests of justice require this; and
(b) the application has a reasonable prospect of success.

(4) If an application is unsuccessful, and did not have a reasonable prospect of success, the Constitutional Court may order the applicants to pay costs.

Section 123. Publication of provincial Acts

A Bill assented to and signed by the Premier of a province becomes a provincial Act, must be published promptly and takes effect when published or on a date determined in terms of the Act.

Section 124. Safekeeping of provincial Acts

The signed copy of a provincial Act is conclusive evidence of the provisions of that Act and, after publication, must be entrusted to the Constitutional Court for safekeeping.

Provincial Executives

Section 125. Executive authority of provinces

(1) The executive authority of a province is vested in the Premier of that province.
(2) The Premier exercises the executive authority, together with the other members of the Executive Council, by –

 (a) implementing provincial legislation in the province;
 (b) implementing all national legislation within the functional areas listed in Schedule 4 or 5 except where the Constitution or an Act of Parliament provides otherwise;
 (c) administering in the province, national legislation outside the functional areas listed in Schedules 4 and 5, the administration of which has been assigned to the provincial executive in terms of an Act of Parliament;
 (d) developing and implementing provincial policy;
 (e) co-ordinating the functions of the provincial administration and its departments;
 (f) preparing and initiating provincial legislation; and
 (g) performing any other function assigned to the provincial executive in terms of the Constitution or an Act of Parliament.

(3) A province has executive authority in terms of subsection (2)(b) only to the extent that the province has the administrative capacity to assume effective responsibility. The national government, by legislative and other measures, must assist provinces to develop the administrative capacity required for the effective exercise of their powers and performance of their functions referred to in subsection (2).
(4) Any dispute concerning the administrative capacity of a province in regard to any function must be referred to the National Council of Provinces for resolution within 30 days of the date of the referral to the Council.
(5) Subject to section 100, the implementation of provincial legislation in a province is an exclusive provincial executive power.
(6) The provincial executive must act in accordance with –

 (a) the Constitution; and
 (b) the provincial constitution, if a constitution has been passed for the province.

Section 126. Assignment of functions

A member of the Executive Council of a province may assign any power or function that is to be exercised or performed in terms of an Act of Parliament or a provincial Act, to a Municipal Council. An assignment –

(a) must be in terms of an agreement between the relevant Executive Council and the Municipal Council;
(b) must be consistent with the Act in terms of which the relevant power or function is exercised or performed; and
(c) takes effect upon proclamation by the Premier.

Section 127. Powers and functions of Premiers

(1) The Premier of a province has the powers and functions entrusted to that office by the Constitution and any legislation.
(2) The Premier of a province is responsible for –

  (a) assenting to and signing Bills;
  (b) referring a Bill back to the provincial legislature for reconsideration of the Bill's constitutionality;
  (c) referring a Bill to the Constitutional Court for a decision on the Bill's constitutionality;
  (d) summoning the legislature to an extraordinary sitting to conduct special business;
  (e) appointing commissions of inquiry; and
  (f) calling a referendum in the province in accordance with national legislation.

Section 128. Election of Premiers

(1) At its first sitting after its election, and whenever necessary to fill a vacancy, a provincial legislature must elect a woman or a man from among its members to be the Premier of the province.
(2) A judge designated by the Chief Justice must preside over the election of the Premier. The procedure set out in Part A of Schedule 3 applies to the election of the Premier.
(3) An election to fill a vacancy in the office of Premier must be held at a time and on a date determined by the Chief Justice, but not later than 30 days after the vacancy occurs.

Section 129. Assumption of office by Premiers

A Premier-elect must assume office within five days of being elected, by swearing or affirming faithfulness to the Republic and obedience to the Constitution, in accordance with Schedule 2.

Section 130. Term of office and removal of Premiers

(1) A Premier's term of office begins when the Premier assumes office and ends upon a vacancy occurring or when the person next elected Premier assumes office.
(2) No person may hold office as Premier for more than two terms, but when a person is elected to fill a vacancy in the office of Premier, the period between that election and the next election of a Premier is not regarded as a term.
(3) The legislature of a province, by a resolution adopted with a supporting vote of at least two thirds of its members, may remove the Premier from office only on the grounds of –

(a) a serious violation of the Constitution or the law;
(b) serious misconduct; or
(c) inability to perform the functions of office.

(4) Anyone who has been removed from the office of Premier in terms of subsection (3)(a) or (b) may not receive any benefits of that office, and may not serve in any public office.

Section 131. Acting Premiers

(1) When the Premier is absent or otherwise unable to fulfil the duties of the office of Premier, or during a vacancy in the office of Premier, an office-bearer in the order below acts as the Premier:

(a) A member of the Executive Council designated by the Premier.
(b) A member of the Executive Council designated by the other members of the Council.
(c) The Speaker, until the legislature designates one of its other members.

(2) An Acting Premier has the responsibilities, powers and functions of the Premier.
(3) Before assuming the responsibilities, powers and functions of the Premier, the Acting Premier must swear or affirm faithfulness to the Republic and obedience to the Constitution, in accordance with Schedule 2.

Section 132. Executive Councils

(1) The Executive Council of a province consists of the Premier, as head of the Council, and no fewer than five and no more than ten members appointed by the Premier from among the members of the provincial legislature.
(2) The Premier of a province appoints the members of the Executive Council, assigns their powers and functions, and may dismiss them.

Section 133. Accountability and responsibilities

(1) The members of the Executive Council of a province are responsible for the functions of the executive assigned to them by the Premier.

(2) Members of the Executive Council of a province are accountable collectively and individually to the legislature for the exercise of their powers and the performance of their functions.

(3) Members of the Executive Council of a province must –

(a) act in accordance with the Constitution and, if a provincial constitution has been passed for the province, also that constitution; and

(b) provide the legislature with full and regular reports concerning matters under their control.

Section 134. Continuation of Executive Councils after elections

When an election of a provincial legislature is held, the Executive Council and its members remain competent to function until the person elected Premier by the next legislature assumes office.

Section 135. Oath or affirmation

Before members of the Executive Council of a province begin to perform their functions, they must swear or affirm faithfulness to the Republic and obedience to the constitution, in accordance with Schedule 2.

Section 136. Conduct of members of Executive Councils

(1) Members of the Executive Council of a province must act in accordance with a code of ethics prescribed by national legislation.

(2) Members of the Executive Council of a province may not –

(a) undertake any other paid work;

(b) act in any way that is inconsistent with their office, or expose themselves to any situation involving the risk of a conflict between their official responsibilities and private interests; or

(c) use their position or any information entrusted to them, to enrich themselves or improperly benefit any other person.

Section 137. Transfer of functions

The Premier by proclamation may transfer to a member of the Executive Council –

(a) the administration of any legislation entrusted to another member; or

(b) any power or function entrusted by legislation to another member.

Section 138. Temporary assignment of functions

The Premier of a province may assign to a member of the Executive Council any power or function of another member who is absent from office or is unable to exercise that power or perform that function.

Section 139. Provincial supervision of local government

(1) When a municipality cannot or does not fulfil an executive obligation in terms of legislation, the relevant provincial executive may intervene by taking any appropriate steps to ensure fulfilment of that obligation, including –

(a) issuing a directive to the Municipal Council, describing the extent of the failure to fulfil its obligations and stating any steps required to meet its obligations; and
(b) assuming responsibility for the relevant obligation in that municipality to the extent necessary –
(i) to maintain essential national standards or meet established minimum standards for the rendering of a service;
(ii) to prevent that Municipal Council from taking unreasonable action that is prejudicial to the interests of another municipality or to the province as a whole; or
(iii) to maintain economic unity.
(c) dissolving the Municipal Council and appointing an administrator until a newly elected Municipal Council has been declared elected, if exceptional circumstances warrant such a step.

(2) If a provincial executive intervenes in a municipality in terms of subsection (1) (b) –

(a) it must submit a written notice of the intervention to-
i. the Cabinet member responsible for local government affairs; and
ii. the relevant provincial legislature and the National Council of Provinces, within 14 days after the intervention began;
(b) the intervention must end if-
i. the Cabinet member responsible for local government affairs disapproves the intervention within 28 days after the intervention began or by the end of that period has not approved the intervention; or
ii. the Council disapproves the intervention within 180 days after the intervention began or by the end of that period has not approved the intervention; and
(c) the Council must, while the intervention continues, review the intervention regularly and make any appropriate recommendations to the provincial executive.

(3) If a Municipal Council is dissolved in terms of subsection (1) (c) -

(a) the provincial executive must immediately submit a written notice of the dissolution to-

i. the Cabinet member responsible for local government affairs; and
ii. the relevant provincial legislature and the National Council of provinces; and

(b) the dissolution takes effect 14 days from the date of receipt of the notice by the Council unless set aside by that Cabinet member or the Council before the expiry of those 14 days.

(4) If a municipality cannot or does not fulfil an obligation in terms of the Constitution or legislation to approve a budget or any revenue-raising measures to give effect to the budget, the relevant provincial executive must intervene by taking any appropriate steps to ensure that the budget or those revenue-raising measures are approved, including dissolving the Municipal Council and-

(a) appointing an administrator until a newly elected Municipal Council has been declared elected; and
(b) approving a temporary budget or revenue-raising measures to provide for the continued functioning of the municipality.

(5) If a municipality, as result of a crisis in its financial affairs, is in serious or persistent material breach of its obligations to provide basic services or to meet its financial commitments, or admits that it is unable to meet its obligations or financial commitments, the relevant provincial executive must-

(a) impose a recovery plan aimed at securing the municipality's ability to meet its obligations to provide basic services or its financial commitments, which-
i. is to be prepared in accordance with national legislation; and
ii. binds the municipality in the exercise of its legislative and executive authority, but only to the extent necessary to solve the crisis in its financial affairs; and
(b) dissolve the Municipal Council, if the municipality cannot or does not approve legislative measures, including a budget or any revenue-raising measures, necessary to give effect to the recovery plan, and-
i. appoint an administrator until a newly elected Municipal Council has been declared elected; and
ii. approve a temporary budget or revenue-raising measures or any other measures giving effect to the recovery plan to provide for the continued functioning of the municipality; or
(c) if the Municipal Council is not dissolved in terms of paragraph (b), assume responsibility for the implementation of the recovery plan to the extent that the municipality cannot or does not otherwise implement the recovery plan.

(6) If a provincial executive intervenes in a municipality in terms of subsection (4) or (5), it must submit a written notice of the intervention to-

(a) the Cabinet member responsible for local government affairs; and

(b) the relevant provincial legislature and the National Council of Provinces, within seven days after the intervention began.

(7) If a provincial executive cannot or does not or does not adequately exercise the powers or perform the functions referred to in subsection (4) or (5), the national executive must intervene in terms of subsection (4) or (5) in the stead of the relevant provincial executive.
(8) National legislation may regulate the implementation of this section, including the processes established by this section.

Section 140. Executive decisions

(1) A decision by the Premier of a province must be in writing if it –

(a) is taken in terms of legislation; or
(b) has legal consequences.

(2) A written decision by the Premier must be countersigned by another Executive Council member if that decision concerns a function assigned to that other member.
(3) Proclamations, regulations and other instruments of subordinate legislation of a province must be accessible to the public.
(4) Provincial legislation may specify the manner in which, and the extent to which, instruments mentioned in subsection (3) must be –

(a) tabled in the provincial legislature; and
(b) approved by the provincial legislature.

Section 141. Motions of no confidence

(1) If a provincial legislature, by a vote supported by a majority of its members, passes a motion of no confidence in the province's Executive Council excluding the Premier, the Premier must reconstitute the Council.
(2) If a provincial legislature, by a vote supported by a majority of its members, passes a motion of no confidence in the Premier, the Premier and the other members of the Executive Council must resign.

Provincial Constitutions

Section 142. Adoption of provincial constitutions

A provincial legislature may pass a constitution for the province or, where applicable, amend its constitution, if at least two thirds of its members vote in favour of the Bill.

Section 143. Contents of provincial constitutions

(1) A provincial constitution, or constitutional amendment, must not be inconsistent with this Constitution, but may provide for –

(a) provincial legislative and executive structures and procedures that differ from those provided for in this chapter; or
(b) the institution, role, authority and status of a traditional monarch, where applicable.

(2) Provisions included in a provincial constitution or constitutional amendment in terms of paragraph (a) or (b) of subsection (1) –

(a) must comply with the values in section 1 and with Chapter 3; and
(b) may not confer on the province any power or function that falls –
(i) outside the area of provincial competence in terms of Schedules 4 and 5; or
(ii) outside the powers and functions conferred on the province by other sections of the Constitution.

Section 144. Certification of provincial constitutions

(1) If a provincial legislature has passed or amended a constitution, the Speaker of the legislature must submit the text of the constitution or constitutional amendment to the Constitutional Court for certification.
(2) No text of a provincial constitution or constitutional amendment becomes law until the Constitutional Court has certified –

(a) that the text has been passed in accordance with section 142; and
(b) that the whole text complies with section 143.

Section 145. Signing, publication and safekeeping of provincial constitutions

(1) The Premier of a province must assent to and sign the text of a provincial constitution or constitutional amendment that has been certified by the Constitutional Court.
(2) The text assented to and signed by the Premier must be published in the national Government Gazette and takes effect on publication or on a later date determined in terms of that constitution or amendment.
(3) The signed text of a provincial constitution or constitutional amendment is conclusive evidence of its provisions and, after publication, must be entrusted to the Constitutional Court for safekeeping.

Conflicting Laws

Section 146. Conflicts between national and provincial legislation

(1) This section applies to a conflict between national legislation and provincial legislation falling within a functional area listed in Schedule 4.
(2) National legislation that applies uniformly with regard to the country as a whole prevails over provincial legislation if any of the following conditions is met:

(a) The national legislation deals with a matter that cannot be regulated effectively by legislation enacted by the respective provinces individually.
(b) The national legislation deals with a matter that, to be dealt with effectively, requires uniformity across the nation, and the national legislation provides that uniformity by establishing –
(i) norms and standards;
(ii) frameworks; or
(iii) national policies.
(c) The national legislation is necessary for –
(i) the maintenance of national security;
(ii) the maintenance of economic unity;
(iii) the protection of the common market in respect of the mobility of goods, services, capital and labour.
(iv) the promotion of economic activities across provincial boundaries;
(v) the promotion of equal opportunity or equal access to government services; or
(vi) the protection of the environment.

(3) National legislation prevails over provincial legislation if the national legislation is aimed at preventing unreasonable action by a province that –

(a) is prejudicial to the economic, health or security interests of another province or the country as a whole; or
(b) impedes the implementation of national economic policy.

(4) When there is a dispute concerning whether national legislation is necessary for a purpose set out in subsection (2)(c) and that dispute comes before a court for resolution, the court must have due regard to the approval or the rejection of the legislation by the National Council of Provinces.
(5) Provincial legislation prevails over national legislation if subsection (2) or (3) does not apply.
(6) A law made in terms of an Act of Parliament or a provincial Act can prevail only if that law has been approved by the National Council of Provinces.
(7) If the National Council of Provinces does not reach a decision within 30 days of its first sitting after a law was referred to it, that law must be considered for all purposes to have been approved by the Council.
(8) If the National Council of Provinces does not approve a law referred to in subsection (6), it must, within 30 days of its decision, forward reasons for not approving the law to the authority that referred the law to it.

Section 147. Other conflicts

(1) If there is a conflict between national legislation and a provincial constitution with regard to –

(a) a matter concerning which this Constitution specifically requires or envisages the enactment of national legislation, the national legislation prevails over the affected provision of the provincial constitution.
(b) national legislative intervention in terms of section 44(2), the national legislation prevails over the provision of the provincial constitution; or
(c) a matter within a functional area listed in Schedule 4, section 146 applies as if the affected provision of the provincial constitution were provincial legislation referred to in that section.

(2) National legislation referred to in section 44(2) prevails over provincial legislation in respect of matters within the functional areas listed in Schedule 5.

Section 148. Conflicts that cannot be resolved

If a dispute concerning a conflict cannot be resolved by a court, the national legislation prevails over the provincial legislation or provincial constitution.

Section 149. Status of legislation that does not prevail

A decision by a court that legislation prevails over other legislation does not invalidate that other legislation, but that other legislation becomes inoperative for as long as the conflict remains.

Section 150. Interpretation of conflicts

When considering an apparent conflict between national and provincial legislation, or between national legislation and a provincial constitution, every court must prefer any reasonable interpretation of the legislation or constitution that avoids a conflict, over any alternative interpretation that results in a conflict.

Schedule 4 Functional Areas of Concurrent National and Provincial Legislative Competence

Part A

Administration of indigenous forests
Agriculture
Airports other than international and national airports
Animal control and diseases
Casinos, racing, gambling and wagering, excluding lotteries and sports pools
Consumer protection
Cultural matters
Disaster management
Education at all levels, excluding tertiary education
Environment
Health services

Housing Indigenous law and customary law, subject to Chapter 12 of the Constitution

Industrial promotion

Language policy and the regulation of official languages to the extent that the provisions of section 6 of the Constitution expressly confer upon the provincial legislatures legislative competence

Media services directly controlled or provided by the provincial government, subject to section 192

Nature conservation, excluding national parks, national botanical gardens and marine resources

Police to the extent that the provisions of Chapter 11 of the Constitution confer upon the provincial legislatures legislative competence

Pollution control

Population development

Property transfer fees

Provincial public enterprises in respect of the functional areas in this Schedule and Schedule 5

Public transport

Public works only in respect of the needs of provincial government departments in the discharge of their responsibilities to administer functions specifically assigned to them in terms of the Constitution or any other law

Regional planning and development

Road traffic regulation

Soil conservation

Tourism

Trade

Traditional leadership, subject to Chapter 12 of the Constitution

Urban and rural development

Vehicle licensing

Welfare services

Part B

The following local government matters to the extent set out in section 155(6)(a) and (7):

Air pollution

Building regulations

Child care facilities

Electricity and gas reticulation

Fire-fighting services

Local tourism

Municipal airports

Municipal planning

Municipal health services

Municipal public transport

Municipal public works only in respect of the needs of municipalities in the discharge of their responsibilities to administer functions specifically assigned to them in terms of the Constitution or any other law

Pontoons, ferries, jetties, piers and harbours, excluding the regulation of international and national shipping and matters related thereto

Storm-water management systems in built-up areas

Trading regulations

Water and sanitation services limited to potable water supply systems and domestic waste-water and sewage disposal systems

Schedule 5 Functional Areas of Exclusive Provincial Legislative Competence

Part A

Abattoirs
Ambulance services
Archives other than national archives
Libraries other than national libraries
Liquor licences
Museums other national museums
Provincial planning
Provincial cultural matters
Provincial recreation and amenities
Provincial sport
Provincial roads and traffic
Veterinary services, excluding regulation of the profession

Part B

The following local government matters to the extent set out for provinces in section 155(6)(a) and (7):

Beaches and amusement facilities
Billboards and the display of advertisements in public places
Cemeteries, funeral parlours and crematoria
Cleansing
Control of public nuisances
Control of undertakings that sell liquor to the public
Facilities for the accommodation, care and burial of animals
Fencing and fences
Licensing of dogs
Licensing and control of undertakings that sell food to the public
Local amenities
Local sport facilities
Markets
Municipal abattoirs

Municipal parks and recreation
Municipal roads
Noise pollution
Pounds
Public places
Refuse removal, refuse dumps and solid waste disposal
Street trading
Street lighting
Traffic and parking

Chapter 2 The Western Cape Constitution

Constitution of the Western Cape (Afrikaans text signed by the Premier)

(Assented to 15 January 1998)

Contents

Preamble

In humble submission to Almighty God,
We, the people of the Western Cape, through our elected representatives –

Recognising and striving to heal the injustices of the past,
Recognising the need for peace, reconciliation and justice,
Endeavouring to promote the development of the Western Cape and a better quality of life for all its people through just and effective government;
Affirming that the Western Cape, a province of the Republic of South Africa, is founded on –

democratic values,
the recognition of human rights,
the recognition of the family,
responsible and accountable government,
the rule of law,
the principles of mutual trust and co-operation, and
loyalty to the national Constitution;
Do now adopt this Constitution for the Western Cape.
May God protect our people.
God seën Suid-Afrika, Nkosi Sikelel' iAfrika, God bless South Africa.

Chapter 1 Founding Provisions

Section 1. Province of the Western Cape

The Western Cape is a Province of the Republic of South Africa as established by the Constitution of the Republic of South Africa.

Section 2. Boundaries of Province

The boundaries of the Western Cape are determined by the national Constitution.

Section 3. Adoption, status and interpretation of this Constitution

(1) This Constitution is adopted for the Western Cape in terms of the national Constitution, the supreme law of the Republic of South Africa.
(2) The legislative and executive powers and functions of the Western Cape recorded in this Constitution emanate exclusively from the national Constitution.
(3) The provisions of this Constitution must not be interpreted as conferring any legislative or executive authority on the Western Cape which is inconsistent with the national Constitution,
(4) In the event of an inconsistency between different texts of this Constitution, the English text prevails.

Section 4. Application of this Constitution

This Constitution applies to the Western Cape. Subject to the national Constitution, it is the highest law in the Western Cape, and the obligations imposed by it must be performed diligently and without delay.

Section 5. Languages

(1) For the purposes of provincial government –

(a) the official languages Afrikaans, English and isiXhosa are to be used; and
(b) these languages enjoy equal status.

(2) The Western Cape government must through legislative and other measures, regulate and monitor its use of Afrikaans, English and isiXhosa.
(3) The Western Cape government must take practical and positive measures to elevate the status and advance the use of those indigenous languages of the people of the Western Cape whose status and use have been historically diminished.

Section 6. Provincial symbols and honours

(1) A provincial Act may provide for

(a) provincial symbols;
(b) the conferral of provincial honours.

(2) A provincial Bill to provide for provincial symbols must be passed by the Provincial Parliament with a supporting vote of at least two thirds of its members,

Chapter 2 Intergovernmental Relations

Section 7. Co-operative government

As part of the provincial sphere of government of the Republic of South Africa, the Western Cape government must –

(a) act in accordance with the principles of co-operative government and intergovernmental relations set out in the national Constitution in all its dealings with the national government, the other provincial governments and the municipalities in the Western Cape;
(b) participate in structures and institutions to promote and facilitate intergovernmental relations, established in terms of the national Constitution; and
(c) make use of mechanisms and procedures for the settlement of intergovernmental disputes, established in terms of the national Constitution.

Section 8. Participation in National Council of Provinces

Delegates to the National Council of Provinces must take an active part in the Council in order to promote the interests of the Western Cape and of the country as a whole in accordance with the principles of co-operative government and intergovernmental relations set out in the national Constitution

Chapter 3 Provincial Parliament

Section 9. Legislative authority

(1) The legislative authority of the Western Cape is vested in the Provincial Parliament.

(2) The Provincial Parliament is bound only by the national Constitution and this Constitution, and must act in accordance with, and within the limits imposed by, these Constitutions.

(3) The Provincial Parliament may –

(a) replace, amend or repeal this Constitution;
(b) pass legislation for the Western Cape in terms of the national Constitution and in accordance with this Constitution;
(c) pass legislation for the Western Cape with regard to any matter assigned to the Western Cape by national legislation; and
(d) assign to a Municipal Council any of its legislative powers referred to in paragraph (b) and, where it is permitted to do so, any of its legislative powers referred to in paragraph (c).

(4) The Provincial Parliament may –

(a) by a resolution recommend to the National Assembly that it passes legislation concerning any matter outside the Provincial Parliament's authority, or in respect of which an Act of Parliament prevails over provincial legislation;
(b) by a resolution recommend to the National Council of Provinces that it passes legislation concerning any other matter; and
(c) by a resolution adopted with a supporting vote of at least two thirds of its members request Parliament to change the name of the Province.

Section 10. Bills to replace, amend or repeal this Constitution

(1) A Bill to replace, amend or repeal this Constitution

(a) must be passed by the Provincial Parliament with a supporting vote of at least two thirds of its members; and
(b) may include only constitutional provisions.

(2) At least 30 days before a Bill referred to in subsection (1) is introduced in the Provincial Parliament, the member or committee intending to introduce the Bill must –

(a) publish, in the official gazette or the Province and in at least three newspapers circulating in the Western Cape, particulars of the proposed Bill for public comment; and
(b) submit, in accordance with the rules of the Provincial Parliament, those particulars to municipalities within the Western Cape for their views.

(3) When a Bill referred to in subsection (1) is introduced, the member or committee introducing the Bill must submit to the Speaker any written comments received from the public and from municipalities for tabling in the Provincial Parliament.

Section 11. Certification

If the Provincial Parliament has replaced or amended this Constitution, the Speaker must submit the text of the new constitution or the constitutional amendment to the Constitutional Court for certification

Section 12. Signing, safekeeping, publication and commencement of provincial constitution

(1) The Premier must assent to and sign the text of a new constitution or any constitutional amendment that has been certified by the Constitutional Court
(2) The text assented to and signed by the Premier must be published in both the national *Government Gazette* and the official gazette of the Province. It takes effect on publication or on a later date determined in terms of the new constitution or the constitutional amendment.
(3) The signed text of a new constitution or a constitutional amendment is conclusive evidence of its provisions. After publication, it must be entrusted to the Constitutional Court for safekeeping.

Section 13. Composition

The Provincial Parliament consists of 42 elected members.

Section 14. Election of Provincial Parliament

The Provincial Parliament consists of persons elected as members in terms of an electoral system that –

(a) is prescribed by national legislation;
(b) is based on the Province's segment of the national common voters roll;
(c) provides for a minimum voting age of 18 years; and
(d) results, in general, in proportional representation.

Section 15. Membership

(1) Every citizen who is qualified to vote for the National Assembly is eligible to be a member of the Provincial Parliament, except –

   (a) anyone who is appointed by, or is in the service of, the state and receives remuneration for that appointment or service, other than
   (i) the Premier and other Provincial Ministers of the Western Cape; and
   (ii) other office-bearers whose functions are compatible with the functions of a member of the Provincial Parliament, and have been declared compatible with those functions by national legislation;
   (b) members of the National Assembly, permanent delegates to the National Council of Provinces or members of a Municipal Council;

(c) unrehabilitated insolvents;
(d) anyone declared to be of unsound mind by a court of the Republic; or
(e) anyone who, after 3 February 1997, has been or is convicted of an offence and sentenced to more than 12 months' imprisonment without the option of a fine, either in the Republic, or outside the Republic if the conduct constituting the offence would have been an offence in the Republic, but no one maybe regarded as having been sentenced until an appeal against the conviction or sentence has been determined, or until the time for an appeal has expired. A disqualification under this paragraph ends five years after the sentence has been completed.

(2) A person who is not eligible to be a member of the Provincial Parliament in terms of subsection (1) (a) or (b) maybe a candidate for the Provincial Parliament, subject to any limits or conditions determined by national legislation.
(3) A person loses membership of the Provincial Parliament if that person –

(a) ceases to be eligible;
(b) resigns as a member; or
(c) is absent from the Provincial Parliament without permission. In circumstances for which the rules and orders of the Provincial Parliament prescribe loss of membership.

(4) Vacancies in the Provincial Parliament must be filled in terms of national legislation.

Section 16. Oath or affirmation

Members of the Provincial Parliament must swear or affirm faithfulness to the Republic and the Western Cape and obedience to the national Constitution and this Constitution, in accordance with Schedule I, before they begin to perform their functions as members.

Section 17. Duration

(1) The Provincial Parliament is elected for a term of five years.
(2) When the Provincial Parliament is dissolved in terms of section 18 or when its term expires, the Premier must, by proclamation, call and set dates for an election, which must he held within 90 days of the date when the Provincial Parliament was dissolved or when its term expired.
(3) If the result of an election of the Provincial Parliament is not declared within the period determined by national legislation, or if an election is set aside by a court, another election must be held in terms of the national Constitution.
(4) The Provincial Parliament remains competent to function from the time it is dissolved or its term expires, until the day before the first day of polling for the next Provincial Parliament.

Section 18. Dissolution of Provincial Parliament before its term expires

(1) The Premier must dissolve the Provincial Parliament if

(a) the Provincial Parliament has adopted a resolution to dissolve with a supporting vote of a majority of all its members, and
(b) three years have passed since the Provincial Parliament was elected.

(2) An Acting Premier must dissolve the Provincial Parliament if there is a vacancy in the office of Premier and the Provincial Parliament fails to elect a new Premier within 30 days after the vacancy occurred.

Section 19. Seat of Provincial Parliament, sittings and recess periods

(1) The seat of the Provincial Parliament is Cape Town.
(2) The Provincial Parliament may determine that it or any of its committees may, when necessary, sit elsewhere in the Western Cape.
(3) After an election, the first sitting of the Provincial Parliament takes place at a time and on a date determined by a judge designated by the President of the Constitutional Court, but not more than 14 days after the election result has been declared.
(4) The Provincial Parliament may determine the times and duration of its other sittings and its recess periods.
(5) The Premier may summon the Provincial Parliament to an extraordinary sitting at any time to conduct special or urgent business.

Section 20. Speaker

(1) The Provincial Parliament must elect a Speaker from amongst its members at the first sitting after its election, or when necessary to fill a vacancy.
(2) A Judge designated by the President of the Constitutional Court must preside over the election of the Speaker. The procedure set out in Schedule 2 to this Constitution applies to the election of the Speaker.
(3) The Provincial Parliament may

(a) elect a Deputy Speaker from among its members; and
(b) elect other presiding officers from among its members to assist the Speaker and the Deputy Speaker.

(4) The Provincial Parliament may remove the Speaker, Deputy Speaker and any other presiding officer by a resolution adopted with a supporting vote of a majority of all its members.

Section 21. Quorum and decisions

(1) Except where this Constitution provides otherwise-

(a) a majority of the members of the Provincial Parliament must be present before a vote may be taken on a Bill or an amendment to a Bill;
(b) at least one third of the members must be present before a vote may be taken on any other question before the Provincial Parliament; and
(c) all questions before the Provincial Parliament are decided by a majority of the votes cast.

(2) The member presiding at a meeting of the Provincial Parliament has no deliberative vote, but –

(a) must cast a deciding vote when there is an equal number of votes on each side of a question; and
(b) may cast a deliberative vote when a question must be decided with a supporting vote of at least two thirds of the members of the Provincial Parliament.

Section 22. Permanent delegates' rights in Provincial Parliament

Permanent delegates to the National Council of Provinces may attend, and speak in, the Provincial Parliament and its committees, but may not vote. The Provincial Parliament may require a permanent delegate to attend the Provincial Parliament or its committees.

Section 23. Powers of Provincial Parliament

(1) In exercising its legislative authority, the Provincial Parliament may

(a) consider, pass, amend or reject any Bill before it; and
(b) initiate or prepare legislation, except money Bills.

(2) Subject to subsection (4), the Provincial Parliament must provide for mechanisms –

(a) to ensure that all provincial organs of state are accountable to it; and
(b) to oversee
(i) the exercise of provincial executive authority, including the implementation of legislation, and
(ii) any provincial organ of state.

(3) The Provincial Parliament may –

(a) determine and control its own internal arrangements, proceedings and procedures; and
(b) make rules and orders concerning its business, with due regard to representative and participatory democracy, accountability, transparency and public participation.

(4) The Provincial Parliament must in its rules and orders provide for –

(a) the establishment, composition, powers, functions, procedures and duration of its committees;
(b) the participation in the proceedings of the provincial Parliament and its committees of minority parties represented in the Provincial Parliament in a manner consistent with democracy;
(c) the conferral on its committees of such powers as are necessary for them to
(i) oversee the activities of the provincial organs of state;
(ii) hold the provincial executive accountable; and
(iii) promote transparency, accountability and the effective management of the provincial economy, provincial budget, provincial debt and the provincial public sector;
(d) a standing committee of the Provincial Parliament to monitor the socioeconomic conditions of the residents of the Western Cape, and to make recommendations to the Provincial Parliament concerning the improvement of these conditions;
(e) co-ordination between the Provincial Parliament and its committees, and the National Council of Provinces;
(f) the receipt of petitions, representations or submissions from any interested person or institution;
(g) the participation of representatives of the different categories of local government in the Western Cape in the deliberations of standing committees on Bills that affect the interests of municipalities in the Western Cape: and
(h) financial and administrative assistance to each party represented in the Provincial Parliament, in proportion to its representation, to enable the party and its leader to perform their functions in the Provincial Parliament effectively.

Section 24. Leader of the Opposition

The rules and orders of the Provincial Parliament must provide for the recognition of the leader of the Opposition in the provincial Parliament.

Section 25. Evidence or information before Provincial Parliament

The Provincial Parliament or any of its committees may

(a) summon any person to appear before it to give evidence on oath or affirmation, or to produce documents;
(b) require any natural or juristic person or provincial organ of state to report to it;
(c) compel, in terms of provincial legislation or the rules and orders of the Provincial Parliament, any person or provincial organ of state to comply with a summons or requirement in terms of paragraph (a) or (b); and
(d) receive petitions, representations or submissions from any interested person or institution.

Section 26. Privilege

Members of the Provincial Parliament and the permanent delegates of the Western Cape to the National Council of Provinces –

(a) have freedom of speech in the Provincial Parliament and in its committees, subject to its rules and orders; and
(b) are not liable to civil or criminal proceedings, arrest, imprisonment or damages for –

(i) anything that they have said in, produced before or submitted to the Provincial Parliament or any of its committees; or

(ii) anything revealed as a result of anything that they have said in, produced before or submitted to the Provincial Parliament or any of its committees,

Section 27. Code of Conduct

Provincial legislation must provide for a code of conduct for the members of the Provincial Parliament.

Section 28. Public access

(1) The proceedings of the Provincial Parliament and its committees take place in public, but reasonable steps may be taken –

    (a) to regulate public access, including access of the media, to the Provincial Parliament and its committees; and
    (b) to provide for the searching of any person and, where appropriate, the refusal of entry to, or the removal of any person.

(2) The public, including the media, may not be excluded from a sitting of a committee of the Provincial Parliament unless it is reasonable and justifiable to do so in an open and democratic society.
(3) The Provincial Parliament must facilitate public participation in its activities and those of its committees.

Section 29. Introduction of Bills

Only a Provincial Minister a committee or member of the Provincial Parliament may introduce a Bill in the Provincial Parliament. If the Bill is a money Bill, only the Provincial Minister responsible for financial matters may introduce it in the Provincial Parliament.

Section 30. Money Bills

(1) A Bill that appropriates money or imposes taxes, levies or duties is a money Bill. A money Bill may not deal with any other matter except a subordinate matter incidental to the appropriation of money or the imposition of taxes, levies or duties.

(2) A provincial Act must provide for a procedure by which the Provincial Parliament may amend a money Bill.

Section 31. Assent to Bills

(1) The Premier of the Western Cape must within 45 days after a Bill has been passed by the Provincial Parliament

(a) assent to and sign the Bill; or
(b) if the Premier has reservations about the constitutionality of the Bill, refer it back to the Provincial Parliament for reconsideration.

(2) If, after reconsideration, the Bill fully accommodates the Premier's reservations, the Premier must, within 45 days of the date of that reconsideration, assent to and sign the Bill; if not, the Premier must, within 49 days of the date of that reconsideration –

(a) assent to and sign the Bill; or
(b) refer it to the Constitutional Court for a decision on its constitutionality.

(3) If the Constitutional Court decides that the Bill is constitutional, the Premier must assent to and sign it within 14 days.

Section 32. Application by members to Constitutional Court

(1) Members of the Provincial Parliament may apply to the Constitutional Court for an order declaring that all or part of a provincial Act is unconstitutional.
(2) An application

(a) must be supported by at least 20 percent of the members of the Provincial Parliament; and
(b) must be made within 30 days of the date on which the Premier assented to and signed the Act.

Section 33. Publication and commencement of provincial Acts

(1) A Bill assented to and signed by the Premier becomes an Act of the Western Cape. It must be published promptly in the official gazette of the Province and takes effect when it is published or on a date determined in terms of the Act.
(2) Provincial legislation must provide for the dissemination and further publication of particulars of provincial Acts.

Section 34. Safekeeping of provincial Acts

The signed copy of an Act is conclusive evidence of its provisions. After publication, the Act must be entrusted to the Constitutional Court for safekeeping.

Chapter 4 Executive

Section 35. Executive authority

(1) The executive authority of Western Cape is vested in the Premier.
(2) The Premier exercises the executive authority, together with the other Provincial Ministers, by –

(a) implementing provincial legislation;
(b) implementing, to the extent that the Western Cape has the administrative capacity to assume effective responsibility, all national legislation within the functional areas listed in Schedule 4 or 5 of the national Constitution except where the national Constitution or an Act of Parliament provides otherwise;
(c) implementing national legislation outside the functional areas listed in Schedules 4 and 5 of the national Constitution, the administration of which has been assigned to the Provincial Cabinet in terms of an Act of Parliament;
(d) developing and implementing provincial policy;
(e) co-ordinating the functions of the provincial administration and its departments;
(f) preparing and initiating provincial legislation: and
(g) performing any other function assigned to the Provincial Cabinet in terms of the national Constitution or an Act of Parliament.

(3) The provincial executive must act in accordance with the national Constitution and this Constitution.

Section 36. Assignment of functions

A Provincial Minister may assign any power or function that is to be exercised or performed in terms of an Act of Parliament, or a provincial Act, to a Municipal Council. An assignment –

(a) must be in terms of an agreement between the relevant Provincial Minister and the Municipal Council;
(b) must be consistent with the Act in terms of which the relevant power or function is exercised or performed; and
(c) takes effect upon proclamation by the Premier in the official gazette of the Province.

Section 37. Powers and functions of Premier

(1) The Premier has the powers and functions entrusted to that office by the national Constitution, this Constitution and any legislation.
(2) The Premier is responsible for –

(a) assenting to and signing Bills;

(b) referring a Bill back to the Provincial Parliament for reconsideration of the Bill's constitutionality;
(c) referring a Bill to the Constitutional Court for a decision on the Bill's constitutionality;
(d) summoning the Provincial Parliament to an extraordinary sitting to conduct special or urgent business;
(e) appointing commissions of inquiry; and
(f) calling a referendum in the Western Cape in accordance with national legislation.

Section 38. Election of Premier

(1) The Provincial Parliament must elect a Premier from among its members at its first siting after its election, or when necessary to fill a vacancy.
(2) A Judge designated by the President of the Constitutional Court must preside over the election of the Premier. The procedure set out in Schedule 2 of this Constitution applies to the election of the Premier.
(3) An election to fill a vacancy in the office of the Premier must be held at a time and on a date determined by the President of the Constitutional Court, but not later than 30 days after the vacancy occurs.

Section 39. Assumption of office by Premier

The Premier-elect must assume office within five days of being elected, by swearing or affirming faithfulness to the Republic and the Western Cape and obedience to the national Constitution and this Constitution, in accordance with Schedule 1.

Section 40. Term of office and removal of Premier

(1) The Premier's term of office begins when the Premier assumes office and ends when a vacancy occurs or when the person next elected Premier assumes office.
(2) No person may hold office as Premier for more than two terms, but when a person is elected to fill a vacancy in the office of Premier the period between that election and the next election of a Premier is not regarded as a term.
(3) The Provincial Parliament, by a resolution adopted with a supporting vote of at least two thirds of its members, may remove the Premier from office only on the grounds of

(a) a serious violation of the national Constitution, this Constitution or the law;
(b) serious misconduct; or
(c) inability to perform the functions of office.

(4) Anyone who has been removed from the office of Premier in terms of subsection (3)(a) or (b) may not receive any benefits of that office, and may not serve in any public office.

Section 41. Acting Premier

(1) When the Premier is absent or otherwise unable to fulfil the duties of the office of Premier, or during a vacancy in the office of Premier, an office-bearer in the order below acts as the Premier –

(a) a Provincial Minister designated by the Premier;
(b) a Provincial Minister designated by the other Provincial Ministers; or
(c) the Speaker, until the Provincial Parliament designates one of its other members.

(2) An Acting Premier has the responsibilities, powers and functions of the Premier.
(3) Before assuming the responsibilities, powers and functions of the Premier, the Acting Premier must swear or affirm faithfulness to the Republic and the Western Cape and obedience to the national Constitution and this Constitution, in accordance with Schedule 1.

Section 42. Provincial Cabinet

(1) The Provincial Cabinet consists of the Premier, as head of the Provincial Cabinet, and no fewer than five and no more than ten Provincial Ministers appointed by the Premier from among the members of the Provincial Parliament.
(2) The Premier appoints the Provincial Ministers, assigns their powers and functions, and may dismiss them.

Section 43. Accountability and responsibilities

(1) The Provincial Ministers are responsible for the functions of the executive assigned to them by the Premier.
(2) Provincial Ministers are accountable collectively and individually to the Provincial Parliament for how they exercise their powers and carry out their functions.
(3) Provincial Ministers must –

(a) act in accordance with the national Constitution and this Constitution; and
(b) provide the Provincial Parliament with full and regular reports concerning matters under their control.

Section 44. Continuation of Provincial Cabinet after elections

When an election of the Provincial Parliament is held, the Provincial Cabinet and its members remain competent to function until the person elected Premier by the next Provincial Parliament assumes office.

Section 45. Oath or affirmation

Before Provincial Ministers begin to perform their functions, they must swear or affirm faithfulness to the Republic and the Western Cape and obedience to the national Constitution and this Constitution, in accordance with Schedule 1.

Section 46. Conduct of members of the Provincial Cabinet

(1) Members of the Provincial Cabinet must act in accordance with the code of ethics prescribed by national legislation.
(2) Members of the Provincial Cabinet may not –

(a) undertake any other paid work;
(b) act in any way that is inconsistent with their office, or expose themselves to any situation involving the risk of a conflict between their official responsibilities and private interests; or
(c) use their position or any information entrusted to them, to enrich themselves or improperly benefit any other person.

Section 47. Transfer of functions

The Premier by proclamation in the official gazette of the Province may transfer to a member of the Provincial Cabinet –

(a) the administration of any legislation entrusted to another member; or
(b) any power or function entrusted by legislation to another member.

Section 48. Temporary assignment of functions

The Premier may temporarily assign to a member of the Provincial Cabinet any power or function of another member who is absent from office or is unable to exercise that power or perform that function.

Section 49. Supervision of local government

(1) When a municipality in the Western Cape cannot or does not fulfil an executive obligation in terms of legislation, the Provincial Cabinet may intervene by taking any appropriate steps to ensure fulfilment of that obligation, including –

(a) issuing a directive to the Municipal Council, describing the extent of the failure to fulfil its obligations and stating any steps required to meet its obligations; and
(b) assuming responsibility for the relevant obligation in that municipality to the extent necessary –
(i) to maintain essential national standards or meet established minimum standards for the rendering of a service;
(ii) to prevent that Municipal Council from taking unreasonable action that is prejudicial to the interests of another municipality or to the Western Cape as a whole; or
(iii) to maintain economic unity.

(2) If the Provincial Cabinet intervenes in a municipality under subsection (1)(b) –

(a) the intervention must end unless it is approved by the national Cabinet member responsible for local government affairs within 14 days of the intervention;
(b) notice of the intervention must be tabled in the Provincial Parliament and in the National Council of Provinces within 14 days of their respective first sittings after the intervention began; and
(c) the intervention must end unless it is approved by the National Council of Provinces within 30 days of its first sitting after the intervention began.

Section 50. Executive decisions

(1) A decision by the Premier must be in writing if it –

(a) is taken in terms of legislation; or
(b) has legal consequences.

(2) A written decision by the Premier must be countersigned by another member of the Provincial Cabinet if that decision concerns a function assigned to that member.
(3) Proclamations, regulations and other subordinate legislation of the Western Cape must be published in the official gazette of the Province and the Western Cape government must take reasonable steps to make them accessible to the public.
(4) Provincial legislation may specify the manner in which, and the extent to which, instruments mentioned in subsection (3) must be tabled in and approved by the Provincial Parliament.

Section 51. Motions of no confidence

(1) If the Provincial Parliament, by a vote supported by a majority of all its members, passes a motion of no confidence in the Provincial Cabinet excluding the Premier, the Premier must reconstitute the Provincial Cabinet.
(2) If the Provincial Parliament, by a vote supported by a majority of all its members, passes a motion of no confidence in the Premier, the Premier and the other Provincial Ministers must resign.

Chapter 5 Local Government

Section 52. Local Government in Western Cape

(1) The local sphere of government in the Western Cape consists of municipalities established in terms of the national Constitution. The ability or right of a municipality to exercise its powers or perform its functions may not be compromised or impeded.
(2) The Western Cape government, by legislative and other measures, must support and strengthen the capacity of municipalities to manage their own affairs, to exercise their powers and to perform their functions.
(3) The Western Cape government must assign to a municipality, by agreement and subject to any conditions, the administration of a matter listed in Part A of Schedule

4 or Part A of Schedule 5 of the national Constitution which necessarily relates to local government, if –

(a) that matter would most effectively be administered locally; and
(b) the municipality has the capacity to administer it.

(4) Provincial legislation must provide for the publication and dissemination of draft provincial legislation that affects the status, institutions, powers or functions of local government, before it is introduced in the Provincial Parliament, in a manner that allows organised local government, municipalities and other interested persons an opportunity to make representations with regard to the draft legislation.
(5) The Western Cape government must publish a municipal by-law in the official gazette of the Province upon request by the municipality.

Section 53. Establishment of municipalities

(1) Provincial legislation must determine the different types of municipality to be established in the Western Cape, as defined by national legislation.
(2) The Western Cape government must establish municipalities in the Western Cape in a manner consistent with national legislation.

Section 54. Monitoring of local government

(1) The Western Cape government must, by legislative or other measures

(a) provide for the monitoring mid support of local government in the Western Cape; and
(b) promote the development of local government capacity to enable municipalities to perform their functions and manage their own affairs.

(2) The Western Cape government has the legislative and executive authority in terms of the national Constitution to see to the effective performance by municipalities of their functions in respect of matters listed in Schedules 4 and 5 of the national Constitution, by regulating the exercise by municipalities of their executive authority.

Chapter 6 Provincial Administration

Section 55. Provincial public servants

The Western Cape government is responsible for the recruitment, appointment, promotion, transfer and dismissal of members of the public service in the administration of the Western Cape within the framework of uniform norms and standards applying to the public service.

Section 56. Basic values and principles governing public administration in the Western Cape

Public administration in the Western Cape must be governed by the democratic values and principles enshrined in the national Constitution.

Chapter 7 Finance

Section 57. Sources of provincial funding

The sources of provincial funding are: –

(a) the equitable share of revenue raised nationally and allocated to the Western Cape in terms of the national Constitution;
(b) other allocations from national government revenue;
(c) additional revenue raised by the Western Cape government; and
(d) other money, resources and assets received by the Western Cape government.

Section 58. Provincial Revenue Fund

(1) All money received by the Western Cape government must be paid into the Provincial Revenue Fund except such money excluded by an Act of Parliament.
(2) Money may be withdrawn from the Provincial Revenue Fund only –

 (a) in terms of an appropriation by a provincial Act; or
 (b) as a direct charge against the Provincial Revenue Fund, when it is provided for in the national Constitution or a provincial Act.

Section 59. Taxes

(1) The Provincial Parliament may impose –

 (a) taxes, levies and duties other than income tax, value-added tax, general sales tax, rates on property or customs duties; and
 (b) flat-rate surcharges on the tax bases of any tax, levy or duty that is imposed by national legislation, other than the tax bases of corporate income tax, value-added tax, rates on property or customs duties.

(2) Provincial legislation may provide for user charges.
(3) The power of the Provincial Parliament to impose taxes, levies, duties and surcharges, as regulated by an Act Parliament, may not be exercised in a way that materially and unreasonably prejudices national economic polices, economic activities across provincial boundaries, or the national mobility of goods, services, capital or labour.

Section 60. Provincial budget

(1) The provincial budget and budgetary process must promote transparency, accountability and the effective financial management of the provincial economy, debt and the public sector.
(2) The provincial budget must comply with national legislation as envisaged by the national Constitution with respect to its form, when it must be tabled, the identification of the sources of revenue and proposed expenditure.
(3) The Provincial Minister responsible for financial matters must in respect of every financial year lay before the Provincial Parliament a budget, containing –

(a) estimates of revenue and expenditure, differentiating between capital and current expenditure;
(b) proposals for financing any anticipated deficit for the period to which they apply; and
(c) an indication of intentions regarding borrowing and other forms of public liability that will increase public debt during the ensuing year.

(4) In prioritising the allocation of funds in the provincial budget, the need to address imbalances, inequities and the development needs of the people of the Western Cape must be taken into consideration.

Section 61. Provincial treasury

(1) Provincial legislation must establish a provincial treasury and may prescribe in accordance with national legislation measures to ensure transparency, accountability and expenditure control, by introducing –

(a) generally recognised accounting practice;
(b) expenditure classifications; and
(c) treasury norms and standards.

(2) The provincial treasury, with the concurrence of the Provincial Minister responsible for financial matters, may stop the transfer of funds to a provincial organ of state only for serious or persistent material breach of the measures prescribed in terms of subsection (1).

Section 62. Procurement

(1) When the Western Cape government contracts for goods or services, it must do so in accordance with a system which is fair, equitable, transparent, competitive and cost-effective.
(2) Subsection (1) does not prevent the Western Cape government, within a framework of national legislation, from implementing a procurement policy providing for

(a) categories of preference in the allocation of contracts; and
(b) the protection or advancement of persons, or categories of persons, disadvantaged by unfair discrimination.

Section 63. Loans

The Western Cape government may raise loans for capital or current expenditure, in accordance with conditions determined by national legislation, but loans for current expenditure –

(a) may be raised only when necessary for bridging purposes during a fiscal year; and
(b) must be repaid within 12 months.

Section 64. Guarantees

(1) The Western Cape government may guarantee a loan in accordance with conditions determined in national legislation only.
(2) The Western Cape government must publish a report annually on the guarantees it has granted.

Section 65. Asset register
Provincial legislation must provide for –

(a) a register of provincial assets; and
(b) the registration of assets in that register.

Chapter 8 Police

Section 66. Policing functions of Western Cape government

(1) The Western Cape government is entitled –

(a) to monitor police conduct;
(b) to assess the effectiveness of visible policing;
(c) to oversee the effectiveness and efficiency of the police service, including receiving reports on the police service;
(d) to promote good relations between the police and the community; and
(e) to liaise with the national Cabinet member responsible for policing with respect to crime and policing in the Western Cape.

(2) In order to perform the functions set out in subsection (1), the Western Cape government –

(a) may investigate, or appoint a commission of inquiry into, any complaints of police inefficiency or a breakdown in relations between the police and any community; and
(b) must make recommendations to the national Cabinet member responsible for policing.

Section 67. Powers of Provincial Parliament

(1) The Provincial Parliament may pass legislation necessary to carry out the functions listed in section 66(1).
(2) The Provincial Parliament may require the provincial commissioner of police for the Western Cape to appear before it or any of its committees to answer questions.
(3) The Provincial Parliament must receive an annual report from the provincial commissioner on policing in the Western Cape.

Section 68. Executive responsibility

(1) The Provincial Cabinet is responsible for policing functions –

(a) vested in it by this Constitution or provincial legislation,
(b) assigned to it in terms of national legislation; and
(c) allocated to it in the national policing policy.

(2) The Provincial Cabinet –

(a) must determine, and convey to the member of the national Cabinet responsible for policing, the policing needs and priorities of the Western Cape;
(b) may lodge a complaint about any misconduct of, or any offence committed by, a member of the police service in the Western Cape, with the national independent police complaints body established by national legislation; and
(c) must participate in the committee composed of the national Cabinet member and the Provincial Ministers responsible for policing established by the national Constitution to ensure effective co-ordination of the police service and effective co-operation between the national and provincial spheres or government.

Section 69. Provincial commissioner of the police service

(1) Before the Provincial Cabinet concurs in the appointment of a provincial commissioner of police, as required by the national Constitution it may require any candidates or nominees for the appointment to appear before it or a committee of its members.
(2) If the provincial commissioner has lost the confidence of the Provincial Cabinet, it may institute appropriate proceedings for the removal or transfer of, or disciplinary action against, that commissioner, in accordance with national legislation: Provided that, save in exceptional circumstances, the Provincial Cabinet must require the provincial commissioner to appear before it or a committee of its members before instituting those proceedings.

Chapter 9 Other Constitutional Institutions

Section 70. Cultural Councils

Provincial legislation must provide for the establishment and reasonable funding, within the Province's available resources, of a cultural council or councils for a community or communities in the Western Cape, sharing a common cultural and language heritage.

Section 71. Establishment of and principles governing Commissioner for Environment

(1) There is a provincial Commissioner for the Environment.
(2) In the exercise of his or her powers and functions the Commissioner must ensure the conservation of the environment in the Western Cape, and must give attention to the need to balance the goals of environmental conservation and sustainable development.
(3) The Commissioner is independent and subject only to the national Constitution, this Constitution and the law, and must be impartial and must exercise the powers and perform the functions of the office of Commissioner without fear, favour or prejudice.
(4) Other provincial organs of state must assist and protect the Commissioner to ensure the independence. impartiality, dignity and effectiveness of the office of Commissioner.
(5) No person or provincial organ of state may interfere with the functioning of the Commissioner.

Section 72. Powers and functions

(1) The Commissioner must

(a) monitor urban and rural development which may impact on the environment;
(b) investigate complaints in respect of environmental administration;
(c) recommend a course of conduct to any provincial organ of state or municipality whose activities have been investigated; and
(d) act in accordance with the principles of co-operative government and intergovernmental relations referred to in Chapter 2.

(2) The Commissioner has the additional powers and functions as may be provided for in provincial legislation.

Section 73. Obligations of provincial organs of state

(1) Where the Commissioner has made recommendations to a provincial organ of state, that organ must report to the Commissioner on its actions in response to those recommendations within a reasonable time.
(2) Any provincial organ of state which refuses or fails to implement the Commissioner's recommendations must upon request furnish the Commissioner with written reasons for that refusal or failure.

Section 74. Reports by the Commissioner

The Commissioner –

(a) must report to the Provincial Parliament annually on his or her activities and on environmental matters in the Western Cape;
(b) must submit any recommendations made by him or her to the Provincial Parliament; and
(c) may report to the Provincial Parliament at any other time.

Section 75. Appointment

(1) The Commissioner must be a South African citizen who –

(a) is ordinarily resident in the Western Cape;
(b) is a fit and proper person with specialised knowledge of, or experience in, environmental matters; and
(c) complies with the requirements imposed by provincial legislation.

(2) The Premier must appoint as the Commissioner a person –

(a) nominated by a committee composed of all parties represented in the Provincial Parliament and which decide to participate; and
(b) approved by the Provincial Parliament by a resolution adopted with a supporting vote of at least 60 percent of the members of the Provincial Parliament.

(3) The rules and orders of the Provincial Parliament must provide for the involvement of civil society in the nomination process.

Section 76. Tenure

The Commissioner is appointed for a tern of three years, renewable once.

Section 77. Removal and suspension

(1) The Commissioner may be removed from office only on –

(a) the ground of misconduct, incapacity or incompetence;
(b) a finding to that effect by a committee composed of all parties represented in the Provincial Parliament and which decide to participate; and
(c) the adoption by the Provincial Parliament of a resolution calling for that person's removal from office with a supporting vote of at least two thirds of the members of the Provincial Parliament.

(2) The Premier –

(a) may suspend the Commissioner from office at any time after the start of the proceedings of a committee of the Provincial Parliament for the removal of that person; and
(b) must remove a person from office upon adoption by the Provincial Parliament of the resolution calling for that person's removal.

Section 78. Establishment of and principles governing Commissioner for Children

(1) There is a provincial Commissioner for Children.
(2) The Commissioner must assist the Western Cape government in protecting and promoting the interests of children in the Western Cape, in particular as regards –

(a) health services;
(b) education;
(c) welfare services:
(d) recreation and amenities; and
(e) sport.

Section 79. Powers and duties

(1) The Commissioner has the power as regulated in provincial legislation to monitor, investigate, research, educate, lobby, advise and report on matters pertaining to children.
(2) The Commissioner –

(a) must report annually to the Provincial Parliament on the measures taken by the Western Cape government to protect and promote the interests of children in the Western Cape; and
(b) may report to the Provincial Parliament at any other time.

Section 80. Appointment and removal

The Commissioner is appointed and removed by the Premier on the recommendation by the Provincial Parliament.

Chapter 10 Directive Principles of Provincial Policy

Section 81. Directive principles

The Western Cape government must adopt and implement policies to actively promote and maintain the welfare of the people of the Western Cape including policies aimed at achieving the following –

(a) safety and security:
(b) the promotion of non-racialism in the Western Cape;
(c) the protection or advancement of persons, or categories of persons disadvantaged by unfair discrimination;

(d) the promotion of respect for the rights of cultural, religious and linguistic communities in the Western Cape;
(e) the creation of job opportunities:
(f) the promotion of a work ethic;
(g) the promotion of a market-oriented economy:
(h) realising the right of access to –

(1) adequate housing;
(2) health care services;
(3) sufficient food and water; and
(4) social security, including appropriate social assistance for people who are unable to support themselves and their dependants:

(i) an environment in which all children –

(1) are given opportunities and facilities to develop in a healthy manner and in conditions of freedom and dignity;
(2) are protected against exploitation, neglect, abuse and abandonment; and
(3) receive basic education under a system of their parents' choice.

(j) the development of rural communities and the promotion of the welfare of rural workers;
(k) a system of taxation which is fair, transparent and accommodates the capacity of people to pay;
(l) an environment in which all frail and elderly persons –

(1) have access to family care or appropriate alternative care when removed from the family environment;
(2) are given basic nutrition, shelter, basic health care services, and social services; and
(3) are protected from maltreatment, neglect, abuse, degradation or involuntary seclusion;

(m) the protection of the environment in the Western Cape, including its unique fauna and flora, for the benefit of present and future generations; and
(n) the protection and conservation of the natural historical, cultural historical, archaeological and architectural heritage of the Western Cape for the benefit of the present and future generations;
(o) the promotional development and enhancement of the youth.

Section 82. Status of directive principles of provincial policy

The directive principles of provincial policy contained in this Chapter are not legally enforceable, but guide the Western Cape government in making and applying laws.

Chapter 11 General Provisions

Section 83. Transitional arrangements

Schedule 3 applies to the transition to the new constitutional order in the Western Cape established by this Constitution, and to matters incidental to that transition.

Section 84. Short title and commencement

(1) This Act is called the Constitution of the Western Cape, 1997, and comes into effect as soon as possible on a date set by the Premier by proclamation in the official gazette of the Province, which may not be later than 1 July 1998.
(2) The Premier may set different dates before the date mentioned in subsection (1) in respect of different provisions of this Constitution, provided that sections 57, 58, 59(1), 60, 61, 63 and 64 come into effect on 1 January 1998.
(3) Unless the context otherwise indicates, a reference in a provision of this Constitution to a time when this Constitution took effect must be construed as a reference to the time when the provision took effect.

Schedule 1 Oaths and Solemn Affirmations

1 Oath or solemn affirmation of members of Provincial Parliament

(1) Members of the Provincial Parliament, before the President of the Constitutional Court or a Judge designated by the President of the Constitutional Court, must swear or affirm as follows:

I, A.B., swear/solemnly affirm that I will be faithful to the Republic of South Africa and the Province of the Western Cape and will obey, respect and uphold the National Constitution, the provincial Constitution and all other law of the Republic, and I solemnly promise to perform my function as a member of the Provincial Parliament to the best of my ability. (In the case of an oath: So help me God.)

(2) Persons filling a vacancy in the Provincial Parliament may swear or affirm in terms of subitem (1) before the presiding officer of the Provincial Parliament.

2 Oath or solemn affirmation of Premier, Acting Premier and Provincial Ministers

The Premier or Acting Premier of the Province and each Provincial Minister, before the President of the Constitutional Court or a Judge designated by the President of the Constitutional Court, must swear or affirm as follows:

I, A.B., swear/solemnly affirm that I will be faithful to the Republic of South Africa and the Province of the Western Cape and will obey, respect and uphold the national Constitution, the provincial Constitution and all other law of the

Republic, and I undertake to hold my office as Premier/Acting Premier/Provincial Minister of the Western Cape with honour and dignity, to be a true and faithful counsellor, not to divulge directly or indirectly any secret matter entrusted to me; and to perform the function of my office conscientiously and to the best of my ability. (In the case of an oath: So help me God.)

Schedule 2 Election Procedures

1 Application

The procedures set out in this Schedule apply whenever the Provincial Parliament meets to elect the Premier of the Western Cape or the Speaker (or Deputy Speaker) of the Provincial Parliament.

2 Nomination

The person presiding at a meeting to which this Schedule applies must call for the nomination of candidates at the meeting.

3 Formal requirements

(1) A nomination must be made on the form prescribed by the rules mentioned in item 9.
(2) The form on which a nomination is made must be signed by two members of the Provincial Parliament, if the Premier of the Province or the Speaker (or Deputy Speaker) of the Provincial Parliament is to be elected.
(3) A person who is nominated must indicate acceptance of the nomination by signing the nomination form or any other form of written confirmation.

4 Announcement of names of candidates

At a meeting to which this Schedule applies, the person presiding must announce the names of the persons who have been nominated as candidates, but may not permit any debate.

5 Single candidate

If only one candidate is nominated, the person presiding must declare the candidate elected.

6 Election procedure

If more than one candidate is nominated –

(a) a vote must be taken at the meeting by secret ballot;

(b) each member present at the meeting may cast one vote; and
(c) the person presiding must declare elected the candidate who receives a majority of the votes.

7 Elimination procedure

(1) If no candidate received a majority of the votes, the candidate who receives the lowest number of votes must be eliminated and a further vote taken on the remaining candidates in accordance with item 6. This procedure must he repeated until a candidate receives a majority of the votes.
(2) When applying subitem (1), if two or more candidates each have the lowest number of votes, a separate vote must be taken on those candidates, and repeated as often as may be necessary to determine which candidates are to be eliminated.

8 Further meetings

(1) If only two candidates are nominated, or if only two candidates remain after an elimination has been applied, and those two candidates receive the same number of votes, a further meeting must be held within seven days, at a time determined by the person presiding.
(2) If a further meeting is held in terms of subitem (1), the procedure prescribed in this Schedule must be applied at that meeting as if it were the first meeting for the election in question.

9 Rules

The rules applicable to the above election procedures are the rules made by the President of the Constitutional Court in terms of the national Constitution.

Schedule 3 Transitional Arrangements

1 Interpretation of existing legislation

Unless inconsistent with the context or clearly inappropriate, a reference in any legislation that existed when this Constitution took effect, to the Provincial Legislature, Premier, Executive Council or member of the Executive Council, must be construed as a reference to the Provincial Parliament, Premier, Provincial Cabinet, or Provincial Minister under this Constitution.

2 Languages

(1) Section 5(1) of the Constitution is subject to the following: The Western Cape government must take reasonable legislative and other measures, within its available resources, to achieve the progressive realisation of the equal status of Afrikaans, English and isiXhosa.

(2) Provincial legislation envisaged in sub-item (1) must be enacted within 12 months of the date when this Constitution took effect.

3 Provincial Parliament

(1) Anyone who is a member or office-bearer of the Provincial legislature when this Constitution takes effect, becomes and holds office as a member or office-hearer of the Provincial Parliament in terms of this Constitution.
(2) The Provincial Parliament as constituted in terms of subitem (1) must be regarded as having been elected under this Constitution for a term that expires on 30 April 1999.
(3) For the duration of its term that expires on 30 April 1999 but subject to section 17(4) of this Constitution, the Provincial Parliament consists of 42 members plus the former senators who became members of the Provincial Parliament in terms of the national Constitution.
(4) The rules and orders of the Provincial Legislature in force when this Constitution takes effect, continue in force, subject to any amendment or repeal.

4 Elections of the Provincial Parliament

(1) Schedule 2 to the Constitution of the Republic of South Africa Act, 1993 (Act 200 of 1993), as amended by Annexure A to Schedule 6 to the national Constitution, applies –

(a) to the first election of the Provincial Parliament under this Constitution;
(b) to the loss of membership of the Provincial Parliament in circumstances other than those provided for in section 15(3) of this Constitution, until the second election of the Provincial Parliament under this Constitution; and
(c) to the filling of vacancies in the Provincial Parliament, and the supplementation, review and use, of party lists for the filling of vacancies, until the second election of the Provincial Parliament under this Constitution.

(2) No election of the Provincial Parliament may be held before 30 April 1999 unless the Provincial Parliament is dissolved in terms of section 8(2) following a motion of no confidence in the Premier in terms of section 51(2).

5 Oaths and affirmations

A person who continues in office in terms or this Schedule and who has taken the oath of office or has made a solemn affirmation under the national Constitution or under the Republic of South Africa Constitution Act, 1993 (Act 200 of 1993), is not obliged to repeat the oath of office or solemn affirmation under this Constitution.

6 Dissolution of Provincial Parliament before expiry of its term

Section 18(1) of this Constitution is suspended until 30 April 1999.

7 Delegates to National Council of Provinces

The Provincial Parliament may, until an Act of Parliament is enacted in terms of section 65(2) of the national Constitution, provide in its rules and orders for the conferral of authority on its delegation to the National Council of Provinces to deliberate, act and cast votes on its behalf in the Council.

8 Provincial Cabinet

(1) Anyone who is the Premier when this Constitution takes effect, continues in and holds office in terms of this Constitution as the Premier.
(2) Subject to section 44 of this Constitution, until the second election of the Provincial Parliament under this Constitution sections 42 and 43 are deemed to read as set out in Annexure A to this Schedule.

9 Enactment of legislation required by this Constitution

(1) Where this Constitution requires the enactment of legislation or rules and orders of the Provincial Parliament, that legislation and those rules and orders must be enacted or adopted, as the case may be, by the relevant authority within a reasonable time after the date when this Constitution took effect.
(2) Provincial legislation envisaged in sections 65 and 70 of this Constitution must be enacted within 12 months of the date when this Constitution took effect.

Annexure A Government of Provincial Unity

1 Section 42 of this Constitution is deemed to read as follows:

(1) The Provincial Cabinet consists of the Premier, as head of the Provincial Cabinet, and:

(a) no fewer than five and no more than ten Provincial Ministers who are members of the Provincial Parliament; and
(b) a maximum of two Provincial Ministers who are eligible to be but are not members of the Provincial Parliament, provided the Premier deems the appointment of such Provincial Ministers expedient.

(3) The Premier appoints the Provincial Ministers, assigns their powers and functions, and may dismiss them.

2 Section 42. Provincial Cabinet

3 Section 43 of this Constitution is deemed to contain the following additional subsection:

(1) A provincial Minister referred to in section 42(1)(b) may attend, and may speak in, the Provincial Parliament, but may not vote, and is entitled to the privilege set out in section 26 of this Constitution.

Selected Bibliography

Although the general part of the literature list that follows (§3) contains references on South African constitutional law in general, the focus of this Bibliography is on sub-national government, and accordingly numerous references on local government (Part III) and on the various topics discussed in Part IV do not appear here.

§1. Legislation

Aliens Control Act 96 of 1991.
Borrowing Powers of Provincial Governments Act 48 of 1996.
Commission for the Promotion and Protection of the Rights of Cultural, Religious and Linguistic Communities Act 19 of 2002.
Constitution of the Republic of South Africa, 1993 (Act 200 of 1993) (*Government Gazette* 15466, 28 January 1994).
Constitution of the Republic of South Africa, 1996 (*Government Gazette* 17737, 24 January 1997).
Division of Revenue Act 3 of 2016.
Electoral Act 73 of 1998.
Executive Members' Ethics Act 82 of 1998.
Financial and Fiscal Commission Act 99 of 1997.
Human Rights Commission Act 54 of 1995.
Intergovernmental Fiscal Relations Act 97 of 1997.
Intergovernmental Relations Framework Act 13 of 2005.
Local Government: Municipal Structures Act 117 of 1998.
Local Government: Municipal Systems Act 32 of 2000.
Local Government: Municipal Finance Management Act 56 of 2003.
Money Bills Amendment Procedure and Related Matters Act 9 of 2009.
National House of Traditional Leaders Act 10 of 1997.
Organized Local Government Act 52 of 1997.
Pan South African Language Board Act 59 of 1995.
Promotion of Administrative Justice Act 3 of 2000.
Provincial Tax Regulation Process Act 53 of 2001.
Public Finance Management Act 1 of 1999 (as amended by Act 29 of 1999).
Public Service Act 103 of 1994.
Refugees Act 130 of 1998.
South African Citizenship Act 88 of 1995.
South African Passports and Travel Documents Act 4 of 1994.
Superior Courts Act 10 of 2013.
Traditional Leadership and Governance Framework Act 41 of 2003.
Use of Official Languages Act 12 of 2012.

Western Cape Constitution, Proc 1/1998 of 16/1/98 (*Western Cape Provincial Gazette* 16/1/98).
Western Cape Cultural Commission and Cultural Councils Act 14 of 1998.
Western Cape Determination of Types of Municipality Act 9 of 2000.
Western Cape Land Administration Act 6 of 1998.
Western Cape Monitoring and Support of Municipalities Act 4 of 2014.
Western Cape Provincial Coat of Arms Act 7 of 1998.
Western Cape Provincial Honours Act 9 of 1999.
Western Cape Provincial Languages Act 13 of 1998.

§2. Table of Cases

African National Congress v. Minister of Local Government and Housing, Kwazulu-Natal 1998 4 BCLR 399 (CC), 1998 1 SA 1 (CC).
Akhil Bharatiya Soshit Karamchari Sangh v. Union of India [1981] 1 SCC 246.
Amod v. Multilateral Motor Vehicle Accidents Fund 1999 4 SA 1319 (SCA).
Bangindawo v. Head of the Nyanda Regional Authority; Hlantlalala v. Head of the Western Tembuland Regional Authority 1998 3 BCLR 314 (Tk), 1998 1 SA 262 (Tk).
Chandra Bhawan Boarding v. State of Mysore AIR [1970] SC 2042.
Dawood v. Minister of Home Affairs; Shalabi v. Minister of Home Affairs; Thomas v. Minister of Home Affairs 2000 8 BCLR 837 (CC).
De Kock NO v. Van Rooyen 2006 6 BCLR 714 (SCA).
De Lille v. Speaker of the National Assembly 1998 7 BCLR 917 (C); 1998 3 SA 430 (C).
Democratic Alliance v. Speaker of National Assembly and Others [2016] ZACC 8.
Democratic Alliance v. Masondo NO 2003 (2) BCLR 128 (CC).
Economic Freedom Fighters v. Speaker of the National Assembly and Others; Democratic Alliance v. Speaker of the National Assembly and Others 2016 (5) BCLR 618 (CC); 2016 (3) SA 580 (CC).
Executive Council of the Western Cape v. Minister for Provincial Affairs and Constitutional Development of the RSA; Executive Council of KwaZulu-Natal v. President of the RSA 1999 12 BCLR 1360 (CC).
Ex Parte President of the RSA In Re: Constitutionality of the Liquor Bill 2000 1 BCLR 1 (CC).
Ex Parte Western Cape Provincial Government: In Re DVB Behuising (Pty) Ltd v. North West Provincial Government 2000 4 BCLR 347 (CC).
Geyser v. Mzunduzi Municipality 2003 (3) BCLR 235 (N).
Government of the Republic of South Africa and Others v. Grootboom and Others 2000 BCLR 1169 (CC).
Head of Department of Education: Mpumalanga v. Hoërskool Ermelo [2009] ZACC 32; 2010 (2) SA 415 (CC); 2010 (3) BCLR 177 (CC);.
In re: Certification of the Amended Text of the Constitution of the Western Cape, 1997 1997 12 BCLR 1653 (CC), 1998 2 SA 655 (CC).
In re: Certification of the Constitution of the Province of KwaZulu-Natal, 1996 1996 11 BCLR 1419 (CC), 1996 4 SA 1098 (CC).

Selected Bibliography

In re: Certification of the Constitution of the Republic of South Africa, 1996 1996 10 BCLR 1253 (CC), 1996 4 SA 744 (CC).

In re: Certification of the Constitution of the Western Cape, 1997 1997 9 BCLR 1167 (CC), 1997 4 SA 795 (CC).

In re: Kwazulu-Natal Amakhosi and Iziphakanyiswa Amendment Bill of 1995: In re: Payment of Salaries, Allowances and other Privileges to the Ingonyama Bill of 1995 1996 7 BCLR 903 (CC), 1996 4 SA 653 (CC).

In re: National Education Policy Bill No 83 of 1995 1996 4 BCLR 518 (CC), 1996 3 SA 289 (CC).

Kham and Others v. Electoral Commission and Another [2015] ZACC 37.

Killian v. Gauteng Provincial Legislature 1999 2 BCLR 225 (T).

Lourens v. Speaker of the National Assembly of Parliament and Others [2016] ZASCA 11.

Minister of Education (Western Cape) v. Mikro Primary School Governing Body [2005] ZASCA 66.

Minister of Police and Others v. Premier of the Western Cape and Others [2013] ZACC 33; 2013 (12) BCLR 1365 (CC); 2014 (1) SA 1 (CC).

National Coalition for Gay and Lesbian Equality v. Minister of Home Affairs 2000 1 BCLR 39 (CC).

Oriani-Ambrosini, MP v. Sisulu, MP Speaker of the National Assembly [2012] ZACC 27; 2012 (6) SA 588 (CC); 2013 (1) BCLR 14 (CC).

Papachristoforou v. MEC for Finance and Economic Affairs, North West Province 1998 10 BCLR 1237 (B).

Premier of KwaZulu-Natal v. President of the Republic of South Africa 1995 12 BCLR 1561 (CC), 1996 1 SA 769 (CC).

Premier of the Province of the Western Cape v. President of the RSA 1999 4 BCLR 382 (CC), 1999 3 SA 657 (CC).

Premier of the Province of the Western Cape v. The Electoral Commission 1999 11 BCLR 1209 (CC).

Premier of the Western Cape v. Overberg District Municipality 2011 (4) SA 441 (SCA).

Prince v. President of the Law Society of the Cape of Good Hope 2002 3 BCLR 231 (CC).

Prinsloo v. Van der Linde 1997 6 BCLR 753 (CC).

Ryland v. Edros 1997 1 BCLR 77 (C), 1997 2 SA 690 (C).

S v. Lawrence; S v. Negal; S v. Solberg 1997 10 BCLR 1348 (CC).

S v. Makwanyane 1995 6 BCLR 665 (CC); 1995 3 SA 391 (CC)

S v. Mhlungu 1995 3 BCLR 793 (CC).

Soobramoney v. Minister of Health, KwaZulu-Natal 1997 12 BCLR 1696 (CC).

The Executive Council of the Western Cape Legislature v. President of the Republic of South Africa 1995 10 BCLR 1289 (CC), 1995 4 SA 877 (CC).

Uthukela District Municipality and Others v. President of the Republic of South Africa and Others 2002 (11) BCLR 1220; 2003 (1) SA 678 (CC).

§3. Literature

General

Selected Bibliography

Basson, D.H. *South Africa's Interim Constitution: Text and Notes.* Kenwyn: Juta 1994.

Brand, D.J. *Financial Constitutional Law – A Comparative Study between Germany and South Africa.* Konrad Adenauer Stiftung, Johannesburg, November 2006.

Burns, Y. *Administrative Law under the 1996 Constitution.* Durban: Butterworths, 1998.

Butler, A. 'The 1996 Constitution Bill, Its Amending Power, and the Constitutional Principles'. *Human Rights and Constitutional Law Journal of Southern Africa* (1996): 24.

Carpenter, G. (ed.) *Suprema Lex: Essays on the Constitution presented to Marinus Wiechers.* Durban: Butterworths, 1998.

Chaskalson, M. & D. Davis. 'Constitutionalism, the Rule of Law, and the First Certification Judgment'. *South African Journal on Human Rights* (1997): 430.

Currie, I. & J. De Waal. *The Bill of Rights Handbook.* 5th edn. Cape Town: Juta, 2005.

Davis, D., H. Cheadle & N. Haysom. *Fundamental Rights in the Constitution: Commentary and Cases.* Cape Town: Juta, 1997.

Department of Provincial and Local Government. *Final Report of the Intergovernmental Relations Audit: Towards a Culture of Co-operative Government.* December 1999.

Devenish, G. *A Commentary on the South African Constitution.* Durban: Butterworths, 1999.

Devenish, G. 'The Making of the Interim Constitution'. *THRHR* (1997): 613.

De Ville, J. & N. Steytler (eds). *Voting in 1999: Choosing an Electoral System.* Durban: Butterworths, 1996.

De Villiers, B. (ed.) *Birth of a Constitution.* Cape Town: Juta, 1994.

De Vos, P. & W. Freedman (eds). *South African Constitutional Law in Context.* Cape Town: Oxford University Press, 2014.

De Waal, J., I. Currie & G. Erasmus. *The Bill of Rights Handbook.* Cape Town: Juta, 1999.

Dlamini, C.M.R. 'The Relationship between Human Rights and Education'. In *Human Rights in South African Education: From the Constitutional Drawing Board to the Chalkboard*, edited by J. De Groof & E.F.J. Malherbe, Leuven: Acco, 1997, 39.

Dube, M.P. *Role of Supreme Court in Indian Constitution.* New Delhi: Deep & Deep Publications, 1988.

Du Plessis, L.M. & H. Corder. *Understanding South Africa's Transitional Bill of Rights.* Cape Town: Juta, 1994.

Electoral Task Team. *Report of the Electoral Task Team.* Cape Town: Electoral Task Team, 2003.

Ebrahim, H. *The Soul of a Nation: Constitution-Making in South Africa.* Cape Town: Oxford University Press, 1998.

Financial and Fiscal Commission (FFC). *Submission on the 2016 Fiscal Framework and Revenue Proposals.* Midrand, 1 March 2016.

Kelly, J.M. *The Irish Constitution.* Dublin: Butterworths, 1994.

Leonardy, U. & D.J. Brand. 'The Defect of the Constitution: Concurrent Powers Are Not Co-Operative or Competitive Powers'. (4) *TSAR* (2010): 657–670.

Madonsela, T.N. 'The Role of the Public Protector in Protecting Human Rights and Deepening Democracy'. Stellenbosch *Law Review* (2012): 1–15.

Selected Bibliography

Mahomed, I. 'The Role of the Judiciary in a Constitutional State'. 115(1) *SALJ* (1998): 111–115.
Malherbe, E.F.J. 'Enkele kwelvrae oor die grondwetlike beskerming van die reg op godsdiensvryheid'. *TSAR* (2006): 636–641.
Malherbe, E.F.J. 'Die sertifisering van die 1996 Grondwet'. *TSAR* (1997): 356.
Malherbe, R. 'The Legal System and the Judiciary,' in *Government and Politics in the New South Africa*, edited by A. Venter. Van Schaik: Pretoria, 1998, 82–108.
Malherbe, R. 'The South African Constitution'. *Zeitschrift für öffentliches Recht* (2000): 61–100.
Malherbe, R. 'A New Beginning: Introducing the South African Constitution and Bill of Rights'. *Netherlands Quarterly of Human Rights* (2000): 45–65.
Malherbe, R. 'Human Rights in South Africa: A Preliminary Assessment'. *Publiekrechtelijke Kronieken* (2000): 150–168.
Murray, C. & R.Simeon. 'From Paper to Practice: The National Council of Provinces after Its First Year'. 14(1) *SA Public Law* (1999): 96–141.
Rautenbach, I.M. 'Introduction to the Bill of Rights',Butterworths editorial team *Bill of Rights Compendium*, Durban: Butterworths, 1996, 1A-1.
Rautenbach, I.M. 'The Right to Access to Sufficient Water and the Two-Stage Approach to the Application of the Bill of Rights'. (74) *THRHR* (2011):107–119.
Rautenbach, I.M. *Rautenbach-Malherbe Constitutional Law*. 6th edn. Johannesburg: LexisNexis, 2012.
Rautenbach I.M. & E.F.J. Malherbe. *Constitutional Law*. 2nd edn. Durban: Butterworths, 1996.
Rautenbach I.M. & E.F.J. Malherbe. *Constitutional Law*. 3rd edn. Durban: Butterworths, 1999.
Rautenbach I.M. & E.F.J. Malherbe. *What does the Constitution say?* Pretoria: Van Schaik, 1998.
Sachs, A. 'The Constitutional Protection of Multiculturalism'. Konrad Adenauer Stiftung, *Seminar Report* (May 1998) 8.
Van Wyk, D.H et al. (eds). *Rights and Constitutionalism: The New South African Legal Order*. Cape Town: Juta, 1994.
Van Wyk, D.H. 'n Paar opmerkings en vrae oor die nuwe Grondwet'. *THRHR* (1997): 377.
Venter, A. (ed.) *Government and Politics in the New South Africa*. Pretoria: Van Schaik, 1998.
Venter, F. 'Aspects of the South African Constitution of 1996. An African Democratic and Social Federal *Rechtsstaat*?' *Zeitschrift für ausländisches öffentliches Recht und Völkerrecht* (1997): 51.
Yacoob, Z. 'The Constitution-Making Process: An Overview'. *Human Rights and Constitutional Law Journal of Southern Africa* (1996): 18.

Sub-national Government

Bennett, T.W. 'The Equality Clause and Customary Law'. *SAJHR* (1994): 122.
Bennett, T.W. *Human Rights and African Customary Law*.Cape Town: Juta 1995.

Selected Bibliography

Besdziek, D. 'Provincial Government'. In *Government and Politics in the New South Africa*, edited by A. Venter. Pretoria: Van Schaik, 1998, 147–192.

Bonthuys, E. & L.M. Du Plessis. 'Whither the Validity of Marriages Concluded Under a System of Religious Law Under the Transitional Constitution?' *SA Public Law* (1995): 200.

Brand, D.J. 'Asymmetry in Federal Systems – Constitutional Arrangements in South Africa'. In *Asymmetries in Constitutional Law*, edited by F. Palermo, C. Zwilling & K. Kössler. Bolzano: EURAC Research, 2009, 117–131.

Brand, D.J. 'Die finansiële krisis in provinsies en munisipaliteite: Verg dit grondwetlike of politieke oplossings?', *LitNet Akademies* 26 Oktober 2012, Jaargang 9(3).

Brand, D.J. 'The Western Cape Provincial Constitution: Comments, Text and Judgements'. Konrad Adenauer Stiftung, *Occasional Papers*, July 1999.

Brand, D.J. 'Development of Concurrent Legislation – a New South African Perspective'. Konrad Adenauer Stiftung, *Seminar Report: Sub-national Constitutional Governance*, 1999, 37.

Brand, D.J. 'The South African Constitution: Three Crucial Issues for Future Development'. *Stellenbosch Law Review* (1998): 182.

Bronstein, V. 'Reconceptualizing the Customary Law Debate in South Africa'. *SAJHR* (1998): 388.

Chaskalson, M. & J. Klaaren. 'Provincial government'. In *Constitutional Law of South Africa*, edited by M. Chaskalson et al., Cape Town: Juta 1998, 4.1–2.

Currie, I. 'Indigenous Law'. In *Constitutional Law of South Africa*, edited by Chaskalson et al., Cape Town: Juta, 1998, 36–1.

De Coning, C. 'The Territorial Imperative: Towards an Evaluation of the Provincial Demarcation Process'. In *Birth of a Constitution*, edited by B. De Villiers. Cape Town: Juta, 1994, 189.

De Ville, J. 'Guidelines for Judicial Review on "Division of Powers" Grounds'. *Stellenbosch Law Review* (1995): 139.

De Villiers, B. (ed.) *Evaluating Federal Systems, Cape Town, Juta.* 1994.

De Villiers, B. 'Intergovernmental Relations in South Africa'. *SA Public Law* (1997): 197.

De Villiers, B. 'Intergovernmental Relations: A Constitutional Framework'. In *Birth of a Constitution*, edited by B. De Villiers. Cape Town: Juta, 1994, 256.

De Villiers, B. 'Intergovernmental Relations: *Bundestreue* and the Duty to Cooperate from a German Perspective'. *SA Public Law* (1994): 430.

De Villiers, B. 'National-Provincial Cooperation: The Potential Role of Provincial Interest Offices: The German Experience'. Konrad Adenauer Stiftung, *Occasional Papers*, January 1999.

De Villiers, B. (ed.) 'Review of Provinces and Local Governments in South Africa: Constitutional Foundations and Practice'. Konrad Adenauer Stiftung, *Occasional Papers*, November 2008.

Department of Constitutional Development and Provincial Affairs. *Intergovernmental Relations: An International Comparative Study*. 1998.

Devenish, G.E. 'The Prospects for Constitutional Litigation in Relation to the Powers of the Central and Provincial Governments as Contained in the Interim Constitution, and Related Issues'. *THRHR* (1996): 34.

Selected Bibliography

Devenish, G.E. 'The Making and Significance of the Draft Kwazulu-Natal Constitution'. *Jahrbuch des Öffentlichen Rechts der Gegenwart* (1999), Band 47.
Erasmus, G. 'Provincial Government Under the 1993 Constitution: What Direction Will It Take?'. *SA Public Law* (1994): 407.
Financial and Fiscal Commission. *Framework Document for Intergovernmental Fiscal Relations in South Africa*, 19 June 1995.
Kerr, A.J. 'The Bill of Rights in the New Constitution and Customary Law'. *SALJ* (1997): 346.
Klaaren, J. 'Federalism'. In *Constitutional Law of South Africa*, edited by M. Chaskalson et al. Cape Town: Juta, 1998, 4.1–2.
Konrad Adenauer Stiftung. *Seminar Report: Sub-national Constitutional Governance*. 1999.
Leonardy, U. 'Constitutional Provisions on Devolution and Federalism'. In *Birth of a Constitution*, edited by B. De Villiers. Cape Town: Juta, 1994, 157.
Maithufi, I.P. 'The Effect of the 1996 Constitution on the Customary Law of Succession and Marriage in South Africa: Some Observations'. *De Jure* (1998): 285.
Malherbe, E.F.J. 'Provinsiale grondwette: 'n barometer van provinsiale outonomie?' *TSAR* (1998): 344.
E.F.J. Malherbe, 'The South African National Council of Provinces: Trojan Horse or White Elephant?' *TSAR* (1998): 77.
Malherbe, E.F.J. 'Die Drankwetsontwerp: vooraf kontrole en grondwetlike gesagsverdeling verder omlyn'. *THRHR* (2000): 321.
Meyer, J. *Local Government Law 1997*. Durban: Butterworths, 1998.
Mokgoro, J. 'Interprovincial Fiscal Equalization: The Role of the Financial and Fiscal Commission'. In *Birth of a Constitution*, edited by B. De Villiers. Cape Town: Juta, 1994, 281.
Mokgoro, Y. 'Traditional Authority and Democracy in the Interim South African Constitution'. Konrad Adenauer Stiftung, *Occasional Papers*, September 1994, 3.
Moosa, N. 'The Interim and Final Constitutions and Muslim Personal Law: Implications for South African Muslim Women'. *Stellenbosch Law Review* (1998): 196.
Murray, C. 'Provincial Constitution-Making in South Africa: The (Non)Example of the Western Cape'. Neue Folge Band 49 *Jahrbuch des öffentlichen Rechts* (2001): 481–512.
National Treasury. *Media statement – Joint ministerial team on Limpopo section 100 intervention*, 19 January 2012.
National Treasury. *Budget Review 2016*.
Pimstone, G. 'The Constitutional Basis of Local Government in South Africa'. Konrad Adenauer Stiftung, *Occasional Papers*, March 1998, 4–5.
Provincial Government Western Cape Department of Finance. *Budget Review 1999*.
RSA Department of Finance. *Budget Review 2000*, Pretoria, 23 February 2000.
RSA Department of Finance. *Intergovernmental Fiscal Review 1999*.
Schlemmer, L. 'Regionalism in South Africa: Opportunities Missed?'. In *Birth of a Constitution*, edited by B. De Villiers, Cape Town: Juta 1994, 243.
Shubane, K. 'Provincial Institutions'. In *Birth of a Constitution*, edited by B. De Villiers. Cape Town: Juta, 1994, 230.

Simeon, R. 'Considerations on the Design of Federations: The South African Constitution in Comparative Context'. *SA Public Law* (1998): 42.
Sinclair, J. 'Family Rights'. In *Rights and Constitutionalism: The New South African Legal Order,* edited by D.H. Van Wyk et al. Cape Town: Juta, 1994, 502.
Tapscott, C. 'Intergovernmental Relations in South Africa: A Comparative Analysis'. In *Intergovernmental Relations: An International Comparative Study.* Department of Constitutional Development and Provincial Affairs, 1998, 9.
Watts, R. 'Provinces, States, *Länder* and Cantons: Content and Variations Among Sub-National Constitutions of the World'. Konrad Adenauer Stiftung, *Seminar Report: Sub-national Constitutional Governance,* 1999, 11.
Wehner, J.H-G. *Fiscal Federalism in South Africa.* Unpublished MA dissertation, University of Stellenbosch, December 1999.
Welsh, D. 'The Provincial Boundary Demarcation Process'. In *Birth of a Constitution,* edited by B. De Villiers. Cape Town: Juta, 1994, 223.
Western Cape Government. *Media statement,* 21 August 2012, www.westerncape.gov.za/news/appointment-commission-inquiry-policing-khayelitsha.
Western Cape Provincial Government Department of Finance. *Budget Review 1999,* Cape Town, 24 February 1999.
Western Cape Government: Provincial Treasury. *Municipal Economic Review and Outlook 2015,* Cape Town, 20 October 2015.
Western Cape Provincial Parliament. *Standing Rules,* www.wcpp.gov.za/standing-rules.

Index

The numbers given here refer to paragraphs.

Index

Index

Made in the USA
Monee, IL
18 October 2026

66037572R10122